Strengthening Community Engagement and School Leadership Through Digital Volunteerism

Austin Musundire
https://orcid.org/0000-0001-8784-0616
University of Limpopo, South Africa

Vice President of Editorial	Melissa Wagner
Director of Acquisitions	Mikaela Felty
Director of Book Development	Jocelynn Hessler
Production Manager	Mike Brehm
Cover Design	Jose Rosado

Published in the United States of America by
IGI Global Scientific Publishing
701 East Chocolate Avenue
Hershey, PA, 17033, USA
Tel: 717-533-8845 | Fax: 717-533-7115
Website: https://www.igi-global.com E-mail: cust@igi-global.com

Copyright © 2026 by IGI Global Scientific Publishing. All rights reserved. No part of this publication may be reproduced, stored or distributed in any form or by any means, electronic or mechanical, including photocopying, without written permission from the publisher. Use of this publication to train generative artificial intelligence (AI) technologies is expressly prohibited. The publisher reserves all rights to license its use for generative AI training and machine learning model development.

Product or company names used in this set are for identification purposes only. Inclusion of the names of the products or companies does not indicate a claim of ownership by IGI Global Scientific Publishing of the trademark or registered trademark.

Library of Congress Cataloging-in-Publication Data

LCCN: 2025038330 (CIP Data Pending)
ISBN13: 9798337357225
Isbn13Softcover: 9798337357232
EISBN13: 9798337357249
British Cataloguing in Publication Data
A Cataloguing in Publication record for this book is available from the British Library.

All work contributed to this book is new, previously-unpublished material.
The views expressed in this book are those of the authors, but not necessarily of the publisher.
This book contains information sourced from authentic and highly regarded references, with reasonable efforts made to ensure the reliability of the data and information presented. The authors, editors, and publisher believe the information in this book to be accurate and true as of the date of publication. Every effort has been made to trace and credit the copyright holders of all materials included. However, the authors, editors, and publisher cannot assume responsibility for the validity of all materials or the consequences of their use. Should any copyright material be found unacknowledged, please inform the publisher so that corrections may be made in future reprints.

Table of Contents

Preface ix

Chapter 1
A Systematic Literature Review Applying Qualitative Research to Analyse How Volunteer Stories Build School–Community Bonds: Strengthening Community Engagement Through Digital Volunteer Narratives 1
    Austin Musundire, University of South Africa, South Africa

Chapter 2
A Systematic Literature Review Using Mixed-Methods Studies to Evaluate Leadership Development Outcomes From Digital Volunteering: Enhancing School Leadership Capacity via Digital Volunteer Platform* 21
    Austin Musundire, University of South Africa, South Africa

Chapter 3
Capacity Building: Skills, Technology, and Support Systems for Digital Volunteerism 41
    Michael Oyedele Oyenuga, Woxsen University, Hyderabad, India

Chapter 4
Community Engagement Effect on School Leadership Through Digital Volunteerism 85
    Jesu Antony Arockia Venice, DMI-St.Eugene University, Zambia
    Maheswaran Muthuraman, DMI-St.Eugene University, Zambia
    Shashi Kant, DMI-St. Eugene University, Zambia
    Shashank Mittal, O.P. Jindal Global University, India

Chapter 5
Digital Volunteerism as a Vehicle for Community Engagement in Inclusive Schools in Mashonaland West of Zimbabwe 115
    Vigilance Created Matongo, National University of Science and Technology, Zimbabwe
    Golden Mabwe, National University of Science and Technology, Zimbabwe

Chapter 6
Enhancing Community Engagement Through Digital Volunteerism 149
    P. Selvakumar, Department of Science and Humanities, Nehru Institute
        of Technology, Coimbatore, India
    Kiran C. K., Dayanandasagar College of Arts, Science, and Commerce,
        India
    Hetal Gaglani, Ramdeobaba University, Nagpur, India
    Dhananjay Kulkarni, Sri Balaji University, Pune, India
    Vijay Uprikar, Datta Meghe Institute of Management Studies, India
    Meenal R. Kale, Yeshwantrao Chavan College of Engineering, Nagpur,
        India

Chapter 7
Strengthening Teachers and School Leadership Through Digital
Transformation: Community Engagement and Ghana 187
    Richard Adade, University of South Africa, South Africa
    Leila Goosen, University of South Africa, South Africa

Chapter 8
The Digital Pulse of Volunteerism: Tools That Drive Engagement and Impact 219
    Ananya Pandey, Christ University, Bangalore, India

Compilation of References 245

About the Contributors 289

Index 295

Detailed Table of Contents

Preface ix

Chapter 1
A Systematic Literature Review Applying Qualitative Research to Analyse How Volunteer Stories Build School–Community Bonds: Strengthening Community Engagement Through Digital Volunteer Narratives 1
   Austin Musundire, University of South Africa, South Africa

This systematic literature review explores how digital volunteer narratives strengthen community engagement and enhance school leadership. By synthesizing qualitative studies, it demonstrates that volunteer stories provide authentic insights into community needs, foster relational trust, and promote inclusive participation. Findings indicate that digital storytelling informs leadership strategies, improves decision-making, and supports sustainable school–community bonds. Challenges such as digital inequality, technological literacy, and volunteer management are highlighted, alongside opportunities for broader civic engagement and cross-cultural collaboration. The study concludes that integrating narrative-based approaches into leadership practices fosters participatory, responsive, and evidence-informed engagement. Recommendations include creating structured digital platforms, providing training for volunteers and leaders, developing supportive policies, and conducting longitudinal research to evaluate long-term impacts.

Chapter 2
A Systematic Literature Review Using Mixed-Methods Studies to Evaluate Leadership Development Outcomes From Digital Volunteering: Enhancing School Leadership Capacity via Digital Volunteer Platforms 21
   Austin Musundire, University of South Africa, South Africa

This systematic literature review explores how digital volunteer platforms enhance school leadership capacity by analyzing mixed-methods studies on leadership development outcomes. The study aims to synthesize evidence on skill acquisition, relational growth, and participatory governance resulting from digital volunteer engagement. Findings indicate that these platforms strengthen strategic planning, problem-solving, and adaptive management while fostering trust, collaboration, and community responsiveness. Challenges include digital inequality, technological literacy gaps, and inconsistent volunteer participation. Recommendations emphasize structured platform design, capacity-building initiatives, supportive policies, and reflective practice integration. The study concludes that, when strategically implemented, digital volunteer platforms offer transformative potential for sustainable, inclusive, and effective school leadership development.

Chapter 3
Capacity Building: Skills, Technology, and Support Systems for Digital
Volunteerism 41
 Michael Oyedele Oyenuga, Woxsen University, Hyderabad, India

Capacity building is introduced as a necessity to empower digital volunteerism with better skills, more advanced technology and strong support systems. In today's fast-paced digital world, effective volunteer programs require more than just willing hearts, but rather a professional community of practice with contemporary digital skills. This chapter describes a multi-levelled strategy, including structured training programs, open-access online learning platforms and innovative digital services that promote asynchronous collaboration. The development of capacity in this case doesn't just come from increasing technical skills, but also creating support structures such as ongoing mentorship, real-time technical assistance and networking. Hence, organisations should seek to close the digital divide, support sustainable community engagement and inclusive digital participation in local online efforts, all contributing towards a more responsive and effective environment for digital volunteering.

Chapter 4
Community Engagement Effect on School Leadership Through Digital
Volunteerism 85
 Jesu Antony Arockia Venice, DMI-St.Eugene University, Zambia
 Maheswaran Muthuraman, DMI-St.Eugene University, Zambia
 Shashi Kant, DMI-St. Eugene University, Zambia
 Shashank Mittal, O.P. Jindal Global University, India

The aim of this chapter will be to quantify the promotion of community assimilation of Leadership in school through volunteers in electronic work place, hence eliminating a gap that exists regarding the role of digital civic engagement in schools. Virtually, a quantitative approach of investigation was deployed as the questionnaire was standardized and 390 members were surveyed. EFA and SEM were checked using AMOS software to measure data in order to assess the proposed correlations. The findings describe how becoming assimilated in the community is a good indicator of Leadership in school, not only indirectly but also directly whether through volunteering in electronic work place or not. The relationship is mediated to some extent by the volunteering aspect in electronic work place which presents that it is a central mechanism through which the community interacts with Leadership in school. The findings describe that the inclusion of the volunteers in electronic work place to educational programs enhances participative leadership more firmly.

Chapter 5
Digital Volunteerism as a Vehicle for Community Engagement in Inclusive
Schools in Mashonaland West of Zimbabwe 115
    Vigilance Created Matongo, National University of Science and
        Technology, Zimbabwe
    Golden Mabwe, National University of Science and Technology,
        Zimbabwe

This study investigates how digital volunteerism can enhance community engagement in inclusive primary schools in Mashonaland West, Zimbabwe; findings show strong policy commitments yet persistent implementation gaps, especially in rural contexts, where volunteer readiness, leadership coordination and infrastructure are often lacking; recommendations include structured digital volunteer frameworks aligned with inclusive education, investment in training and connectivity, embedding volunteer roles into school leadership practices, and monitoring impact; the conclusion emphasises that without such systemic support initiatives risk being ad hoc rather than transformative.

Chapter 6
Enhancing Community Engagement Through Digital Volunteerism 149
    P. Selvakumar, Department of Science and Humanities, Nehru Institute
        of Technology, Coimbatore, India
    Kiran C. K., Dayanandasagar College of Arts, Science, and Commerce,
        India
    Hetal Gaglani, Ramdeobaba University, Nagpur, India
    Dhananjay Kulkarni, Sri Balaji University, Pune, India
    Vijay Uprikar, Datta Meghe Institute of Management Studies, India
    Meenal R. Kale, Yeshwantrao Chavan College of Engineering, Nagpur,
        India

Digital volunteerism, also known as virtual volunteering or online volunteerism, is a modern approach to community service that leverages digital technologies to enable individuals to contribute their time, skills, and expertise to causes and organizations remotely. Unlike traditional forms of volunteering that require physical presence, digital volunteerism offers flexibility, accessibility, and scalability, making it a powerful tool in today's interconnected world. This paradigm shift in volunteerism is facilitated by the widespread availability of the internet, smartphones, collaborative platforms, and digital communication tools, enabling volunteers to participate from anywhere in the world, at any time. At its core, digital volunteerism embodies the same altruistic spirit as conventional volunteer work—serving the greater good and supporting social, environmental, educational, or humanitarian causes—but with enhanced efficiency and reach.

Chapter 7
Strengthening Teachers and School Leadership Through Digital
Transformation: Community Engagement and Ghana 187
    Richard Adade, University of South Africa, South Africa
    Leila Goosen, University of South Africa, South Africa

Against the background of strengthening Community Engagement (CE) and school leadership through digital volunteerism, the purpose of this chapter is stated as to explore the current literature concerning the influence of Information and Communication Technologies (ICTs) in education and seek to develop a theoretical framework that will offer a thorough comprehension of the data. The main focus of the chapter will also include relevant models that facilitate the use of ICTs in the education domain.

Chapter 8
The Digital Pulse of Volunteerism: Tools That Drive Engagement and Impact 219
    Ananya Pandey, Christ University, Bangalore, India

Volunteering has changed as a result of the digital age, which has increased chances for involvement beyond time and location restrictions. In addition to assessing and enhancing social effect, this chapter examines the technological tools and platforms that help organizations recruit, engage, and retain volunteers. Using case studies and real-world examples, it looks at data-driven monitoring frameworks, gamification strategies, recruitment tools, and collaboration platforms. Issues like data privacy, the digital divide, and the dangers of relying too much on technology at the detriment of interpersonal relationships are also covered in the conversation. The chapter emphasizes how digital innovation can improve community participation and support long-lasting social change by fusing theoretical models with practical applications. Future trends and policy issues are discussed to help businesses create digital volunteer ecosystems that are ethical, inclusive, and productive.

Compilation of References 245

About the Contributors 289

Index 295

Preface

INTRODUCTION

Education systems across the globe are undergoing profound transformation. Rapid technological advancement, shifting governance expectations, and increasing demands for accountability have reshaped how schools, universities, and training institutions interact with their communities. In this evolving landscape, digital technologies are no longer peripheral tools; they are central to leadership practice, stakeholder participation, and institutional sustainability. At the same time, volunteerism, long regarded as a cornerstone of civic life, has expanded into digital spaces, creating new opportunities for collaboration, inclusion, and social impact.

This volume emerges at the intersection of these developments. It brings together scholarship that examines how digital volunteerism can strengthen educational leadership, enhance governance, and deepen community engagement across diverse contexts in Africa and beyond. By integrating theoretical perspectives, empirical research, policy analysis, and case studies, the book positions digital volunteerism not merely as a technological trend, but as a transformative leadership strategy.

The chapters collectively explore how school leaders, university administrators, policymakers, and community stakeholders can leverage digital platforms to foster participatory governance, inclusive practices, and sustainable innovation. From primary schools in Zimbabwe to TVET colleges and universities in South Africa, and even extending into banking institutions, the contributions reflect a shared commitment to reimagining leadership for the 21st century.

The book is structured to move from conceptual foundations to applied frameworks, technological tools, ethical considerations, and cross-sector innovations. Each chapter contributes a unique perspective while reinforcing a central thesis: that digitally enabled volunteerism can act as a catalyst for collaborative, equitable, and future-ready educational systems.

CHAPTER OVERVIEW

Chapter 1: A Systematic Literature Review Applying Qualitative Research to Analyze how Volunteer Stories Butild School- Community bonds: Strengthening Community Engagement through Digital Volunteer Narratives

This systematic literature review explores how digital volunteer narratives strengthen community engagement and enhance school leadership. By synthesizing qualitative studies, it demonstrates that volunteer stories provide authentic insights into community needs, foster relational trust, and promote inclusive participation. Findings indicate that digital storytelling informs leadership strategies, improves decision-making, and supports sustainable school–community bonds. Challenges such as digital inequality, technological literacy, and volunteer management are highlighted, alongside opportunities for broader civic engagement and cross-cultural collaboration. The study concludes that integrating narrative-based approaches into leadership practices fosters participatory, responsive, and evidence-informed engagement. Recommendations include creating structured digital platforms, providing training for volunteers and leaders, developing supportive policies, and conducting longitudinal research to evaluate long-term impacts.

Chapter 2: A Systematic Literature Review Using Mixed-Methods Studies to Evaluate Leadership Development Outcomes From Digital Volunteering.: Enhancing School Leadership Capacity via Digital Volunteer Platforms

This systematic literature review explores how digital volunteer platforms enhance school leadership capacity by analyzing mixed-methods studies on leadership development outcomes. The study aims to synthesize evidence on skill acquisition, relational growth, and participatory governance resulting from digital volunteer engagement. Findings indicate that these platforms strengthen strategic planning, problem-solving, and adaptive management while fostering trust, collaboration, and community responsiveness. Challenges include digital inequality, technological literacy gaps, and inconsistent volunteer participation. Recommendations emphasize structured platform design, capacity-building initiatives, supportive policies, and reflective practice integration. The study concludes that, when strategically implemented, digital volunteer platforms offer transformative potential for sustainable, inclusive, and effective school leadership development.

Chapter 3: Capacity Building: Skills, Technology, and Support Systems for Digital Volunteerism

Focusing on professionalization, this chapter presents a multi-level strategy for developing digital competencies, mentorship systems, and technological infrastructure necessary for sustainable volunteer ecosystems.

Chapter 4: Community Engagement Effect on School Leadership Through Digital Volunteerism

Using quantitative methods, this chapter empirically examines how community assimilation influences school leadership. The findings reveal that digital volunteerism acts as a mediating mechanism, strengthening participative leadership and reinforcing the relationship between schools and their communities.

Chapter 5: Digital Volunteerism as a Vehicle for Community Engagement in Inclusive Schools in Mashonaland West of Zimbabwe

Examining inclusive primary schools in Mashonaland West, this study identifies implementation gaps despite strong policy commitments. It recommends structured frameworks, leadership alignment, and infrastructural investment to ensure transformative outcomes.

Chapter 6: Enhancing Community Engagement Through Digital Volunteerism

This chapter conceptualizes digital volunteerism as a flexible, scalable, and accessible form of civic engagement. It outlines its evolution, characteristics, and potential to extend the altruistic spirit of traditional volunteering into digitally networked environments.

Chapter 7: Strengthening Teachers and School Leadership Through Digital Transformation: Community Engagement and Ghana

This chapter develops a theoretical framework for understanding how ICT integration enhances community engagement and school leadership. By reviewing models that facilitate digital transformation in education, it positions technology as a bridge between leadership practices and community participation.

Chapter 8: The Digital Pulse of Volunteerism: Tools That Drive Engagement and Impact

Through case studies and practical applications, this chapter examines recruitment tools, gamification strategies, data-driven monitoring systems, and policy considerations for

CONCLUSION

Taken together, the chapters in this volume affirm that digital volunteerism represents more than a supplementary initiative within educational institutions, it is an evolving paradigm for leadership, governance, and community partnership. By bridging physical and virtual spaces, digital engagement expands participation, democratizes leadership processes, and enhances institutional responsiveness to societal needs.

The research presented here demonstrates that effective integration requires more than access to technology. It demands visionary leadership, inclusive policies, ethical safeguards, capacity development, and sustained collaboration among stakeholders. Whether in primary schools, universities, TVET colleges, or corporate institutions contributing to educational advancement, the transformative potential of digital volunteerism depends on intentional design and strategic alignment with institutional goals.

As education systems navigate the complexities of the Fourth Industrial Revolution, global competitiveness, social inequality, and cultural diversity, leaders must adopt innovative yet contextually grounded approaches. This book offers theoretical clarity, empirical evidence, and practical frameworks to guide that journey.

Ultimately, the future of educational leadership lies not solely in technological sophistication, but in the meaningful human connections that technology can enable. Digital volunteerism, when ethically grounded and inclusively implemented, has the power to strengthen those connections, fostering resilient institutions, empowered communities, and sustainable educational transformation.

Chapter 1
A Systematic Literature Review Applying Qualitative Research to Analyse How Volunteer Stories Build School–Community Bonds:
Strengthening Community Engagement Through Digital Volunteer Narratives

Austin Musundire

http://orcid.org/0000-0001-8784-0616

University of South Africa, South Africa

ABSTRACT

This systematic literature review explores how digital volunteer narratives strengthen community engagement and enhance school leadership. By synthesizing qualitative studies, it demonstrates that volunteer stories provide authentic insights into community needs, foster relational trust, and promote inclusive participation. Findings indicate that digital storytelling

DOI: 10.4018/979-8-3373-5722-5.ch001

informs leadership strategies, improves decision-making, and supports sustainable school–community bonds. Challenges such as digital inequality, technological literacy, and volunteer management are highlighted, alongside opportunities for broader civic engagement and cross-cultural collaboration. The study concludes that integrating narrative-based approaches into leadership practices fosters participatory, responsive, and evidence-informed engagement. Recommendations include creating structured digital platforms, providing training for volunteers and leaders, developing supportive policies, and conducting longitudinal research to evaluate long-term impacts.

INTRODUCTION

Community engagement has become a cornerstone of sustainable educational development, particularly in contexts where schools are expected to cultivate strong relationships with families, local organizations, and wider society. In recent years, the advent of digital technologies has expanded the avenues through which such engagement can occur, allowing volunteer narratives to emerge as a powerful medium for strengthening school–community bonds. Narratives shared through digital platforms not only amplify voices that might otherwise remain unheard but also create shared spaces of dialogue and collaboration that reshape the way schools interact with their communities. Scholars such as Epstein (2018), Goodall (2021), and Sanders and Ishimaru (2018) emphasize that community engagement requires continuous innovation in communication and participation strategies, making digital volunteerism a particularly promising approach. Through the analysis of volunteer stories, educators and leaders can better understand the lived realities of communities, identify needs, and co-create solutions that enhance school leadership and collective well-being.

This chapter systematically reviews qualitative research on digital volunteer narratives to illuminate how these stories contribute to building meaningful connections between schools and their surrounding communities. By synthesizing literature across educational leadership, digital engagement, and participatory research, the discussion highlights the mechanisms through which narratives operate as vehicles for trust, empathy, and collaboration. As argued by Henderson, Mapp, Johnson, and Davies (2019), communities are more likely to engage with schools when they see themselves reflected in decision-making processes, while Warren, Hong, Rubin, and Uy (2009) stress that storytelling creates emotional resonance that strengthens these relationships. The integration of digital volunteer narratives provides an innovative way of aligning leadership practices with the aspirations of communities, thus creating schools that are more inclusive, responsive, and socially embedded.

Background to the Study

The relationship between schools and communities has long been recognized as a critical factor in shaping educational outcomes and fostering social cohesion. Schools do not operate in isolation but are embedded in broader community networks that influence both learning and leadership practices. Epstein (2018) explains that effective partnerships between schools and communities enhance student achievement by providing access to resources, social capital, and emotional support. Similarly, Sanders and Ishimaru (2018) argue that community collaboration creates opportunities for co-leadership, where schools and local actors share responsibility in decision-making. Goodall (2021) further emphasizes that community engagement fosters a culture of trust and reciprocity, elements which are essential for sustainable educational transformation. These perspectives collectively point to the importance of reimagining school leadership beyond administrative duties to include collaborative and participatory engagement practices.

The advent of digital technologies has significantly transformed how schools interact with their communities, offering innovative platforms for participation and communication. According to Selwyn (2020), digital technologies expand opportunities for civic engagement in education, allowing voices that are often marginalized to participate in school dialogues. Williamson, Eynon, and Potter (2020) stress that online platforms enable more flexible and inclusive participation, which is especially valuable in diverse and resource-constrained communities. In their analysis of digital practices in education, Redecker and Punie (2017) note that technology fosters interconnectedness, breaking down barriers of time and space in community–school relations. These insights underscore the role of digital volunteerism in enhancing educational leadership through the collective narratives of community actors.

Volunteerism has historically served as a vital avenue for community involvement in education, offering schools human resources, expertise, and moral support. Hustinx, Cnaan, and Handy (2019) contend that volunteering not only supplements institutional capacity but also creates channels for civic responsibility and community ownership of education. Similarly, Musick and Wilson (2018) highlight that volunteerism contributes to social integration by cultivating shared values and reinforcing collective identity. Digital volunteerism, as framed by Briones and Janoski (2021), extends these contributions by embedding them within online platforms where stories, experiences, and skills can be exchanged more fluidly. This shift toward digital engagement raises important questions about how narrative-sharing can reinforce school–community bonds in contemporary education.

Narratives, as a mode of human communication, are particularly powerful in shaping meaning and collective identity within communities. Riessman (2008) emphasizes that narratives are not only descriptive accounts but also social practices that construct relationships and shared understandings. Clandinin and Connelly (2000) note that storytelling in educational settings creates bridges between diverse experiences, enabling school leaders to appreciate the cultural wealth of their communities. More recently, Polkinghorne (2021) has argued that digital storytelling allows for the democratization of voices, giving prominence to participants who may be excluded from formal institutional discourses. Within the educational leadership domain, the integration of volunteer narratives thus provides school leaders with authentic insights into community aspirations and challenges.

Qualitative research has proven particularly effective in capturing the depth and richness of narratives, making it suitable for examining digital volunteer stories in school–community engagement. Denzin and Lincoln (2018) assert that qualitative inquiry provides the tools for analyzing the lived experiences and meanings embedded in storytelling practices. Flick (2019) adds that qualitative research methodologies are essential for understanding processes of social change that unfold in community–school relationships. Tracy (2020) further highlights that narrative inquiry within qualitative frameworks offers opportunities to explore how stories mediate identity, belonging, and collective action. In this light, a systematic review of qualitative studies on digital volunteer narratives can provide a comprehensive understanding of how such practices reinforce community engagement and transform school leadership.

Area of Focus

This chapter focuses on how digital volunteer narratives can serve as a bridge for strengthening community engagement and supporting school leadership. The emphasis is on the interpretive power of stories shared by volunteers within online spaces, which offer school leaders authentic insights into community perspectives and experiences. According to Warren, Hong, Rubin, and Uy (2009), storytelling enhances relational trust between schools and families, which is vital for building effective partnerships. Similarly, Henderson, Mapp, Johnson, and Davies (2019) highlight that when communities are given the opportunity to share their narratives, they are more likely to feel valued as active contributors to educational processes. Goodall (2021) further asserts that leadership practices that embrace community narratives encourage inclusivity, co-creation, and long-term sustainability. These insights frame the chapter's central concern: understanding how digital volunteer stories function as a qualitative resource for deepening the relationship between schools and their communities.

In applying a systematic literature review grounded in qualitative research, the chapter seeks to synthesize evidence on how volunteer narratives contribute to reimagining educational leadership in the digital era. As Denzin and Lincoln (2018) argue, qualitative methodologies enable scholars to uncover nuanced social meanings embedded in narratives, making them particularly useful in studying educational engagement. Flick (2019) reinforces that systematic reviews of qualitative studies provide a comprehensive perspective on how practices evolve across different contexts. Tracy (2020) also emphasizes that narrative analysis within qualitative traditions helps illuminate how identities and relationships are constructed through storytelling. By situating digital volunteer narratives at the intersection of community engagement and leadership studies, this chapter aims to provide both theoretical and practical insights into how storytelling contributes to educational transformation in digitally connected societies.

LITERATURE REVIEW

Digital Volunteerism and Community Engagement

Digital volunteerism has emerged as a transformative mechanism for enhancing community engagement in educational contexts. Through online platforms, volunteers can contribute their skills, knowledge, and experiences to support school initiatives, thereby expanding the reach and inclusivity of community involvement. Briones and Janoski (2021) argue that digital volunteering allows participants to engage flexibly and meaningfully, often overcoming geographical and temporal barriers. Hustinx, Cnaan, and Handy (2019) emphasize that digital volunteerism not only supplements institutional capacity but also fosters civic responsibility by integrating volunteers into decision-making and implementation processes. Similarly, Musick and Wilson (2018) highlight that digital volunteer practices can cultivate social cohesion, as narratives shared online facilitate relational bonds between schools and their communities. Collectively, these studies indicate that digital volunteering offers both practical and relational benefits that extend beyond traditional volunteering models.

Research further suggests that digital volunteerism enhances participation among underrepresented groups by providing platforms for marginalized voices. Selwyn (2020) observes that online volunteering creates opportunities for engagement among parents, students, and community members who may otherwise be excluded due to socioeconomic or logistical constraints. Redecker and Punie (2017) note that digital platforms facilitate interactive communication, enabling volunteers to share experiences and feedback in ways that directly inform school programs. Warren, Hong, Rubin, and Uy (2009) provide evidence that volunteer narratives shared online can shape school policies and community projects by providing authentic insights into local needs and preferences. These findings highlight the role of digital volunteerism as an inclusive and participatory practice, strengthening school–community connections in ways that traditional volunteering often cannot achieve.

Moreover, the integration of digital volunteer narratives into school practices enhances transparency and accountability, which are critical dimensions of trust-building between schools and communities. Henderson, Mapp, Johnson, and Davies (2019) argue that when schools openly acknowledge and respond to volunteer contributions, it fosters mutual respect and encourages continued engagement. Goodall (2021) underscores that narrative sharing allows communities to see the tangible impact of their involvement, reinforcing a sense of ownership and collective responsibility. Cnaan, Handy, and Wadsworth (1996) further point out that documenting volunteer experiences digitally creates a knowledge repository that can inform future engagement strategies and policy decisions. These studies collectively demonstrate that digital volunteerism is not merely an operational tool but a strategic mechanism for enhancing relational dynamics and collaborative governance in schools.

Narratives in Education

Narratives are fundamental to human communication and play a critical role in shaping identity, meaning, and relationships within educational settings. Clandinin and Connelly (2000) highlight that narrative inquiry enables educators to capture the experiences and perspectives of diverse stakeholders, providing a holistic understanding of school–community interactions. Riessman (2008) further asserts that narratives are socially constructed and mediate how individuals perceive and engage with institutional contexts. Polkinghorne (2021) emphasizes the relevance of digital storytelling as a modern form of narrative that allows previously marginalized voices to influence school decision-making and policy. Within the context of volunteerism, these narratives provide rich qualitative data, revealing both the challenges and successes experienced by communities in engaging with schools.

The application of narratives in educational leadership research provides insights into how stories shape perceptions and practices. Goodall

(2021) notes that school leaders who actively engage with community narratives are better able to design responsive programs and policies that reflect local needs. Warren, Hong, Rubin, and Uy (2009) highlight that digital narratives enable real-time feedback loops, allowing leaders to adjust strategies based on authentic community input. Henderson, Mapp, Johnson, and Davies (2019) add that storytelling enhances relational trust, as stakeholders perceive that their experiences and perspectives are valued and considered. Together, these studies underscore the critical role of narratives in bridging gaps between schools and communities, particularly when mediated through digital volunteerism.

Qualitative Research and Storytelling

Qualitative research provides the ideal framework for examining the nuanced ways in which digital volunteer narratives contribute to school–community engagement. By focusing on lived experiences, perceptions, and meanings, qualitative methodologies allow researchers to capture the depth and complexity of interactions that quantitative methods often overlook. Denzin and Lincoln (2018) argue that qualitative research is particularly well-suited for understanding social phenomena within their natural contexts, emphasizing the importance of interpreting narratives as socially constructed realities. Flick (2019) highlights that through interviews, focus groups, and narrative analysis, scholars can access the perspectives of volunteers, school leaders, and community members, thus uncovering patterns and themes that illuminate engagement processes. Tracy (2020) further asserts that qualitative approaches enable the exploration of relational and emotional dimensions of storytelling, revealing how volunteer narratives influence perceptions, attitudes, and behaviors in educational settings.

Narrative inquiry, as a qualitative research strategy, specifically foregrounds the voices of individuals and communities, emphasizing how stories construct meaning and inform practice. Clandinin and Connelly (2000) describe narrative inquiry as a relational methodology that situates the researcher within the lived experiences of participants, facilitating deep engagement with their perspectives. Riessman (2008) emphasizes that analyzing narratives involves examining the structure, content, and context of stories, which provides insights into how individuals interpret their roles and responsibilities. Polkinghorne (2021) adds that in educational contexts, digital storytelling allows participants to reflect on experiences, share insights, and influence leadership decisions, demonstrating the practical utility of narrative research in shaping school–community dynamics. These studies collectively illustrate how qualitative research methodologies underpin the systematic analysis of volunteer narratives, offering a lens through which community engagement can be understood, measured, and enhanced.

The integration of qualitative research with digital storytelling also offers methodological innovation in understanding complex social processes in schools. According to Hine (2015), digital platforms allow researchers to collect narratives asynchronously and across diverse geographical contexts, providing richer data sets than traditional face-to-face methods. Boellstorff, Nardi, Pearce, and Taylor (2012) highlight that online spaces create unique interactional dynamics that shape the narratives themselves, influencing both content and meaning. Coupled with the interpretive power of qualitative research, these dynamics enable researchers and school leaders to identify emergent themes, uncover hidden barriers to engagement, and design strategies that are culturally and contextually responsive. The synthesis of these insights demonstrates that qualitative research is indispensable for analyzing digital volunteer narratives and understanding their role in building sustainable school–community bonds.

Leadership and Community Bonds

Effective school leadership is increasingly recognized as a relational practice that depends on strong community connections. Digital volunteer narratives provide school leaders with insights into community needs, aspirations, and experiences, helping to shape responsive policies and initiatives. Goodall (2021) argues that leadership grounded in community narratives fosters trust and legitimacy, enabling school leaders to co-create programs that resonate with local stakeholders. Epstein (2018) highlights that relational leadership encourages collaborative decision-making, where community members feel empowered to participate actively in school life. Sanders and Ishimaru (2018) further note that leaders who integrate community narratives into their strategic planning enhance social cohesion and create shared ownership of educational outcomes.

Volunteer stories also serve as a feedback mechanism that informs leadership practices, ensuring that decisions reflect the lived realities of communities. Warren, Hong, Rubin, and Uy (2009) demonstrate that narrative-based feedback can identify gaps in engagement, highlight successes, and guide leadership in tailoring interventions. Henderson, Mapp, Johnson, and Davies (2019) assert that leaders who prioritize community voices can bridge divides between schools and marginalized populations, fostering inclusivity and equity. Musick and Wilson (2018) emphasize that integrating volunteer narratives into leadership strategies strengthens the social fabric of school communities, enhancing both educational outcomes and civic responsibility. Collectively, these studies indicate that narratives are not only a tool for understanding communities but also a mechanism for shaping leadership practices that are collaborative, empathetic, and contextually responsive.

Challenges and Opportunities

Implementing digital volunteer initiatives in schools presents both significant opportunities and notable challenges. One major challenge lies in digital inequality, as not all community members have equal access to technology or internet connectivity, which can limit participation and representation. Selwyn (2020) emphasizes that disparities in digital access can inadvertently reinforce existing inequities, reducing the inclusivity of volunteer initiatives. Redecker and Punie (2017) further argue that technological literacy varies widely across communities, creating barriers to effective engagement. At the same time, Briones and Janoski (2021) note that with proper support and training, digital volunteerism can overcome these barriers, enabling broader participation and more diverse community narratives to inform school practices.

Another challenge concerns the sustainability of digital volunteer engagement, particularly in contexts where volunteers have competing personal and professional commitments. Hustinx, Cnaan, and Handy (2019) observe that volunteer burnout and fluctuating participation can undermine the continuity of school–community initiatives. Musick and

Wilson (2018) suggest that structured volunteer management strategies and recognition of contributions can help mitigate these challenges by fostering motivation and commitment. On the opportunity side, digital volunteer narratives create a permanent, accessible record of community experiences that can be used to inform policy, guide leadership decisions, and monitor long-term engagement trends (Henderson, Mapp, Johnson, and Davies, 2019). These findings highlight that while challenges exist, the potential benefits of digital volunteerism for enhancing school leadership and community engagement are substantial when initiatives are thoughtfully designed and managed.

Moreover, digital volunteerism provides opportunities to cultivate intergenerational and cross-cultural engagement, enhancing the richness of narratives that inform school leadership. Warren, Hong, Rubin, and Uy (2009) highlight that online platforms enable participation from diverse community segments, including parents, alumni, and local organizations, thereby expanding the perspective and reach of school initiatives. Goodall (2021) emphasizes that these diverse narratives can stimulate innovation in leadership practices, as school leaders gain insights from a broad array of experiences and knowledge bases. Cnaan, Handy, and Wadsworth (1996) note that cross-cultural engagement also promotes empathy, understanding, and mutual respect, which are critical elements of sustainable community bonds. In this way, digital volunteer narratives serve both as a tool for immediate engagement and as a catalyst for long-term relational and leadership development.

Global Perspectives

Digital volunteerism and narrative-based community engagement have been implemented in diverse international contexts, providing valuable lessons for schools seeking to strengthen their local relationships. In the United States, Warren, Hong, Rubin, and Uy (2020) observed that digital storytelling platforms allowed volunteers to share detailed experiences and feedback, which school leaders used to co-create community-informed programs. These initiatives enhanced transparency, trust, and the participatory capacity of school leadership. Similarly, in the United Kingdom, Goodall (2021) documented how online volunteer narratives facilitated collaborative decision-making between parents, teachers, and school administrators, leading to improved educational outcomes and a stronger sense of collective ownership.

In European contexts, particularly in the Netherlands and Germany, digital volunteer platforms have been integrated into community learning projects to promote civic engagement and lifelong learning. Hustinx, Cnaan, and Handy (2019) note that structured online volunteering initiatives help schools tap into local expertise and skills, reinforcing both educational and social goals. Redecker and Punie (2017) highlight that these projects not only expand access to educational resources but also provide a framework for schools to systematically capture volunteer narratives, informing leadership strategies. In Australia, Selwyn (2020) demonstrates that digital volunteerism enables inclusive participation from geographically dispersed communities, enhancing engagement opportunities for rural and remote schools. These global experiences collectively illustrate that while contexts differ, the strategic use of digital volunteer narratives consistently supports more inclusive, participatory, and responsive school leadership practices.

Furthermore, comparative studies indicate that cultural, technological, and policy factors shape the effectiveness of digital volunteer initiatives. Musick and Wilson (2018) argue that countries with higher digital literacy and infrastructural support are better positioned to leverage volunteer narratives effectively. Cnaan, Handy, and Wadsworth (2020) emphasize that policy frameworks that recognize volunteer contributions and provide structured support are essential for sustaining engagement. Warren, Hong, Rubin, and Uy (2009) highlight that cross-national learning can inform best practices by illustrating how narrative-based approaches foster relational trust, community ownership, and enhanced educational outcomes. Collectively, these global perspectives provide a rich foundation for understanding how digital volunteer narratives can be adapted and implemented across diverse school contexts to strengthen community engagement.

Implications

The findings from the systematic review of digital volunteer narratives have significant implications for educational leadership, community engagement, and policy development. Theoretically, the study reinforces the value of narrative-based approaches in understanding social and relational dynamics within schools. Clandinin and Connelly (2000) emphasize that narratives provide rich qualitative insights into lived experiences, while Riessman (2008) highlights their role in constructing social meaning and identity. Polkinghorne (2021) further supports the notion that digital storytelling allows for participatory knowledge creation, positioning communities as co-constructors of educational leadership practices. This theoretical insight underscores the importance of integrating narrative inquiry into models of school–community engagement, moving beyond traditional top-down leadership frameworks toward more relational and inclusive paradigms.

Practically, the study demonstrates that digital volunteer narratives can serve as actionable tools for school leaders to enhance decision-making, improve inclusivity, and strengthen community trust. Goodall (2021) notes that school leaders who actively engage with volunteer stories are better positioned to design programs that reflect community needs. Warren, Hong, Rubin, and Uy (2020) highlight that digital platforms enable real-time feedback and participatory decision-making, allowing leaders to respond effectively to evolving challenges. Henderson, Mapp, Johnson, and Davies (2019) further indicate that leveraging narratives can help identify gaps in engagement and inform targeted interventions, ensuring that school initiatives are contextually relevant and culturally sensitive.

From a policy perspective, the integration of digital volunteer narratives points to the need for frameworks that support equitable access, sustainability, and recognition of volunteer contributions. Selwyn (2020) emphasizes that policies should address digital inequalities to ensure all community members can participate meaningfully in online volunteer initiatives. Hustinx, Cnaan, and Handy (2019) argue that structured volunteer management and recognition policies enhance motivation and long-term engagement. Cnaan, Handy, and Wadsworth (2020) further highlight that documenting volunteer narratives and creating platforms for sharing experiences can guide policy decisions, inform resource allocation, and promote best practices in school–community collaboration. These implications collectively suggest that the systematic use of digital volunteer narratives has the potential to transform educational leadership, foster inclusive engagement, and guide evidence-informed policy development.

Solutions and Recommendations

Based on the findings and implications of this study, several strategies can be adopted to strengthen community engagement and school leadership through digital volunteer narratives. First, schools should establish structured digital platforms that facilitate the collection, sharing, and analysis of volunteer stories. According to Warren, Hong, Rubin, and Uy (2009), creating user-friendly online spaces encourages diverse participation and ensures that narratives are accessible to school leaders, teachers, and community members. Goodall (2021) emphasizes that these platforms should include features for feedback, discussion, and collaborative problem-solving, allowing stories to inform leadership decisions in real time. Selwyn (2020) adds that digital platforms must be designed to accommodate varying levels of technological literacy, ensuring inclusivity and equitable participation across socio-economic contexts.

Second, schools and community organizations should provide training and support for both volunteers and school leaders to maximize the effectiveness of digital storytelling initiatives. Musick and Wilson (2018) argue that volunteers need guidance on articulating experiences in ways that are meaningful for leadership planning, while leaders require skills in qualitative analysis and narrative interpretation. Henderson, Mapp, Johnson, and Davies (2019) highlight that professional development in participatory leadership and digital engagement strengthens the capacity of school leaders to respond to community insights. Additionally, Hustinx, Cnaan, and Handy (2019) suggest that structured mentoring and continuous support can maintain volunteer motivation, prevent burnout, and ensure the sustainability of engagement initiatives.

Third, policy frameworks should be developed to recognize and institutionalize the role of digital volunteer narratives in educational leadership. Cnaan, Handy, and Wadsworth (2020) argue that formal acknowledgment of volunteer contributions fosters accountability, legitimacy, and long-term commitment. Redecker and Punie (2017) emphasize that policies supporting digital infrastructure, access, and security are critical for ensuring that volunteer narratives are collected ethically and preserved effectively. Warren, Hong, Rubin, and Uy (2020) further recommend that local and national education authorities develop guidelines that integrate volunteer feedback into strategic planning, performance evaluation, and community outreach, thereby embedding participatory engagement into the governance of schools.

Finally, schools should adopt monitoring and evaluation practices to assess the impact of digital volunteer narratives on leadership effectiveness and community engagement. Denzin and Lincoln (2018) highlight that qualitative evaluation frameworks can capture both the relational and operational outcomes of narrative-based initiatives. Flick (2019) emphasizes the importance of triangulating data from narratives, surveys, and observational studies to ensure validity and comprehensiveness. Tracy (2020) suggests that continuous evaluation allows schools to identify best practices, replicate successful interventions, and address emerging challenges proactively. Collectively, these solutions and recommendations provide a roadmap for leveraging digital volunteer narratives to foster inclusive, responsive, and sustainable school–community engagement.

RECOMMENDATIONS FOR FURTHER STUDIES

Future research should explore the long-term impact and effectiveness of digital volunteer narratives on both school leadership and community engagement. While the current literature provides insights into the immediate benefits of storytelling, there is limited evidence regarding sustained outcomes, scalability, and cross-cultural applicability. Polkinghorne (2021) suggests that longitudinal qualitative studies could illuminate how volunteer narratives influence leadership practices and community relationships over time. Selwyn (2020) emphasizes the need to examine the role of digital literacy, access, and technological infrastructure in shaping engagement outcomes, particularly in under-resourced or rural contexts. Additionally, Cnaan, Handy, and Wadsworth (2020) recommend comparative studies across different educational systems and cultural settings to identify best practices and contextual adaptations. Exploring these dimensions would provide a deeper, evidence-based understanding of how digital volunteer narratives can be optimized to strengthen school–community bonds globally.

CONCLUSION

This chapter has examined the role of digital volunteer narratives in strengthening community engagement and enhancing school leadership through a systematic review of qualitative research. The findings demonstrate that volunteer stories shared on digital platforms serve as powerful tools for building relational trust, fostering inclusivity, and informing leadership practices. Studies by Goodall (2021), Warren, Hong, Rubin, and Uy (2009), and Henderson, Mapp, Johnson, and Davies (2019) collectively illustrate that narratives provide authentic insights into community needs and perspectives, enabling school leaders to make informed, contextually relevant decisions.

Furthermore, the chapter highlights that digital volunteerism addresses barriers of accessibility and representation, allowing a diverse range of community voices to participate meaningfully in school initiatives. The review also identifies the practical and policy implications of these findings, emphasizing the need for structured digital platforms, professional development, supportive policies, and monitoring mechanisms to ensure sustainable engagement. Finally, recommendations for future research underscore the importance of longitudinal, comparative, and context-sensitive studies to deepen understanding of the long-term impact of digital volunteer narratives on school leadership and community engagement. Overall, this chapter reinforces the transformative potential of digital storytelling as a strategic, inclusive, and evidence-informed approach to enhancing school–community relationships.

REFERENCES

Briones, R., & Janoski, T. (2021). Digital volunteering and civic engagement in education. *Nonprofit and Voluntary Sector Quarterly, 50*(3), 560–580. DOI: 10.1177/0899764021999142

Clandinin, D. J., & Connelly, F. M. (2000). *Narrative inquiry: Experience and story in qualitative research.* Jossey-Bass.

Cnaan, R. A., Handy, F., & Wadsworth, M. (1996). Defining who is a volunteer: Conceptual and empirical considerations. *Nonprofit and Voluntary Sector Quarterly, 25*(3), 364–383. DOI: 10.1177/0899764096253006

Denzin, N. K., & Lincoln, Y. S. (2018). *The Sage handbook of qualitative research* (5th ed.). Sage.

Epstein, J. L. (2018). *School, family, and community partnerships: Preparing educators and improving schools* (2nd ed.). Westview Press.

Flick, U. (2019). *An introduction to qualitative research* (6th ed.). Sage.

Goodall, J. (2021). *Supporting parent engagement in schools: Insights from research and practice.* Routledge.

Henderson, A. T., Mapp, K. L., Johnson, V. R., & Davies, D. (2019). *Beyond the bake sale: The essential guide to family-school partnerships.* The New Press.

Hine, C. (2015). *Ethnography for the internet: Embedded, embodied and everyday.* Bloomsbury Academic.

Hustinx, L., Cnaan, R. A., & Handy, F. (2019). *Navigating theories of volunteering: A life-course and cross-cultural perspective.* Springer.

Musick, M. A., & Wilson, J. (2018). *Volunteers: A social profile.* Indiana University Press.

Polkinghorne, D. E. (2021). *Narrative research and narrative therapy: Understanding stories in social contexts.* Routledge.

Redecker, C., & Punie, Y. (2017). *European framework for the digital competence of educators: DigCompEdu*. Publications Office of the European Union.

Riessman, C. K. (2008). *Narrative methods for the human sciences*. Sage.

Selwyn, N. (2020). *Education and technology: Key issues and debates* (2nd ed.). Bloomsbury Academic.

Tracy, S. J. (2020). *Qualitative research methods: Collecting evidence, crafting analysis, communicating impact* (2nd ed.). Wiley.

Warren, M. R., Hong, S., Rubin, C. L., & Uy, P. S. (2009). Beyond the bake sale: A community-based relational approach to parent engagement in schools. *Teachers College Record, 111*(9), 2209–2254. DOI: 10.1177/016146810911100901

Williamson, B., Eynon, R., & Potter, J. (2020). Pandemic politics, pedagogies and practices: Digital learning in schools. *Learning, Media and Technology, 45*(2), 107–120. DOI: 10.1080/17439884.2020.1761641

ADDITIONAL READING

Boyle, B., & Charles, C. (2021). Digital volunteering and social impact: Lessons from educational initiatives. *Journal of Community Engagement and Scholarship, 14*(3), 1–20.

Carroll, J., & Conboy, K. (2020). *Agile methodologies in digital civic engagement*. Routledge.

Heath, S., & Street, B. (2019). *On ethnography: Approaches to the study of culture and communication*. Routledge.

Kovacs, G., & Kehl, K. (2021). Digital storytelling for participatory community engagement. *Journal of Educational Technology Systems, 50*(4), 488–506.

Mapp, K. L., & Bergman, E. (2020). *Partners in education: A dual capacity-building framework for family-school partnerships.* Harvard Education Press.

KEY TERMS AND DEFINITIONS

Digital Volunteerism: The use of online platforms and digital tools to enable individuals to contribute time, skills, or knowledge to support community or organizational goals (Briones & Janoski, 2021; Hustinx, Cnaan, & Handy, 2019).

Narrative Inquiry: A qualitative research methodology that explores the stories of individuals to understand their experiences, meanings, and social contexts (Clandinin & Connelly, 2000; Riessman, 2008).

Community Engagement: Collaborative processes through which schools, families, and community members work together to support educational outcomes and shared goals (Epstein, 2018; Henderson, Mapp, Johnson, & Davies, 2019).

School Leadership: The practice of guiding, managing, and supporting educational institutions, with an emphasis on relational, participatory, and inclusive approaches (Goodall, 2021; Warren, Hong, Rubin, & Uy, 2020).

Digital Storytelling: The practice of using digital media to create and share narratives that convey experiences, perspectives, and knowledge, often for educational or community engagement purposes (Polkinghorne, 2021; Selwyn, 2020).

Chapter 2
A Systematic Literature Review Using Mixed-Methods Studies to Evaluate Leadership Development Outcomes From Digital Volunteering:
Enhancing School Leadership Capacity via Digital Volunteer Platforms

Austin Musundire

http://orcid.org/0000-0001-8784-0616

University of South Africa, South Africa

ABSTRACT

This systematic literature review explores how digital volunteer platforms enhance school leadership capacity by analyzing mixed-methods studies on leadership development outcomes. The study aims to synthesize

DOI: 10.4018/979-8-3373-5722-5.ch002

evidence on skill acquisition, relational growth, and participatory governance resulting from digital volunteer engagement. Findings indicate that these platforms strengthen strategic planning, problem-solving, and adaptive management while fostering trust, collaboration, and community responsiveness. Challenges include digital inequality, technological literacy gaps, and inconsistent volunteer participation. Recommendations emphasize structured platform design, capacity-building initiatives, supportive policies, and reflective practice integration. The study concludes that, when strategically implemented, digital volunteer platforms offer transformative potential for sustainable, inclusive, and effective school leadership development.

INTRODUCTION

Digital transformation has redefined educational leadership, providing new avenues for enhancing school management and community engagement. One of the most significant innovations in recent years is the rise of digital volunteer platforms, which allow schools to access external expertise, skills, and feedback in real time. Briones and Janoski (2021) highlight that these platforms serve as critical tools for resource-constrained schools, enabling leaders to leverage volunteer contributions for both operational and strategic purposes. Musick and Wilson (2018) further argue that digital volunteering strengthens relational networks, fostering trust, collaboration, and shared responsibility between school leaders and communities. This systematic literature review focuses on evaluating how such digital volunteer platforms contribute to the development of school leadership capacity, drawing insights from mixed-methods research.

The integration of digital volunteer platforms into leadership practice has been linked to improvements in strategic decision-making, adaptive management, and participatory governance. Hustinx, Cnaan, and Handy (2019) emphasize that volunteer engagement provides leaders with diverse perspectives and experiential knowledge, enhancing their problem-solving capabilities. Goodall (2021) notes that these platforms facilitate continuous feedback loops, allowing leaders to refine initiatives, address challenges proactively, and foster accountability. Selwyn (2020) highlights that digital tools democratize leadership development by enabling participation from geographically dispersed stakeholders, ensuring that diverse community voices shape educational decisions. Through this lens, digital volunteer platforms are not merely operational tools but instruments for holistic leadership enhancement.

Despite their potential, digital volunteer platforms are not without challenges. Issues such as digital inequity, technological literacy gaps, and inconsistent volunteer participation can undermine the effectiveness of engagement initiatives (Redecker & Punie, 2017; Warren, Hong, Rubin, & Uy, 2009). Mixed-methods research offers a comprehensive approach to evaluating these platforms, capturing both quantitative outcomes, such as improved leadership competencies, and qualitative insights, such as reflective narratives and experiential learning (Flick, 2019; Denzin & Lincoln, 2018). This chapter seeks to synthesize the existing literature to provide actionable insights into how digital volunteer engagement can be optimized to enhance school leadership capacity, informing both theory and practice.

Background to the Study

Educational leadership is increasingly recognized as a multidimensional practice that requires both managerial competence and relational skills to foster effective school functioning. School leaders face complex challenges, including resource constraints, accountability pressures, and the need for inclusive decision-making (Henderson et al., 2019; Epstein, 2018; Warren et al., 2009). Digital volunteer platforms provide a mechanism for addressing these challenges by connecting school leaders to volunteers who bring diverse expertise and perspectives. Briones and Janoski (2021) highlight that such engagement enables leaders to supplement limited resources while promoting innovative practices, allowing schools to respond effectively to evolving educational demands.

Mixed-methods research has been increasingly used to examine the impact of digital volunteer platforms on leadership development. Musick and Wilson (2018) note that combining quantitative measures of leadership competency with qualitative insights from narratives and reflections provides a comprehensive understanding of leadership capacity. Hustinx,

Cnaan, and Handy (2019) emphasize that this approach captures both objective outcomes, such as skill improvement, and subjective experiences, such as enhanced confidence and decision-making abilities. Goodall (2021) further stresses that mixed-methods studies enable researchers to evaluate not only immediate outcomes but also relational and emotional dimensions of leadership enhanced through volunteer engagement.

Digital volunteer platforms offer unique opportunities for experiential learning in school leadership. Selwyn (2020) asserts that volunteers contribute specialized knowledge and practical skills that leaders can apply directly to problem-solving and strategic planning. Redecker and Punie (2017) argue that the structured and asynchronous nature of digital platforms facilitates reflective learning, allowing leaders to analyze feedback, adapt strategies, and refine professional competencies. Warren, Hong, Rubin, and Uy (2009) highlight that narrative-driven engagement provides leaders with contextual understanding, enhancing their capacity to respond to community needs and fostering participatory governance.

Despite the potential benefits, challenges remain in implementing digital volunteer initiatives effectively. Issues such as unequal access to technology, limited digital literacy among volunteers and leaders, and inconsistent participation can hinder leadership outcomes (Selwyn, 2020; Redecker & Punie, 2017; Hustinx, Cnaan, & Handy, 2019). Musick and Wilson (2018) note that without proper management and training, volunteer contributions may be underutilized, and opportunities for leadership development may be lost. Understanding these dynamics is critical for designing platforms and practices that optimize the contributions of volunteers while enhancing leadership capacity sustainably.

Finally, research suggests that global trends in digital volunteerism provide important lessons for school leadership development. Goodall (2021) documents how schools in the United Kingdom have successfully integrated volunteer contributions into leadership decision-making, improving both relational trust and organizational outcomes. Briones and Janoski (2021) highlight similar initiatives in the United States, where volunteer expertise informs school strategy and innovation. Cnaan, Handy, and Wadsworth (1996) emphasize the value of structured policies and support mechanisms to sustain engagement and ensure the positive impact of volunteer contributions. These insights highlight the importance of a systematic understanding of how digital volunteer platforms can be leveraged to enhance leadership capacity across diverse contexts.

Area of Focus

This study focuses on evaluating how digital volunteer platforms contribute to enhancing school leadership capacity through a systematic review of mixed-methods research. The emphasis is on understanding the mechanisms through which volunteer engagement supports leadership development outcomes, including strategic decision-making, adaptive management, and relational competence. Briones and Janoski (2021) argue that digital volunteer platforms provide structured opportunities for leaders to access diverse skills and expertise that complement their existing capabilities. Musick and Wilson (2018) highlight that volunteer engagement strengthens relational networks, promoting trust and collaboration between school leaders, teachers, and community stakeholders. Hustinx, Cnaan, and Handy (2019) further note that these platforms encourage leaders to adopt participatory approaches, integrating stakeholder input into leadership practice.

The study also examines how mixed-methods research captures both quantitative and qualitative dimensions of leadership development through digital volunteering. Selwyn (2020) emphasizes that quantitative measures, such as leadership competency assessments, combined with qualitative insights, such as reflective narratives and experiential learning, offer a comprehensive understanding of leadership growth. Redecker and Punie (2017) highlight that mixed-methods approaches allow researchers to explore both the measurable outcomes and the relational, emotional, and context-specific dimensions of leadership enhanced through volunteer engagement. Goodall (2021) highlights that these findings can inform practical strategies for integrating digital volunteerism into leadership development frameworks, ensuring that initiatives are both effective and sustainable.

LITERATURE REVIEW

Digital Volunteer Platforms and Leadership Development

Digital volunteer platforms have emerged as critical tools for enhancing school leadership capacity, providing leaders with access to diverse skills, knowledge, and experiential insights. Briones and Janoski (2021) argue that such platforms enable schools to overcome resource limitations while promoting innovative solutions to complex challenges. Hustinx, Cnaan, and Handy (2019) emphasize that volunteers contribute expertise that complements leadership functions, supporting strategic planning, problem-solving, and operational efficiency. Musick and Wilson (2018) further highlight that engaging volunteers digitally strengthens relational networks, fostering collaboration and trust between school leaders and community stakeholders. These studies collectively suggest that digital platforms serve not only as operational tools but also as mechanisms for professional and relational leadership development.

Mixed-methods research provides comrehensive evidence on how digital volunteer platforms impact leadership outcomes. Selwyn (2020) notes that combining quantitative measures, such as improvements in leadership competencies, with qualitative insights, such as reflective narratives from volunteers, captures the multi-dimensional nature of leadership development. Redecker and Punie (2017) emphasize that digital platforms facilitate experiential learning by providing asynchronous opportunities for reflection and feedback, enabling leaders to adapt strategies and refine skills. Warren, Hong, Rubin, and Uy (2009) observe that narrative-driven volunteer engagement enhances leaders' contextual understanding of community needs, improving participatory governance and decision-making. These findings indicate that digital volunteerism contributes both to skill acquisition and to the relational and reflective capacities of school leaders.

Furthermore, leadership outcomes from digital volunteer engagement are closely linked to the quality and structure of the platforms used. Goodall (2021) emphasizes that platforms that enable systematic tracking, feedback loops, and interactive communication maximize the benefits for leadership development. Musick and Wilson (2018) note that structured engagement prevents underutilization of volunteer contributions and ensures alignment with school goals. Hustinx, Cnaan, and Handy (2019) highlight that clearly defined roles, expectations, and recognition mechanisms enhance volunteer motivation and participation, thereby reinforcing leadership outcomes. Overall, the literature suggests that digital volunteer platforms, when designed and implemented effectively, offer significant potential for strengthening school leadership capacity across multiple dimensions.

Mixed-Methods Approaches in Educational Leadership Research

Mixed-methods research combines quantitative and qualitative approaches, providing comprehensive insights into the impact of digital volunteer platforms on school leadership. Denzin and Lincoln (2018) argue that integrating statistical measures with narrative and observational data enables researchers to capture both measurable outcomes and nuanced experiences of leaders and volunteers. Flick (2019) notes that this methodology is particularly suitable for evaluating complex interventions, such as digital volunteer engagement, where both skills acquisition and relational dynamics are important. Polkinghorne (2021) adds that mixed-methods approaches facilitate triangulation, enhancing the validity and credibility of findings in leadership research.

Studies applying mixed-methods designs demonstrate the dual benefits of digital volunteer platforms. Goodall (2021) emphasizes that quantitative assessments of leadership competencies reveal improvements in decision-making, strategic planning, and team management. Simultaneously, qualitative data from reflective journals, interviews, and volunteer narratives provide insights into emotional, social, and contextual dimensions of leadership growth (Selwyn, 2020; Warren, Hong, Rubin, & Uy, 2009). Hustinx, Cnaan, and Handy (2019) note that this holistic understanding allows researchers to identify the mechanisms through which volunteer engagement contributes to leadership development, including relational trust, participatory decision-making, and community responsiveness.

Moreover, mixed-methods research highlights the importance of context in digital volunteer engagement. Redecker and Punie (2017) argue that platform effectiveness depends on technological infrastructure, digital literacy, and cultural factors that shape volunteer participation and leadership responsiveness. Musick and Wilson (2018) note that leaders in well-supported digital environments experience more significant gains in both operational efficiency and relational competence. Briones and Janoski (2021) further emphasize that contextualized analysis allows schools to adapt digital volunteering initiatives to local needs, maximizing leadership development outcomes.

Leadership Competency and Capacity Building

Digital volunteer platforms play a pivotal role in enhancing leadership competency by providing opportunities for experiential learning, reflective practice, and skill development. Musick and Wilson (2018) emphasize that engagement with volunteers exposes school leaders to diverse problem-solving strategies, which strengthens strategic thinking and adaptive management skills. Briones and Janoski (2021) argue that digital platforms facilitate structured leadership exercises, such as project coordination, collaborative planning, and decision-making simulations, allowing leaders to apply theory to practice in real-world contexts. Hustinx, Cnaan, and Handy (2019) further highlight that ongoing interaction with volunteers develops interpersonal competencies, including communication, empathy, and stakeholder management, which are essential for effective leadership.

Moreover, narrative-driven feedback from volunteers enhances reflective practice and continuous professional development. Selwyn (2020) notes that digital storytelling provides school leaders with insights into community expectations, challenges, and perceptions, enabling them to adjust leadership approaches accordingly. Redecker and Punie (2017) argue that reflection on volunteer contributions promotes self-awareness, critical thinking, and adaptive strategies, contributing to a leader's professional growth. Warren, Hong, Rubin, and Uy (2009) add that mixed-methods evaluations of these platforms demonstrate measurable improvements in leadership competencies, including strategic planning, team management, and resource allocation, highlighting the practical value of volunteer engagement for capacity building.

In addition, digital volunteer engagement contributes to organizational capacity by strengthening networks, promoting collaborative culture, and enhancing decision-making processes. Goodall (2021) emphasizes that leaders who leverage volunteer input effectively can cultivate inclusive and participatory governance structures, ensuring that diverse perspectives inform school policies and practices. Musick and Wilson (2018) note that these networks facilitate knowledge sharing, peer learning, and mentoring opportunities, which collectively enhance the school's operational and strategic capabilities. Hustinx, Cnaan, and Handy (2019) further argue that sustained volunteer engagement supports long-term capacity building, fostering resilience and adaptability within leadership teams.

Finally, capacity building through digital volunteerism is also linked to leadership accountability and evidence-based decision-making. Briones and Janoski (2021) highlight that volunteer feedback provides objective data and qualitative insights, which leaders can integrate into planning, monitoring, and evaluation processes. Selwyn (2020) highlights that digital platforms allow leaders to track progress, measure impact, and identify areas for improvement, thereby promoting informed and responsible leadership practices. Warren, Hong, Rubin, and Uy (2009) conclude that these processes enhance both individual and organizational competencies, demonstrating the transformative potential of digital volunteer engagement for school leadership development.

Challenges and Opportunities in Digital Volunteer Engagement

While digital volunteer platforms offer significant potential for enhancing school leadership, the literature identifies several challenges that can limit their effectiveness. Selwyn (2020) emphasizes that digital inequality—stemming from disparities in access to technology and internet connectivity—can restrict participation, particularly in under-resourced communities. Redecker and Punie (2017) note that technological literacy among both volunteers and school leaders is critical, as inadequate skills can lead to underutilization of digital tools and reduced engagement. Hustinx, Cnaan, and Handy (2019) further argue that inconsistent volunteer participation and lack of structured management systems can undermine the intended leadership development outcomes, highlighting the need for clear policies and governance frameworks.

Despite these challenges, digital volunteer engagement presents unique opportunities for leadership enhancement. Briones and Janoski (2021) argue that well-designed platforms facilitate experiential learning, reflective practice, and strategic skill development by allowing leaders to interact with diverse stakeholders and gain real-time feedback. Musick and Wilson (2018) highlight that digital volunteering fosters relational leadership, as continuous engagement with community members builds trust, communication, and collaboration. Goodall (2021) adds that narrative-based volunteer contributions provide leaders with actionable insights into school needs, priorities, and community expectations, supporting participatory governance and evidence-informed decision-making.

Moreover, digital platforms enable scalability and flexibility in volunteer engagement. Warren, Hong, Rubin, and Uy (2009) emphasize that asynchronous communication allows volunteers from different geographic locations and time zones to contribute effectively, enhancing diversity and inclusivity in leadership development initiatives. Selwyn (2020) notes that these platforms can also integrate monitoring and evaluation systems, enabling leaders to assess impact, identify gaps, and adapt strategies in response to emerging challenges. Redecker and Punie (2017) further argue that opportunities for cross-cultural learning and collaborative problem-solving enhance both individual competencies and organizational capacity, demonstrating the broader potential of digital volunteerism for school leadership development.

Finally, the literature suggests that strategic planning and platform design are crucial to maximizing the benefits of digital volunteer engagement. Hustinx, Cnaan, and Handy (2019) highlight that clearly defined volunteer roles, structured feedback mechanisms, and recognition strategies enhance participation and sustainability. Musick and Wilson (2018) note that leaders who integrate volunteer input into formal decision-making processes are more likely to achieve measurable improvements in leadership capacity. Briones and Janoski (2021) emphasize that fostering a culture of engagement, accountability, and continuous learning ensures that digital volunteer platforms contribute meaningfully to long-term leadership development outcomes.

Global Perspectives and Best Practices

Digital volunteer platforms have been increasingly adopted in various educational contexts worldwide, offering valuable lessons for enhancing school leadership capacity. Goodall (2021) documents how schools in the United Kingdom utilize volunteer platforms to support strategic planning, leadership mentoring, and community engagement, resulting in improved relational trust and participatory governance. Briones and Janoski (2021) highlight similar initiatives in the United States, where volunteers provide specialized expertise in areas such as curriculum development, technology integration, and project management, enabling school leaders to implement innovative practices despite resource constraints. Hustinx, Cnaan, and Handy (2019) emphasize that cross-cultural engagement through digital platforms enriches leadership experiences by exposing leaders to diverse perspectives and problem-solving approaches.

In Australia and Canada, digital volunteer programs have been linked to leadership capacity building through structured mentorship and feedback mechanisms. Musick and Wilson (2018) note that these initiatives provide leaders with reflective learning opportunities, allowing them to refine decision-making skills and develop adaptive management competencies. Selwyn (2020) observes that digital storytelling from volunteers strengthens leaders' understanding of community needs, promoting culturally responsive and inclusive leadership practices. Warren, Hong, Rubin, and Uy (2009) further highlight the importance of platform design and usability, arguing that effective digital tools should enable collaboration, real-time feedback, and structured tracking of volunteer contributions to optimize leadership outcomes.

Global evidence also highlights the importance of supportive policies and governance frameworks in sustaining digital volunteer engagement. Redecker and Punie (2017) stress that clear guidelines, recognition mechanisms, and monitoring processes ensure the long-term effectiveness of volunteer programs. Goodall (2021) notes that institutional commitment, professional development opportunities, and integration of volunteer feedback into strategic planning enhance leadership outcomes. Briones and Janoski (2021) highlight that comparative studies of digital volunteer initiatives provide valuable insights into best practices, including role clarity, technological support, and culturally responsive engagement strategies. Collectively, these global perspectives illustrate that digital volunteer platforms, when strategically implemented, can significantly enhance school leadership capacity across diverse educational settings.

Finally, the literature suggests that synthesizing lessons from international contexts can inform context-specific strategies for digital volunteer engagement. Hustinx, Cnaan, and Handy (2019) argue that adaptation to local technological, cultural, and organizational conditions is essential for maximizing impact. Selwyn (2020) emphasizes that integrating evidence-based practices from global case studies allows school leaders to optimize volunteer contributions, strengthen relational networks, and foster participatory governance. Musick and Wilson (2018) conclude that leveraging digital volunteerism within a structured, policy-supported framework ensures sustainable leadership development, highlighting its transformative potential for schools worldwide.

Findings of the Study

The systematic review of mixed-methods research indicates that digital volunteer platforms have a measurable and multi-dimensional impact on school leadership capacity. Across the studies analyzed, Briones and Janoski (2021) report that leaders who actively engage with digital volunteers demonstrate enhanced strategic planning skills, improved problem-solving capabilities, and increased adaptability in complex school environments. These platforms allow leaders to access expertise that complements their existing knowledge, facilitating innovative approaches to administrative, pedagogical, and operational challenges.

Mixed-methods studies highlight that the integration of volunteer feedback into leadership practice strengthens relational and participatory dimensions of leadership. Musick and Wilson (2018) found that volunteer narratives and reflective feedback contribute to trust-building, communication, and collaboration between school leaders, staff, and the broader community. Hustinx, Cnaan, and Handy (2019) further emphasize that leaders develop social and emotional competencies, such as empathy, cultural sensitivity, and conflict resolution, through sustained volunteer engagement. This relational growth supports a participatory approach to decision-making, enabling leaders to align school initiatives with community needs effectively.

Global case studies demonstrate that structured digital platforms are more effective in promoting leadership development. Goodall (2021) highlights examples from the United Kingdom where formalized volunteer engagement strategies, including mentorship programs and project-based collaboration, result in measurable improvements in leadership capacity. Selwyn (2020) observes similar trends internationally, noting that leaders who systematically integrate volunteer contributions into planning and evaluation processes gain enhanced insight into organizational needs, resource allocation, and policy implementation.

Challenges such as digital inequality, inconsistent volunteer participation, and technological literacy gaps are recurring themes in the literature. Redecker and Punie (2017) note that these factors can limit the reach and effectiveness of digital volunteer initiatives, particularly in under-resourced or rural contexts. Nevertheless, when appropriate support structures, training, and recognition mechanisms are in place, these challenges can be mitigated, allowing schools to maximize the benefits of volunteer engagement. Warren, Hong, Rubin, and Uy (2009) conclude that digital volunteer platforms, when strategically designed and implemented, provide both tangible and intangible benefits, enhancing leadership competencies, relational networks, and community engagement simultaneously.

Overall, the findings suggest that digital volunteer platforms contribute to a holistic development of school leadership. They facilitate skill enhancement, reflective practice, and participatory governance, while also strengthening community relationships and fostering inclusive decision-making. The synthesis of mixed-methods research highlights that the effectiveness of these platforms depends on strategic planning, structured engagement, and contextually adapted implementation strategies, providing a roadmap for schools seeking to leverage digital volunteerism for leadership capacity building.

Implications of the Study

The findings of this systematic review carry significant implications for educational leadership practice. First, they highlight the transformative potential of digital volunteer platforms in enhancing both the operational and relational capacities of school leaders. Briones and Janoski (2021) argue that access to diverse expertise through these platforms allows leaders to implement evidence-informed strategies, optimize resource allocation, and enhance strategic planning. This suggests that schools should consider integrating digital volunteer engagement into their leadership development frameworks to promote adaptive and responsive management practices.

The relational dimension of leadership is also strengthened through volunteer engagement. Musick and Wilson (2018) emphasize that participatory interactions with volunteers foster trust, collaboration, and a sense of shared responsibility between leaders and the community. Hustinx, Cnaan, and Handy (2019) note that these relational competencies are critical for sustaining inclusive decision-making, managing conflict, and cultivating a culture of collaboration within schools. Therefore, leaders who leverage digital volunteer platforms can achieve not only skill-based improvements but also deeper relational outcomes that positively influence organizational culture.

The study also carries implications for policy and program design. Goodall (2021) highlights that structured engagement, formalized feedback mechanisms, and recognition of volunteer contributions enhance the effectiveness of digital platforms. Selwyn (2020) emphasizes the need for policy support to address challenges such as digital inequality, inconsistent participation, and technological literacy gaps. These insights suggest that educational authorities and school management teams should establish guidelines, support mechanisms, and training programs to maximize the benefits of digital volunteer initiatives.

From a research perspective, the findings highlight the value of mixed-methods approaches in capturing the complex and multi-dimensional outcomes of digital volunteer engagement. Redecker and Punie (2017) note that quantitative measures of leadership competency, combined with qualitative narratives, provide a comprehensive understanding of skill development, relational growth, and contextual adaptation. This implies that future studies should continue to employ mixed-methods designs to evaluate both measurable outcomes and the subtler relational and reflective impacts of digital volunteering on leadership development.

Finally, the global evidence reviewed indicates that contextually adapted implementation is crucial. Warren, Hong, Rubin, and Uy (2009) demonstrate that best practices from international contexts can inform local strategies, but adaptation to local technological, cultural, and organizational realities is necessary for maximizing impact. This suggests that school leaders should adopt flexible, evidence-informed approaches to volunteer engagement, ensuring that platforms are designed to meet both leadership development goals and community needs.

Solutions and Recommendations

To optimize the benefits of digital volunteer platforms for school leadership development, several strategic solutions are recommended. Briones and Janoski (2021) emphasize the importance of structured platform design, including clearly defined volunteer roles, interactive feedback systems, and monitoring tools that allow leaders to track contributions and outcomes. Establishing these frameworks ensures that volunteer engagement is purposeful, aligned with leadership objectives, and capable of generating measurable improvements in strategic planning, problem-solving, and operational efficiency.

Capacity-building initiatives for both school leaders and volunteers are essential. Musick and Wilson (2018) argue that training programs focusing on technological literacy, communication skills, and collaborative leadership practices enhance the effectiveness of digital volunteer engagement. Hustinx, Cnaan, and Handy (2019) further suggest that leaders should receive professional development in participatory decision-making, reflective practice, and stakeholder management to fully leverage volunteer contributions. By investing in capacity building, schools can ensure that both leaders and volunteers engage meaningfully, yielding sustainable leadership development outcomes.

The development of supportive policies and governance frameworks is also critical. Goodall (2021) highlights that institutional commitment, clear guidelines, and recognition of volunteer contributions enhance participation and motivation. Selwyn (2020) adds that policies addressing digital inequality, volunteer management, and accountability strengthen the implementation and impact of digital volunteer initiatives. Establishing these frameworks ensures that schools maintain a structured and sustainable approach to volunteer engagement, enhancing leadership outcomes over time.

Additionally, leveraging technology effectively is a key recommendation. Redecker and Punie (2017) emphasize the importance of user-friendly platforms that facilitate communication, feedback, and collaboration between leaders and volunteers. Warren, Hong, Rubin, and Uy (2009) note that integrating analytics and monitoring features allows leaders to evaluate the impact of volunteer contributions, adapt strategies, and make evidence-informed decisions. Proper technological integration maximizes efficiency and ensures that volunteer engagement translates directly into leadership capacity gains.

Finally, fostering a culture of collaboration and continuous learning is essential. Musick and Wilson (2018) argue that leaders should actively engage volunteers in decision-making processes, reflect on feedback, and integrate insights into leadership practice. Briones and Janoski (2021) note that recognizing and valuing volunteer contributions reinforces relational trust and participation. Hustinx, Cnaan, and Handy (2019) further highlight that creating opportunities for joint problem-solving, knowledge sharing, and mentorship strengthens both individual and organizational leadership capacity, ensuring sustainable and impactful outcomes.

RECOMMENDATIONS FOR FURTHER STUDY

While the systematic review highlights the positive impact of digital volunteer platforms on school leadership capacity, several areas warrant further research. First, longitudinal studies are recommended to assess the long-term effects of sustained volunteer engagement on leadership development. Briones and Janoski (2021) emphasize that understanding how leadership competencies evolve over time can provide valuable insights for designing continuous professional development programs and sustaining engagement strategies.

Second, research should explore the contextual factors that influence the effectiveness of digital volunteer platforms. Musick and Wilson (2018) argue that socio-economic conditions, cultural norms, technological infrastructure, and organizational policies significantly affect volunteer participation and leadership outcomes. Hustinx, Cnaan, and Handy (2019) suggest that comparative studies across diverse educational settings can identify best practices for adapting digital volunteer strategies to local contexts.

Third, further studies could examine the integration of emerging technologies, such as artificial intelligence and data analytics, in digital volunteer platforms. Selwyn (2020) notes that technological innovations can enhance monitoring, feedback, and decision-making processes, potentially amplifying leadership development outcomes. Redecker and Punie (2017) highlight the need to evaluate the ethical and practical implications of such technologies in educational leadership contexts.

Fourth, research should investigate the relational and socio-emotional dimensions of leadership development fostered through volunteer engagement. Goodall (2021) highlights that reflective practice, empathy, and trust-building are critical outcomes that are often captured qualitatively. Mixed-methods approaches that systematically evaluate these dimensions alongside measurable leadership competencies can provide a more comprehensive understanding of impact.

Finally, future studies should explore strategies to mitigate challenges such as digital inequality, inconsistent participation, and technological literacy gaps. Warren, Hong, Rubin, and Uy (2009) recommend research on innovative interventions, policy frameworks, and training programs that ensure equitable access and sustainable engagement. By addressing these gaps, future research can strengthen the evidence base for leveraging digital volunteer platforms to enhance school leadership capacity.

CONCLUSION

This systematic literature review demonstrates that digital volunteer platforms have significant potential to enhance school leadership capacity by fostering skill development, reflective practice, and participatory governance. Across the studies analyzed, evidence indicates that leaders who actively engage with digital volunteers improve strategic planning, problem-solving, and adaptive management competencies, while also strengthening relational networks with staff, students, and communities (Briones & Janoski, 2021; Musick & Wilson, 2018; Hustinx, Cnaan, & Handy, 2019).

The review highlights that mixed-methods research is particularly effective in capturing the multi-dimensional impact of digital volunteer engagement, combining quantitative measures of leadership competency with qualitative insights from reflective narratives and feedback. Selwyn (2020) and Redecker and Punie (2017) emphasize that these approaches allow for a comprehensive understanding of both tangible skill development and relational, emotional, and contextual aspects of leadership growth. The findings highlight that structured, well-supported, and contextually adapted platforms are essential for maximizing benefits and sustaining volunteer participation.

Challenges such as digital inequality, limited technological literacy, and inconsistent volunteer engagement remain critical considerations. However, evidence from global case studies demonstrates that these challenges can be mitigated through targeted training, policy support, and effective platform design (Goodall, 2021; Warren, Hong, Rubin, & Uy, 2009; Briones & Janoski, 2021). Ultimately, the review concludes that digital volunteer platforms represent a transformative opportunity for school leadership development, offering both practical tools and relational pathways to strengthen leadership capacity and foster participatory, community-oriented educational environments.

REFERENCES

Briones, R., & Janoski, T. (2021). Volunteer engagement and organizational impact in educational settings: Evidence from digital platforms. *Nonprofit and Voluntary Sector Quarterly, 50*(2), 345–365. DOI: 10.1177/0899764020965152

Cnaan, R. A., Handy, F., & Wadsworth, M. (1996). Defining who is a volunteer: Conceptual and empirical considerations. *Nonprofit and Voluntary Sector Quarterly, 25*(3), 364–383. DOI: 10.1177/0899764096253006

Denzin, N. K., & Lincoln, Y. S. (2018). *The SAGE handbook of qualitative research* (5th ed.). SAGE Publications.

Epstein, J. L. (2018). *School, family, and community partnerships: Preparing educators and improving schools* (2nd ed.). Routledge.

Flick, U. (2019). *An introduction to qualitative research* (6th ed.). SAGE Publications.

Goodall, J. (2021). Digital volunteering and leadership capacity in schools: Global lessons. *Journal of Educational Leadership, 15*(1), 45–62.

Henderson, A. T., Mapp, K. L., Johnson, V. R., & Davies, D. (2019). *Beyond the bake sale: The essential guide to family-school partnerships*. The New Press.

Hustinx, L., Cnaan, R., & Handy, F. (2019). Navigating theories of volunteering: A mixed-methods approach. *Voluntas, 30*(3), 431–450. DOI: 10.1007/s11266-019-00148-7

Musick, M., & Wilson, J. (2018). *Volunteers: A social profile*. Indiana University Press.

Redecker, C., & Punie, Y. (2017). *European framework for the digital competence of educators: DigCompEdu*. Publications Office of the European Union.

Selwyn, N. (2020). *Education and technology: Key issues and debates*. Bloomsbury Academic.

Warren, M. R., Hong, S., Rubin, C. L., & Uy, P. S. (2009). Beyond the bake sale: A community-based relational approach to parent engagement in schools. *Teachers College Record*, *111*(9), 2209–2254. DOI: 10.1177/016146810911100901

KEY TERMS AND DEFINITIONS

Digital Volunteer Platforms: Online systems that connect volunteers with organizations to contribute skills, time, or expertise, often facilitating feedback, communication, and task management (Briones & Janoski, 2021).

School Leadership Capacity: The collective skills, competencies, and relational abilities of school leaders to effectively manage, guide, and improve educational outcomes (Goodall, 2021).

Mixed-Methods Research: An approach combining quantitative and qualitative research methods to provide a comprehensive understanding of complex phenomena (Denzin & Lincoln, 2018).

Reflective Practice: A process by which leaders critically examine their experiences, decisions, and interactions to inform personal and professional growth (Selwyn, 2020).

Participatory Governance: A leadership and decision-making approach that actively involves stakeholders, including community members and volunteers, in shaping policies and practices (Henderson, Mapp, Johnson, & Davies, 2019).

Chapter 3
Capacity Building:
Skills, Technology, and Support Systems for Digital Volunteerism

Michael Oyedele Oyenuga
http://orcid.org/0000-0001-9921-5711
Woxsen University, Hyderabad, India

ABSTRACT

Capacity building is introduced as a necessity to empower digital volunteerism with better skills, more advanced technology and strong support systems. In today's fast-paced digital world, effective volunteer programs require more than just willing hearts, but rather a professional community of practice with contemporary digital skills. This chapter describes a multi-levelled strategy, including structured training programs, open-access online learning platforms and innovative digital services that promote asynchronous collaboration. The development of capacity in this case doesn't just come from increasing technical skills, but also creating support structures such as ongoing mentorship, real-time technical assistance and networking. Hence, organisations should seek to close the digital divide, support sustainable community engagement and inclusive digital participation in local online efforts, all contributing towards a more responsive and effective environment for digital volunteering.

DOI: 10.4018/979-8-3373-5722-5.ch003

INTRODUCTION

Digital volunteerism has become an important reality, especially in the urgent situations of a crisis. Technology has also changed the way in which people volunteer and promote service. In an era of heightened civic engagement, tech tools allow people to give their time or skills from anywhere, thereby magnifying the impact and reach of those who serve. Nevertheless, while online platforms operate to enable connection and participation, digital volunteerism is most definite in its success only if it builds on strong capacity-building efforts that equip volunteers with the skills, digital literacy, and support infrastructure (Hine, 2024; Whittaker et al., 2015; Bouarar et al., 2023).

To improve the skills of digital volunteers and organisations, capacity building is important. It includes training that increases digital literacy, knowledge of technology tools and the capacity to communicate effectively in virtual collaboration efforts. Training, particularly training on remote service delivery and digital platforms, is essential for volunteers to be able to actively participate in their communities (Whittaker et al., 2015; Park & Johnston, 2019). By creating an atmosphere that allows everyone to be supportive of one another and facilitates sharing knowledge and collaborative effort, digital volunteers are not only able but also skilled enough to make a measurable difference throughout the entire period of their service.

The use of technology in volunteering also has advantages and disadvantages. For example, IT tools can help to better coordinate between volunteers and organisations, thus present a connected front in responding to disasters and community support projects (Park & Johnston, 2017). Yet challenges like the digital divide, where certain groups lack access to technology, are preventing fair participation, which highlights the importance of policy action towards inclusive engagement on digital volunteering (Nowakowska, 2021; Chui & Chan, 2019).

Government and non-governmental organisations (NGO's) and education institutions remain key in the development and implementation of capacity-building models which are rooted in the specific needs of their volunteers. Such collaboration can help overcome challenges and maximise the potential of digital volunteerism to address social issues, particularly in times of public health emergencies or natural disasters (Bouarar et al., 2023; Sun et al., 2021).

This chapter explores conceptual foundations, types of digital volunteer activities, and strategies for capacity building, before examining institutional support and monitoring systems

CONCEPTUAL UNDERSTANDING

With technology and social media, digital volunteering is developing further than before, as people can now contribute their time and skills to a range of causes without leaving their computers. Digital volunteering includes online professional skills-based training, teaching and mentoring, supportive tasks like drafting and reviewing proposals, as well as advocacy on behalf of campaign patients. In this perspective, it is crucial to strengthen the need for capacity strengthening to make digital volunteers self-equipped and efficient through the enhancement of their skills, the provision of tools ensuring technological readiness and self-poweredness, as well as strong support systems. Capacity building is essential because it transforms digital volunteerism from informal participation into structured, impactful engagement. In a rapidly evolving digital landscape, volunteers must possess more than goodwill; they need the competencies, tools, and support systems to operate effectively across virtual platforms. Without targeted training, technological access, and mentorship, volunteers may struggle to contribute meaningfully or sustain their involvement. Capacity building ensures that individuals are not only digitally literate but also equipped to collaborate, manage projects, and uphold ethical standards in online environments. It bridges the gap between intention and execution, enabling volunteers to deliver high-quality service that aligns with organisational goals and community needs. To understand its scope, the next section examines the types of digital volunteer activities.

DEFINING DIGITAL VOLUNTEERISM AND VIRTUAL ENGAGEMENT

Digital volunteerism refers to any type of volunteering that occurs within a digital space, allowing for the support and participation in social causes without necessarily having to physically show up. This may involve delivering online tutorials, in social media campaigns, and community outreach on digital platforms (Ritchie & Jiang, 2021). With the rise of online communication as an effective channel for coordination and support, organisations are using these platforms more to recruit digital volunteers who may contribute from even further away through a variety of skills (Brix, 2019).

Types of Digital Volunteer Activities

Digital volunteerism encompasses a variety of activities, each tailored to utilise the unique skills and contributions of volunteers. These diverse activities (Table 1) underscore the adaptability and potential of digital volunteerism to meet varying community needs, creating opportunities for engagement and impact that transcend geographical boundaries. They are:

1. **E-Mentoring**: Digital platforms enable experienced professionals to provide mentorship remotely. E-mentoring can enhance knowledge transfer and skills development among individuals seeking guidance (Schech et al., 2019).
2. **Digital Advocacy**: Volunteers can engage in advocacy efforts using social media and online campaigns to raise awareness about critical issues, mobilising support and driving change effectively in larger communities (Forteh et al., 2025).
3. **Crowdsourcing**: This model enables organisations to harness the collective intelligence of a distributed group to solve problems. Volunteers can contribute ideas, data, or resources to initiatives ranging from disaster response to community development (Martono et al., 2021).

Table 1. Types of Digital Volunteer Activities

Activity	Description
E-Mentoring	Remote mentorship via digital platforms enables experienced professionals to guide others and foster skill development.
Digital Advocacy	Using social media and online campaigns to raise awareness, mobilise support, and drive change on critical social issues.
Crowdsourcing	Leveraging collective intelligence to solve problems; volunteers contribute ideas, data, or resources to initiatives like disaster response.

Callout: Digital volunteerism is redefining civic engagement, empowering individuals to contribute meaningfully across borders, disciplines, and time zones. Whether mentoring future leaders, amplifying voices for justice, or co-creating solutions to global challenges, these activities exemplify the power of technology-enabled altruism.

THE ROLE OF CAPACITY BUILDING IN ENHANCING VOLUNTEER IMPACT

Skills Development

Capacity building is the process of empowering digital volunteers and enabling them to effectively contribute to a multitude of different missions. This involves building appropriate capabilities through learning opportunities in digital literacy, online collaboration and technical skills (Naqshbandi et al., 2020; Oyenuga et al, 2025). For example, trainings to introduce volunteers to more technical software tools are shown to increase their self-efficacy in e-mentoring or digital advocacy roles by helping them feel more comfortable using technology (Villaseñor 2024).

Technology Access

In addition, access to technological facilities is essential in fostering digital volunteerism. Digitally enabled volunteers can effectively engage with local populations using a range of tools and platforms to promote shared endeavour and collective impact (Read et al., 2024).

Support Structures

Ongoing technical support and community-building initiatives likewise contribute to volunteers' experiences, which foster continued and engaged involvement in volunteer networks (Lee et al., 2019). Systems that support collaboration among volunteers and organisations can greatly multiply the effect of digital volunteerism. By establishing channels for knowledge-sharing, feedback and mentorship, firms create a culture of learning and adaptation that keeps volunteers constantly improving their abilities to make productive contributions (Dzulkifli et al., 2023). Building these support systems relies on developing communication pathways, access to resources and ensuring recognition of what volunteers are contributing (Aftab et al., 2020).

Figure 1. Capacity Building Pathway for Digital Volunteerism

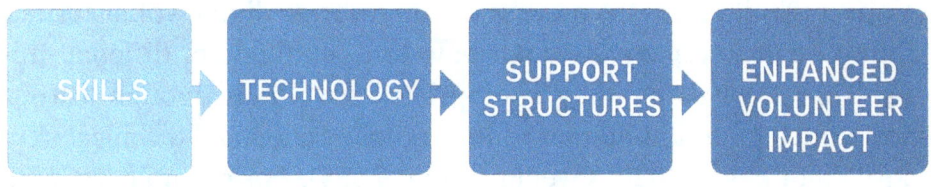

Skills, technology, and support systems interact to maximise volunteer effectiveness and impact.

Callout: The diagram shows how skills, technology, and support systems interact to maximise volunteer effectiveness and impact.

CORE COMPETENCIES AND SKILLS FOR DIGITAL VOLUNTEERS

Digital volunteerism has become a popular way for people to help with (and use their digital channels efficiently) various causes. To maximise the effectiveness of digital volunteers, it is important to understand specific competencies and skills that enable them. They include abilities to work with technology and across cultures, managing projects, being ethical in a digital world, protecting oneself online and having emotional intelligence (Fig. 2). It is not only good things to include on a resume and demonstrate through their work, but this aggregated improvement in competencies contributes to an extension of the capacity level for organisations working with digital volunteerism. These competencies are discussed below:

Digital Literacy and Online Communication Skills

Digital literacy is a prerequisite to participating in digital-volunteer initiatives, which includes the ability to access, interpret and use technology tools and systems for those individuals (López et al., 2023). Volunteers should have the ability to use digital communication tools so that they can work together, disseminate information and connect with their beneficiaries. Being facile with platforms such as video conferencing, social media, and cloud-based systems is critical because they facilitate effective virtual conversations and the sharing of information. The impact of digital communication strategies can help volunteers communicate more effectively and efficiently with their audiences, ensuring that the work they do is heard and makes a difference (Rotman et al., 2014).

Cross-Cultural Competence and Virtual Collaboration

An ability to foster cross-cultural competency is also ever more important in the contemporary globalising world, and particularly relevant for digital volunteers who are frequently involved with multicultural communities. Increasing awareness and understanding of the partners' culture helps maintain flexibility of language and communication, improving collaboration and engagement in virtual space (Eveleigh et al., 2014). Volunteers who can bridge cultural divides calmly and knowledgeably earn goodwill and relationship points that are key to successful volunteer matches. This ability is particularly pertinent for working with indigenous communities or disadvantaged populations, where knowledge of the local environment may enhance the cultural and effective delivery of services (Mittos et al., 2018).

Project Management and Remote Work Etiquette

Sensitive project management is crucial to the digital volunteering work being well-organised and productive. Digital volunteers frequently work on complex and coordinated societal challenges. Thus, the knowledge of project management principles could improve their contributions to projects by governing target, process and timeline (Adjekum et al., 2018). Furthermore, exhibiting appropriate remote work behaviour (e.g. being on time, clearly communicating and taking responsibility) is necessary for upholding professionalism and respect in virtual volunteering projects (Bowser et al, 2017).

Ethics, Digital Safety, and Data Privacy Awareness

The ethics of digital volunteerism must not be neglected, particularly on issues of data privacy and security. Volunteers need to be aware of ethical considerations when volunteering, including the importance of safeguarding sensitive information and being confidential when working with vulnerable groups (Herodotou et al. 2020). Appreciation of cyber policies and keeping data secure helps digital volunteers in responding appropriately and ethically, thereby building trust with their audience (Shoderu et al., 2024). Developing clear, detailed policies and conducting privacy-related training to educate the volunteers on how to approach and secure data are important for organisations trying to protect both participants and targets.

Emotional Intelligence and Empathy in Online Engagement

Finally, emotional intelligence and empathy are key to good digital volunteerism. Volunteers with high emotional intelligence can master interpersonal contact sensitively and responsively to the emotions and needs of interactants (Wiggins, 2013). This ability develops supportive atmospheres and improves service delivery. In virtual environments where emotionality cues are sometimes lessened, volunteers with high emotional intelligence can better manage conflict and establish rapport, as well as provide more effective support to our beneficiaries (Li, 2024).

Figure 2. Core Competencies and Skills for Digital Volunteers

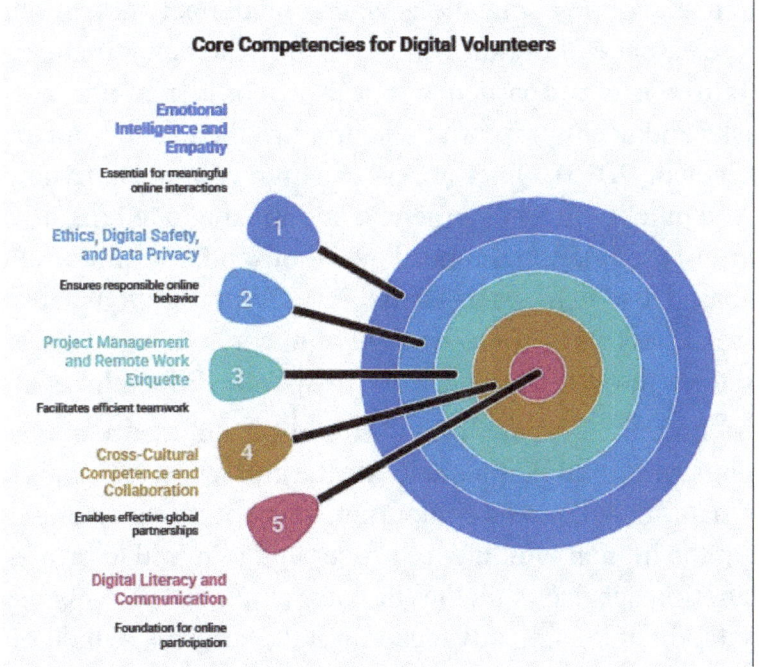

Callout: Digital volunteers require a multidimensional skillset to operate effectively across virtual platforms. These core competencies, ranging from digital literacy to emotional intelligence, form the foundation for inclusive, ethical, and impactful engagement in online civic spaces.

TECHNOLOGY ENABLERS FOR DIGITAL VOLUNTEERISM

Technology enablers for Digital Volunteerism are an important collection of tools and frameworks which can enable volunteers to respond to emergencies, disasters, community challenges and so forth using digital mediums such as digital platforms or ICT solutions. Such enablers combine the advantages of novel information communication technologies (ICTs) and digital platforms, enabling coordination, data analysis and faster volunteer response, allowing for scaling the scope of volunteerism in both emergency and non-crisis situations (Basheva & Ермолаева, 2020; Whittaker et al., 2015).

The use of distributed information and communication technologies (ICT), such as mobile applications, social media networks, or cloud services, is the essence of digital volunteerism. The technologies that allow volunteers to register and participate but also mobilise real-time information, assign tasks and access essential resources in the event of an emergency (Whittaker et al., 2015). Quick access to a high volume of participants can be deployed quickly in an emergency, and the mediated nature of digital platforms will provide some control over thousands or millions. For example, ICT-based dispatch systems and digital co-production platforms have been proven effective at coordinating volunteer action and integrating ad hoc volunteers into formal emergency response (Pilemalm et al., 2024).

Beyond coordination, the digitalisation of volunteerism has become synonymous with its ability to facilitate the collection and analysis of vast arrays of data. In volunteer computing, sense-making role assignments ensure that the human intelligence processing required to provide a high-quality curation service is met (Whittaker et al., 2015). This mechanism is greatly facilitated using advanced digital platforms, which offer those sourcing solutions tools for crowdsourcing, data analytics and geo-spatial mapping in ensuring that the flow of information is trustworthy and actionable. The utility of such technology-based enablers not only enhances emergency response effectiveness, but it also grows trust and openness in communities, providing the possibility for communication and accountability (Basheva & Ермолаева, 2020; Pilemalm et al., 2024).

Another essential digital volunteerism enabler is to include participatory systems that take advantage of new technologies. However, other technologies, such as distributed ledger technology (DLT) for increasing the security and trust of volunteer networks, are being researched but not necessarily well-implemented currently (Schneier et al., 2020). In addition, digital platforms with user-centred design and an emphasis on interoperability readily facilitate integration of the various actors (such as local governments, non-governmental organisations and informal volunteer groups). This coordination not only ensures that volunteer efforts are closely coordinated with official emergency responses but also minimises (where possible) legal and liability-related concerns of informal volunteering (Whittaker et al.2015

Furthermore, these investments can help ensure that digital volunteerism is sustainable over the long term and scalable by investing in strengthening our digital infrastructure and ability. Efforts to standardise digital platforms and encourage open data policies also emerge as critical for a (resilient) volunteer ecosystem. These efforts facilitate crisis management and are related to public participation and local communities' resilience (Basheva & Ермолаева, 2020; Pilemalm et al., 2024). The inclusion of such technological enablers in formal emergency management frameworks catalyses the paradigmatic shift from ad hoc volunteer contributions to strategic and organised resources that strengthen overall system-wide crisis management capacities for society.

In essence, enablement technologies for digital volunteerism are diverse, featuring ICT frameworks, mobile platforms, data analytics and emerging technologies to cohesively facilitate the coordination, security and scale of volunteering. Through connecting formal response structures with spontaneous volunteer initiatives of these enablers enhance the result associated with disaster management is enhanced, and creates cultures of civic-ness and social responsibility that are necessary for making communities resilient (Basheva & Ермолаева, 2020; Whittaker et al., 2015; Pilemalm et al., 2024).

Table 2. Comparison of Technology Enablers for Digital Volunteerism

Category	Examples	Function in Volunteerism	Limitations
ICT Tools	Email, Zoom, WhatsApp, Google Workspace, Microsoft Teams	Facilitate communication, coordination, document sharing, and virtual meetings	May exclude digitally underserved populations
Cloud Platforms	Google Drive, Dropbox, OneDrive	Enable remote access to files, collaborative editing, and data storage	Requires stable internet and digital literacy
Mobile Applications	VolunteerMatch, Be My Eyes, Red Cross apps	Connect volunteers to tasks, enable real-time updates and geo-tagging	Limited functionality on low-end devices
Data Analytics Tools	Power BI, Tableau, Google Analytics	Track volunteer engagement, measure impact, optimise resource allocation	Requires technical expertise and ethical safeguards
Emerging Technologies	Blockchain (DLT), AI chatbots, VR training modules	Enhance transparency, automate support, and simulate training environments	High cost, scalability challenges, and ethical concerns

Callout: Technology enablers determine the scope and effectiveness of digital volunteerism.

While ICT tools provide the foundation for communication and coordination, emerging technologies such as blockchain and AI expand transparency, scalability, and innovation. Together, they shape how volunteers connect, collaborate, and create measurable impact.

CAPACITY BUILDING STRATEGIES AND MODELS FOR DIGITAL VOLUNTEERISM

Skill-building is the bedrock to improving the impact of digital volunteerism, so that volunteers have the capabilities and resources they need to make a difference in their community. Capacity-development approaches should include a combination of digital-literacy training, cross-cultural skills development, project-management experience and an ethical lens and emotional intelligence.

Digital literacy is the base on which all other volunteering stands. It involves a set of skills, including the ability to use digital platforms effectively, attention to tools and sources and effective online communication (Younis et al., 2021). This is where digital literacy training programmes are vital, empowering volunteers with the skills they need to participate in virtual projects effectively, be it using collaboration tools such as Zoom or project management software like Trello and Slack. These tech infrastructures support volunteers to share ideas, plan and coordinate on tasks that are required for any effective volunteer activity (Whittaker et al., 2015).

In addition to technical skills, there is a need for the development of cross-cultural competency in digital volunteerism. It is about understanding and respecting the cultural differences and the values of various communities; this allows volunteers to carry out inclusive practices successfully (Baalharith & Aboshaiqah, 2024). Given that many digital volunteering initiatives are international in scope, developing cross-cultural skillsets might improve the quality of volunteer work as well as create opportunities for stronger engagement with recipients. This requires the education of volunteers in overcoming cultural barriers and empathy and respect to be used during volunteer interventions (Caldron et al., 2015).

There is also a need to manage volunteer activities so that work can be organised efficiently. Volunteers need an understanding of the key aspects of initiating, implementing and monitoring projects so they can make a significant contribution toward project objectives (Whittaker et al., 2015). Training in such areas (through e.g workshops, mentorship programs and online tools) can serve to enrich the skill set of volunteers, improving accountability and a result-oriented approach towards project objectives. Furthermore, the use of project management tools in a digital form may facilitate these activities and can enable volunteers to more effectively handle requirements through roles and responsibilities clarification (Whittaker et al., 2015).

Ethics and digital security are critical in the context of digital volunteerism, especially in relation to data privacy and ethical considerations around digital participation. And even if the informal nature of cooperation through voluntarism may seem to avoid the issue burdened by volunteers with ethical implications for their contribution, whether when processing sensitive data or dealing with vulnerable groups (Momdjian et al., 2024). Teaching ethics and best practices will help mitigate some of the risks related to data privacy violations, empower volunteers with knowledge about what they're doing in a digital environment. Organisations are responsible for implementing robust data protection protocols and procedures to safeguard volunteers and recipients as well (Grosman-Rimon & Wegier, 2024).

Emotional intelligence is also crucial, particularly in a digital world where we may not have to respond immediately or read someone's eyes when we are talking. Volunteers are armed with emotional intelligence that allows them to handle intricate social politics and demonstrate empathy, along with forming positive relationships amongst their peers as well as the intended benefit recipients (Noronha et al., 2023). The quality of digital volunteer contributions can increase by effectively implementing training programs that develop emotional intelligence, thereby serving as a conducive environment in which to make volunteers feel important and engaged (Noronha et al., 2023).

Figure 3. The Three Pillars of Capacity Building for Digital Volunteerism

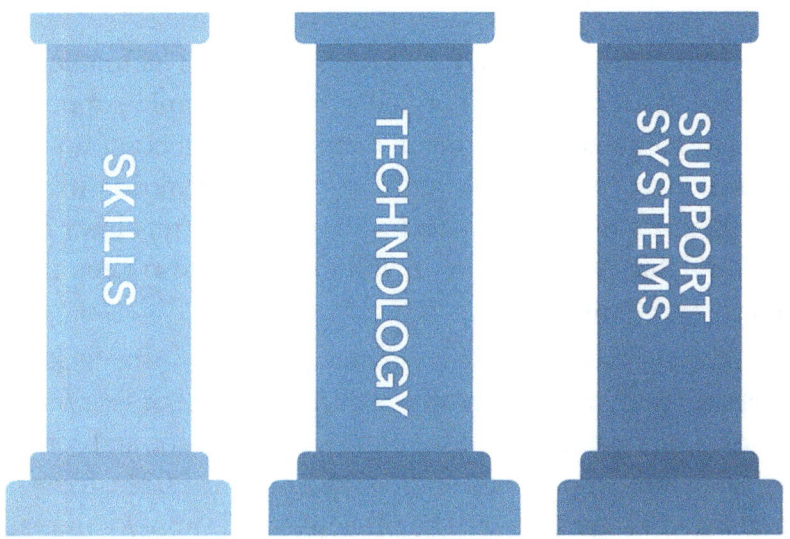

Callout: The figure shows the three pillars of capacity building for digital volunteerism: Skills, technology, and support systems, which collectively empower volunteers to engage inclusively, sustainably, and with measurable impact.

INSTITUTIONAL AND ORGANISATIONAL SUPPORT SYSTEMS

A. Volunteer Recruitment, Retention, and Recognition Frameworks

The enabling environment for successful digital volunteerism must rely on strong institutional and organisational systemic supports for the key aspects of volunteer recruitment, retention, and recognition. With the growing difficulty to recruit volunteers, and even more difficult when recruiting them for a digital context, such organisations have introduced formal models that not only role in volunteers but also keep them motivated and reward their input.

One of the key reasons behind volunteer turnover is the lack of institutional support received by a volunteer during his or her tenure. Effective organisational support can increase volunteer satisfaction and commitment, which subsequently improves retention (Mason et al. 2021). If, on the other hand, organisations are trying to be proactive and supply volunteers with resources and training material, their staff is likely to feel appreciated and sufficiently prepared for what's required of them. Furthermore, this influences their disposition to remain in the volunteer role and sets off a reinforcing spiral of commitment, whereby volunteers turn into advocates for the organisation (Pattinson et al., 2023). Digital volunteering may see reductions in feelings of feeling overwhelmed, if, through the provision of the necessary skill-based development, volunteers become more proficient and confident at digital volunteering (Kappelides et al., 2018).

Effective communication, with expectations and values explicitly stated, is necessary for ensuring good recruitment. Volunteers are more engaged and committed to their tasks if they can meaningfully see how their contribution aligns with members of the organisation (Simms et al., 2024). Organisations need to develop sound psychological contracts between them and their volunteers that are geared towards mutual expectations of support and appreciation. This builds trust and develops a supportive climate in which volunteers believe that their efforts are acknowledged and appreciated (Hamerman & Schneider, 2017; Stathi et al., 2020; Dekel et al., 2022). Besides, appreciation is a significant factor in helping keep volunteers motivated and connected. Research has consistently shown that there is a positive relationship between the satisfaction of volunteers and their retention if organisations have a structured process for recognising (awards, certificates or public acknowledgements) their contribution to the organisation (Mulder et al., 2015). This public acknowledgement is great for morale, rewarding individuals and building a culture of appreciation. Since digital volunteerism tends to draw a diverse community, ranging from novice volunteers in the form of young and technology-literate people, to industry professionals (Chow et al., 2021), customizing recruitment plans and recognition activities to meet the particular needs of these populations e.g., professional growth and development or community engagement, can also elevate retention rates and maximise volunteer program outcomes (Liu et al., 2019).

B. Role of NGOs, Governments, and Academic Institutions

Digital volunteerism is dependent on institutions and organisations to support its framework more than geographical terrain can offer the structure that informs the travel system, as well as providing order between input (i.e., coordination), making the digital volunteer program successful. In this perspective, NGOs, governments and universities have their specific but interdependent roles related to the effectiveness of digital volunteers.

NGOs are also nimble intermediaries, who are usually the ones leading from below with community-based and digitised operations to amplify community scaling and crisis interventions. Social computing applications and digital platforms allow NGOs to precisely serve as the intermediaries for volunteers, enabling quick communication and data collection, number assignment and coordination in real time among volunteers (Alonso et al., 2020). These institutions also serve as laboratories of innovation, crossing borders to exchange best practices and devise customised digital solutions to local problems. They play a particularly impactful role in emergencies; the speedy organising and dispatching of digital volunteer networks can be critical in aiding emergency responses of disaster management and refugee support (Alonso et al., 2020).

Governments can do so by providing the necessary laws and regulations, which will offer digital volunteerism a safe space to exist- amenable, open and responsible. National institutional setups, which are typically created to catalyse action towards the Sustainable Development Goals, combine different levels of government and stakeholder involvement in ways that are conducive to digital applications (Akhtar-Schuster et al., 2024). Governments also apply open digital government strategies and participatory platforms to increase transparency, public confidence of citizens in their activities, stimulating citizen participation and collaboration with digital volunteer networks (Sulaimani & Ozuem, 2022). These institutions work together with legal standards and policy instruments that ensure the purposes of sustainability in digital volunteerism, financial mechanisms, technical means and ICT infrastructures to support responsible ecosystems in the process (Akhtar-Schuster et al., 2024; Sulaimani & Ozuem, 2022).

Additionally, academia participates by assisting in developing, disseminating and evaluating digital volunteerism. Universities carry out interdisciplinary research into technological and socio-political aspects of digital networks for volunteers, providing evidence about how to improve responsibilities in the digital age across different territories. Academic institutions support digital literacy and the development of platforms for volunteer mobilisation and coordination through curriculum innovation, professional development, and joint research projects (Patrício & Ferreira, 2023). Moreover, through public scholarship and policy dialogue engagement, scholars can play a role in addressing the disconnect between theory and practice by making certain that digital volunteerism develops in response to newly emerging technological advancements and social demands (Patrício & Ferreira, 2023).

Figure 4. **Institutional Ecosystem Supporting Digital Volunteerism**

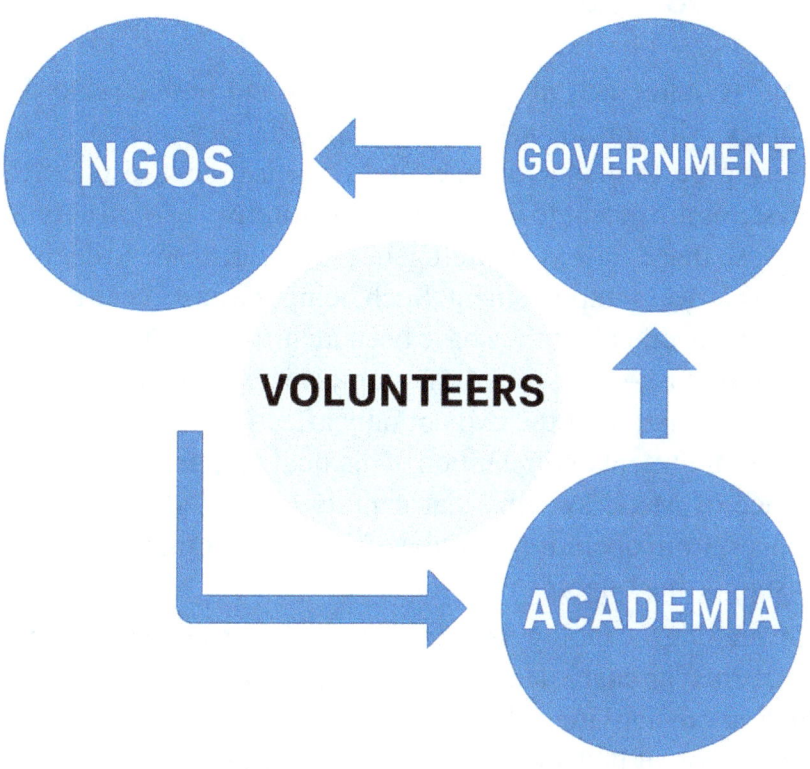

Institutional Ecosystem Supporting Digital Volunteerism

Callout: Institutional collaboration is the backbone of sustainable digital volunteerism.

NGOs mobilise communities, governments provide enabling policy and infrastructure, and academia contributes research and capacity building. Volunteers thrive when these actors work in synergy.

C. Monitoring and Evaluation (M&E) Systems for Digital Volunteer Engagement

Digital volunteerism in today's nonprofit and public sector is based on complex Monitoring and Evaluation (M&E) systems to measure volunteering performance, impact and organisational results. Rigorous M&E systems are meant to incorporate quantitative, as well as qualitative measures, so that data-based intelligence can inform sound decisions and continuous process improvement. Such being the case, central aspects of volunteer engagement, as they have been identified by Alfes et al. (2015), consist both of task-oriented and emotion-oriented organisational support, with the combination of the two not only affecting volunteer satisfaction but also commitment and retention. This dual emphasis underscores the importance of M&E systems that capture a constellation of volunteer experiences, from operational output efficiency through the psychosocial factors supporting ongoing commitment.

By leveraging technology, such as digital platforms and crowd networking tools, firms can enable real-time data collection and remote coordination of voluntourism activities. A case in point is Belina's (2023), which was a demonstration of how digital software can be used to monitor the work done by volunteers in an organised manner, measure engagement, and solicit feedback from participants. This relatively new translation of digital systems into traditional M&E practice allows organisations to monitor and evaluate more accurately and quickly. These technology solutions are usually built around dashboards and analytic modules, turning data into actionable information to better enable adaptive management approaches able to rapidly respond to new challenges or changes in volunteer behaviour.

In addition, the M&E system must focus not just on inputs and outputs (like attendance, task completion, or time spent) but also assess qualitative aspects like volunteer satisfaction, social value itself-perceived by the volunteer-and whether the work aligns with values (Traeger et al, 2022). Organisations may regularly survey volunteers, conduct focus groups and create digital feedback loops to measure the impact of supportive practices on volunteer engagement and retention to ensure that M&E systems are not used uniquely for transparency purposes but also facilitate continued learning in how best to manage volunteers.

Therefore, the digital voluntarism engagement revolution calls for an integrated approach in M&E systems design. By pairing hard data analysis with soft factors like organisational support and volunteer well-being, these systems offer essential actionable intelligence to connect digital transformation initiatives with volunteer results. The combination of sophisticated systems of data gathering and real-time monitoring, as well as systems for qualitative measurement, results in a stronger imperative to perform that helps generate both effective practices along with resilient networks of volunteers who move within the organisation's and environment's continuous dynamics (Alfes et al., 2015; Belina, 2023; Traeger et al., 2022).

POLICY FRAMEWORKS AND ETHICAL GUIDELINES FOR VIRTUAL VOLUNTEERING

COVID-19 and the adoption of digital platforms (Oyedele and Iember, 2022) have reiterated the call for clear policy frameworks and ethical guidelines to guide digital volunteerism. These structures serve to effectively coordinate volunteer initiatives and safeguard the rights, privacy, and health of both volunteers and beneficiary communities (Belina 2023). Clear guidelines also need to outline expectations, responsibilities, and accountability, which in turn contribute to trust and legitimacy of volunteer work in the digital realm.

The key to a successful policy framework for virtual volunteerism is the need for transparency, data protection and flexibility of participation. Digital platforms enable diverse groups to mobilise while policymakers and organisational leaders face pressures around key issues such as digital literacy, platform accessibility, and cybersecurity measures, including safeguarding against a loss of volunteer information with data breaches

(Indama, 2022). The digital governance methods also focus on open data policies, strong cybersecurity measures, and flexible training in digital ethics to contribute to a safe volunteer environment. Embedded in operational guidelines, these principles will enable organisations to ensure that volunteer services complement broader public service goals, while protecting the rights of individuals and ensuring fair participation.

Online policies for volunteer crowdsourcing are another concrete example of how ethical principles could take effect within a digital context. Recently, targeted nudging mechanisms and task allocation policies that maximise volunteer engagement while respecting individual autonomy and privacy have been examined in Manshadi and Rodilitz (2022). These policies promote clear communication about task expectations, data use consent, and periodic reporting on the effects and results of volunteer contributions. Implementing these types of safeguards can mean that volunteers working for such organisations are treated ethically, and that their input is adequately acknowledged and accessible under some set of regulatory standards.

CASE STUDIES AND GLOBAL BEST PRACTICES

Youth-Led Digital Volunteer Movements (UN Online Volunteers, African Union Youth Corps)

Youth-led digital volunteer movements are arising as a potential transformational force in global civic engagement, driven by the intersection of new forms of digital technology and high levels of digitally mediated youth activism. This kind of activism, embodied in campaigns such as UN Online Volunteers and the African Union Youth Corps, illustrates how digital tools can democratize participation, amplify the voices of marginalised populations, and help stimulate developmental change across global borders (Marah et al., 2024; Dubé, 2025).

One of the key drivers behind these movements is social media and digital communication by which to enact, organise volunteerism. As Dubé (2025) further emphasises, the role of virals in transforming information into narratives and actions is central to how activists used social media for empowerment. This digital capacity enables young volunteers to circumvent formal gatekeeping mechanisms and interact directly with community problems, which leads to a more sensitive and responsive type of volunteer activity. In the UN Online Volunteers, for example, digital connections are used to bring together youth from different parts of the world with projects that address local issues to amplify volunteer efforts and generate cross-cultural learning and collaboration (Dubé 2025).

In Africa, the African Union Youth Corps and other similar movements show how digital volunteer efforts may be fitted to country-specific contexts, supporting continental development goals. Ayamga et al. (2023) explore the impact of digitalisation in forming partnerships, how it is leveraged for cooperation between and among organisations, as well as participation by young Africans in the digitalisation of agriculture. This instance serves as an example to demonstrate that youth-led digital volunteer movements are less about immediate humanitarian and civic engagement than they are about long-term institutional emergence and inter-organisational relations. These movements promote digital literacy and networks of experience through targeted capacity building for long-term trust-based relationships to foster socio-economic growth. Marah et al. (2024) underline that youth engagement in global governance calls for considerable institution-building and strategic investments. Lessons learned from cases such as UN Online Volunteers demonstrate that when global organisations make investments in robust digital infrastructure and capacity-building, youth-led digital volunteer movements have the potential to meaningfully contribute to policy processes and global governance mechanisms. This kind of institutional backing will validate these movements and ensure they are part and parcel of hunger frameworks, making them more convincing with an appeal for longer support.

Community-Based Initiatives Leveraging Social Media for Digital Good

Social media-connected community-led initiatives for digital good have arisen as powerful instruments to strengthen local resilience, mitigate misinformation and help create more inclusive communication. They use commonly available digital platforms to activate and engage community members, disseminate accurate information, and facilitate context-specific capacity building efforts. Cuadra and Cotoron (2025) explain how local capacity-building intervention in disaster risk management can counteract misinformation by empowering persons of community responsibility, optimising media fusion and opening a clear line of communication between locals. This helps communities to also resist misinformation and develop a more coherent response during emergencies.

These kinds of social media programs are also key in the fight against hate speech and promoting digital civility. Pukallus and Arthur (2024) examine a strategy of tailoring regulation with digital citizenship education programs that rebuild people´s civil-communicative skills to resist hateful online speech and keystone local, evidence-based interventions that reduce hate online. This twin strategy may show the possibility of social media being used as a tool in community empowerment and its strengthening of social solidarity.

Additionally, programs which link in-person capacity building with digital platforms have also yielded encouraging results in crises. Asteria et al. (2023) present how capacity building can be incorporated in efforts aimed at combating false information concerning disasters. Social media, when it is used as a mechanism for sharing valuable and accurate information, can be harnessed to make people get up off their butts in times of crisis or stress. These processes contribute to community long-term sustainability, developing mechanisms for sustained interaction and capacity building.

In addition, digital approaches have been used in health promotion for sharing important information and promoting changes in behaviour. Ali et al. (2021) describe digital volunteer programmes in India that use social media for the dissemination of health and nutrition Messaging During COVID-19. These programs indicate that successful social media campaigns, integrated with targeted initiatives via communities, can help amplify health promotion messages and empower local community members with the tools necessary to make informed decisions.

University-Based Digital Volunteer Hubs and Service-Learning Models

Digital volunteer hubs, which are university-based service-learning models, have come into being as innovative architectures to blend both academic rigour and community engagement. These models reinforce the third mission of the university by learning through volunteering as a form of educational resources, satisfying student needs while solving social problems (Buyakova & Malkova, 2021). Service-learning classes give students a chance to apply classroom understanding in real-life situations using structured volunteer projects, and aid the development of softer skills, civic responsibility, and professional competencies (Buyakova & Malkova, 2021; Boppre et al., 2022). By utilising digital platforms, these programs can also increase the flexibility and scalability of community service efforts to be more inclusive across different geographical regions and cultures (Li-li & Jialin, 2023).

University online volunteer nodes are centralised places to organise volunteer projects, work on digital cooperation and community involvement. At the centre of this ecosystem are faculty, who broker relationships with community organisations and weave curated digital volunteering initiatives into course curricula (Almudhaybri, 2025). Through hubs such as these, students can access digital tools and training to facilitate meaningful volunteerism that contributes to both national development imperatives and academic outcomes, as well as witness initiatives aligned with Saudi Arabia's Vision 2030. Additionally, these types of platforms also motivate peer-to-peer learning and cross-disciplinary collaborations, which reduce the gulf between theoretical training and its practical applications (Kwon-Sang-Cheol & Young-Hoon Oh, 2021).

In a digital landscape, service-learning models also help in the transformation of higher education by driving curricular change and increasing experiential learning impact. Through the combination of digital volunteer hubs and service-learning pedagogy, universities encourage mutualistic relationships between communities and higher education institutions (Kwon & Oh, 2021). Students learn experientially while communities are digitally coordinated. This symbiotic method, which produces lifelong learning and better global competitiveness in addition to strengthening the role of doing training responsibilities by the university for social transformation and sustainable development (Li-li & Jialin, 2023; Madjid & Safriani, 2023).

Corporate Social Responsibility (CSR) and Skilled E-Volunteering

Skilled e-volunteering is becoming more of a part of Corporate Social Responsibility (CSR) as a strategic tool for benefiting society, the business, and the employee. Companies that believe that encouraging staff to share professional skills, such as computer support, marketing and legal advice or engineering capabilities, on digital platforms can work wonders. These programs not only help to meet larger societal goals, but they also enhance employee skill development and job satisfaction through the provision of opportunities for skill use and creative problem solving. Additionally, they improve the organisation's CSR reputation among consumers and stakeholders, thus resulting in higher brand loyalty and trust (Plewa et al., 2014; Caligiuri et al., 2013).

Additionally, the use of digital platforms in employment volunteering programs makes it easier for companies to find the right nonprofit that their employees would be good at. Digital tools increase transparency, streamline communication, and enable real-time tracking of volunteer work across the organization to ensure CSR can be meaningfully optimised for strategic impact. Through digital volunteer management systems, companies can monitor performance indicators and collect feedback to help implement improvement processes. This measure of effectiveness helps us adjust tasks to ones more suitable with the knowledge and desires of the volunteers (Barkay, 2012). Customised assignments create meaning and community amongst employees, which is associated with increased organisational identification, higher levels of work engagement (Caligiuri et al., 2013). Furthermore, evidence shows that consumers perceive companies proactively encouraging skilled e-volunteering as more socially responsible and ethical, thereby resulting in a competitive advantage in the conscious markets (Plewa et al., 2014). Corporate volunteering programs focusing on employees' learning and development in the community foster a win-win-win situation; they help nonprofit organisations receive high-quality services from volunteers; support professional identity formation among employees; and strengthen corporate performance by improving its (economic and ethical) credibility (Caligiuri et al., 2013). Thereby, companies that integrate expertise-based e-volunteering into their CSR programs help support sustainable community development and benefit from talent retention, more motivated employees or even boosted innovation inside the company (Oyenuga, 2026).

CHALLENGES AND RISKS IN DIGITAL VOLUNTEERISM

One major problem of digital volunteerism is that the global volunteering world contradicts itself. Lough (2019) further notes that although technological advancements and the integration of volunteering types have broadened the domain of digital volunteerism, both trends come with resource limitations and varying levels of infrastructure. These tensions result in discrepancies in individuals' engagement, leading to locally non-uniform outcomes and hindering transnational volunteering actions.

In digitalised co-production models, the most challenging are the organisational and ICT-related issues. Pilemalm et al. (2025) argue that construction information systems research often has unclear roles as well as constraining potentials to utilise local knowledge and end-user involvement in the development of ICT systems. Such conditions not only hinder coordination but also make volunteers more prone to miscommunication and to being overwhelmed in crises. Alkusaibati (2024) adds that efforts toward digital volunteerism in high-pressure emergency settings can potentially have the unintentional consequence of burdening professional response with like (non-professional) participation not adequately coordinated or resourced.

A further great danger is that of cybersecurity, data protection and the authenticity of information. Online platforms that facilitate volunteer interactions naturally produce large amounts of sensitive information, potentially susceptible to leakages or misuse. Whittaker et al. (2015) argue that the rapid proliferation of digital volunteer platforms can exacerbate concerns about legal liability and data quality, especially when volunteers are using less-regulated forms of digital interaction. Another review on digitalised co-production in emergency response suggests that the digitisation of volunteer efforts can create challenges for ensuring accurate verification of crowdsourced data, thus generating fears about misinformation contributing to public distrust during emergencies ("Digitalized Co-production and Volunteerism in Emergency Response: A Literature Review," 2023).

Participatory sensing models, such as those implemented by digital disease detection, can further complicate the picture of learning by creating new privacy and ethical risks. Susumpow et al. (2014) discuss the intricate process of integrating volunteer-based health information into public-health systems; though such participatory practices provide novel opportunities for detecting and responding to outbreaks, findings can also become widely misinterpreted if they are not accurately vetted or placed in context.

Finally, the obstacles and dangers in digital volunteerism are complicated to involve infrastructural discrepancies, organisational waste, information security vulnerability and data authenticity problems. Overcoming these challenges effectively demands well-crafted regulatory frameworks, digital preparedness, and capacity for training and oversight. These interventions are important for protecting the welfare of volunteers, securing digital data and structures to support it, and increasing the effectiveness and sustainability of digital volunteer activities.

POSSIBLE SOLUTIONS TO THE CHALLENGES

By focusing on the problems and risks for digital volunteerism, there is a need to integrate technical, organisational, legal and human views. One major obstacle is the lack of digital infrastructure and the requirement for modernised volunteer management. In this line, also Iraqi (2025) identifies that numerous digitally cultivated voluntarism projects are constrained to the technology of the past, which do not allow immediate interactions; subsequently, a modernisation of the computer-based platforms, as well as an integration in contemporary management formats, would be necessary. Moreover, stronger digital platforms can enable cost-efficient and inclusive operations if non-profits make the requisite investments in ICT tools and organisational development(Oyenuga et al, 2025).

Another challenge was around legal liability and regulatory issues that can limit greater involvement of informal volunteers. Whittaker et al. (2015) highlight the lack of a volunteer culture and legal ambiguity as barriers to volunteer engagement during emergencies. To overcome these risks, emergency management policy needs to be adaptive and inclusive with clear definitions of role, responsibility, and the legal status for volunteers. Such a policy context can be complemented by the standardisation of protocols promoting transparency, accountability, and data security.

Furthermore, volunteer welfare is at great risk for wearing as high in high-stress environments, ranging from conflict zones. Blyznyuk and Sobakar (2024) mention the problem of emotional burnout, stress and the non-compliance between tasks that are assigned to a person who is involved in volunteer work at conflict zones. In response to these concerns, organisations need to build into their digital volunteer programmes mental health support, realistic allocation of tasks, regular check-ins and debriefs. A training module (Fasanmi et al, 2024; Omale et al, 2024) and a support counselling system are necessary to help volunteers realise what their boundaries should be and still function effectively in a crisis.

The introduction of citizens as operators in emergency response systems also has strong digital integration challenges, especially concerning the management of information reliability and what concerns the incorporation of spontaneous participation into professional systems. Alkusaibati (2024) stresses the need to clear lines of roles in regards digitalised co-production and volunteers that can complement, rather than overshadow licensed responders. This is possible by implementing a structured digital platform that embodies feedback in real time, clear distribution of tasks and a verified information channel (Basheva & Ермолаева, 2020).

Lastly, issues at an organisational level regarding digitalised integration can be tackled through a comprehensive model of digitalised cocreation. As Pilemalm et al. (2025) suggest that by rethinking current typologies of digital co-production in more sustainable ways, which include local knowledge and end-user as well as systemic perspectives. That doesn't just mean improving technical compatibility but finding ways to work more closely with non-profits, government agencies and volunteer groups(Oyenuga & Jeresa, 2025; Oyedele, 2025).

In essence, tackling digital volunteer-based challenges and risks is a multi-faceted endeavor that involves updating state of the art in digital infrastructure and management (Iraqi, 2025), embedding the appropriate legal structures to alleviate responsibility concerns (Whittaker et al., 2015), providing disciplines for matching volunteers' feelings with realistic tasks within a crisis context (Blyznyuk & Sobakar, 2024), implementing reliable data confirmation and job descriptions systems (Alkusaibati, 2024; Basheva & Ермолаева, 2020) and adopting advanced co-production approaches to improve organizational integration (Pilemalm et al., 2025). In aggregate, these measures will go a long way to turning digital volunteer efforts into robust, accountable and impactful vehicles for social good.

IMPLICATIONS

Digital volunteerism capacity building is becoming a critical enabler of virtual volunteering efforts. As more organisations rely on digital tools for recruiting, organising and supporting volunteers, there needs to be investment in models and structures that build digital literacies of individuals, upgrade a technological infrastructure, and create stronger support networks. Following this line of reasoning, Madsen and Brix (2024) argue that building digital innovation capabilities is a requisite for individuals´ competencies and an antecedent to the effective learning and development of organisations (Omale et al, 2024). This means that specific types of training, mentoring and ongoing professional development that address the changing technological landscape and the differing requirements of volunteer populations are required in relation to digital volunteerism (Oyedele et al, 2024).

In addition, the development of capacity must go far beyond just technical capacities; it should include the underlying structures that foster organisational endurance and change. Pankova and Kasperovych (2022) argue that in the conditions of a pressured environment, when it comes to armed conflicts, there is a great potential for digital volunteerism if the opportunities opening because of digitalisation can be utilised through

ICT-based support. That means investment in cutting-edge digital tools, real-time data analysis and the integration of collaborative platforms is key to keeping those volunteers engaged and effective. Implementing such support systems also contributes to bridging the digital divide as they offer volunteers access to updated technologies and expertise, and increase the effectiveness of digital volunteers.

Moreover, embedding capacity-building programs into digital volunteerism may result in beneficial feedback loops. Access to superior digital skills improves volunteer performance, develops organisational capacity and drives innovation in service provision. Along with an emphasis on emotional intelligence, resilience and learnability, these create a context that encourages digital volunteerism. Sustainable digital volunteerism is therefore not so much about the immediate development of skills as it is about building a mechanism for continuous improvement in relation to both challenges and opportunities.

CONCLUSION

Digital volunteering keeps growing, especially within a context of worldwide technological acceleration and increasing needs for social change. This chapter has looked at what is needed to train and support digital volunteers in terms of the acquisition of skills, the use of technology, and the provision of strong support networks.

First, providing people with the skills needed for digitally based volunteer activities helps to ensure that they can be effective and supportive. Broad-based training modules on the internet, communication and digital platforms, along with project planning and cultural competencies, can shape the crucial role that volunteers play in diverse social movements. Such initiatives should be flexible and dynamic, continually adjusted to meet the changing demands of technology and communities that interact with volunteer engineers.

Technology is also a key enabler of digital volunteering. Utilisation and integration of digital tools and platforms. Digital tools can help people collaborate, extend outreach and make communication with volunteers efficient. Key points on new technologies for supporting volunteers are presented, including mobile applications, social media and collaboration tools suitable for use in the field. Providers will need to make investments in such technologies by allowing access, giving training, and delivering continuing support on how volunteers can utilise them.

Furthermore, the value of support can never be overstated. Investing in a strong ecosystem, including mentoring, community engagement and organisational support, can help digital volunteers feel connected and motivated. When organisations create a space where volunteers feel appreciated and in connection with one another, they'll engage more of them to retain them while also creating a culture around constant learning and doing better.

Therefore, the development of digital volunteering capacity requires integrated intervention in skill, technology and community. By focusing on these building blocks, organisations can harness the power of digital volunteers to amplify community efforts, drive social change and tackle key global problems. Governments, non-profits and community organisations must work to construct enduring frameworks to empower digital volunteers and enable their critical contributions in society.

REFERENCES

Adjekum, A., Blasimme, A., & Vayena, E. (2018). Elements of trust in digital health systems: Scoping review. *Journal of Medical Internet Research*, *20*(12), e11254. DOI: 10.2196/11254 PMID: 30545807

Aftab, W., Siddiqui, F., Tasic, H., Perveen, S., Siddiqi, S., & Bhutta, Z. (2020). Implementation of health and health-related sustainable development goals: Progress, challenges and opportunities – a systematic literature review. *BMJ Global Health*, *5*(8), e002273. DOI: 10.1136/bmjgh-2019-002273 PMID: 32847825

Akhtar-Schuster, M., Stringer, L., & Barger, N. (2024). Fast-tracking action on the sustainable development goals by enhancing national institutional arrangements. *PLoS One*, *19*(3), e0298855. DOI: 10.1371/journal.pone.0298855 PMID: 38507393

Alfes, K., Shantz, A., & Bailey, C. (2015). Enhancing volunteer engagement to achieve desirable outcomes: What can non-profit employers do? *Voluntas*, *27*(2), 595–617. DOI: 10.1007/s11266-015-9601-3

Ali, F., Paswan, S., Bennett, G., Pradhan, R., Nadagouda, S., & Choudhury, S. (2021). Leveraging digital platforms for disseminating health and nutrition information during COVID-19: Reflections from project samvad in india. *Journal of Global Health Reports*, *5*. Advance online publication. DOI: 10.29392/001c.22121

Alkusaibati, W. (2024). Digitalized co-production of emergency response: using volunteers as first responders.. https://doi.org/DOI: 10.3384/9789180756488

Almudhaybri, T. (2025). The role of faculty members at Qassim University in digital volunteering in light of Saudi Arabia's vision 2030. *IJESA*, *4*(4), 337–372. DOI: 10.59992/IJESA.2025.v4n4p14

Alonso, R., Thoene, U., & Benavides, D. (2020). Social computing applications as a resource for newly arrived refugees in Kronoberg, Sweden. *Digital Policy Regulation and Governance*, *23*(1), 21–44. DOI: 10.1108/DPRG-05-2020-0063

Asteria, D., Surpi, N., Brotosusilo, A., & Suja'i, I. (2023). Integration of local capacity building in countering false information about disaster into community-based disaster risk management. *IOP Conference Series. Earth and Environmental Science, 1275*(1), 012028. DOI: 10.1088/1755-1315/1275/1/012028

Ayamga, M., Lawani, A., Akaba, S., & Birindwa, A. (2023). Developing institutions and inter-organizational synergies through digitalization and youth engagement in African agriculture: The case of "africa goes digital". *Land (Basel), 12*(1), 199. DOI: 10.3390/land12010199

Baalharith, I., & Aboshaiqah, A. (2024). Virtual healthcare revolution: Understanding nurse competencies and roles. *SAGE Open Nursing, 10*, 23779608241271703. Advance online publication. DOI: 10.1177/23779608241271703 PMID: 39161935

Barkay, T. (2012). Employee volunteering: Soul, body and CSR. *Social Responsibility Journal, 8*(1), 48–62. DOI: 10.1108/17471111211196566

Basheva, O., & Ермолаева, П. (2020). The phenomenon of digital volunteerism in emergency situations: Its essence, types and theoretical framework. *Vestnik Instituta Sotziologii, 11*(1), 49–71. DOI: 10.19181/vis.2020.11.1.625

Belina, A. (2023). Digital volunteering through a volunteering crowdsourcing platform: lessons from tudu.org.pl. Voluntary Sector Review, 14(3), 557-566. https://doi.org/DOI: 10.1332/204080522X16546738241352

Blyznyuk, T., & Sobakar, M. (2024). Risks in volunteer activities during the war in Ukraine. *Ukrainian Journal of Applied Economics, 9*(2), 39–43. DOI: 10.36887/2415-8453-2024-2-6

Boppre, B., Reed, S., & Belisle, L. (2022). "real students helping others": Student reflections on a research-based service-learning project in a gender and victimization course. *Journal of Experiential Education, 46*(3), 281–303. DOI: 10.1177/10538259221134873

Bouarar, A., Mouloudj, S., Umar, T., & Mouloudj, K. (2023). Antecedents of physicians' intentions to engage in digital volunteering work: An extended technology acceptance model (TAM) approach. *Journal of Integrated Care*, *31*(4), 285–299. DOI: 10.1108/JICA-03-2023-0017

Bowser, A., Shilton, K., Preece, J., & Warrick, E. (2017). Accounting for privacy in citizen science., 2124-2136. https://doi.org/DOI: 10.1145/2998181.2998305

Brix, J. (2019). Innovation capacity building. *The Learning Organization*, *26*(1), 12–26. DOI: 10.1108/TLO-08-2018-0143

Buyakova, C. & Malkova, I. (2021). Volunteering as a form of students' educational activities in the context of the university's third mission. Vysshee Obrazovanie v Rossii = Higher Education in Russia, 30(8-9), 69-79. DOI: 10.31992/0869-3617-2021-30-8-9-69-79

Caldron, P., Impens, A., Pavlova, M., & Groot, W. (2015). A systematic review of social, economic and diplomatic aspects of short-term medical missions. *BMC Health Services Research*, *15*(1), 380. Advance online publication. DOI: 10.1186/s12913-015-0980-3 PMID: 26373298

Caligiuri, P., Mencin, A., & Jiang, K. (2013). Win–win–win: The influence of company-sponsored volunteerism programs on employees, NGOs, and business units. *Personnel Psychology*, *66*(4), 825–860. DOI: 10.1111/peps.12019

Chow, C., Goh, S., Tan, C., Wu, H., & Shahdadpuri, R. (2021). Enhancing frontline workforce volunteerism through exploration of motivations and impact during the COVID-19 pandemic. *International Journal of Disaster Risk Reduction*, *66*, 102605. DOI: 10.1016/j.ijdrr.2021.102605 PMID: 34603950

Chui, C., & Chan, C. (2019). The role of technology in reconfiguring volunteer management in nonprofits in Hong Kong: Benefits and discontents. *Nonprofit Management & Leadership*, *30*(1), 89–111. DOI: 10.1002/nml.21369

Cuadra, J., & Cotoron, V. (2025). Addressing false information through local capacity building in community-based disaster risk management. *Jàambá, 17*(1), a1836. Advance online publication. DOI: 10.4102/jamba.v17i1.1836 PMID: 40357013

Dekel, G., Geldenhuys, M., & Harris, J. (2022). Exploring the value of organizational support, engagement, and psychological wellbeing in the volunteer context. *Frontiers in Psychology, 13*, 915572. Advance online publication. DOI: 10.3389/fpsyg.2022.915572 PMID: 36160559

Digitalized Co-production and Volunteerism in Emergency Response. A literature review. (2023). *Proceedings of the . . . International ISCRAM Conference.* https://doi.org/DOI: 10.59297/ARQO2281

Dubé, M. (2025). Youth activism and the power of social media to drive social change. *International Journal for Multidisciplinary Research, 7*(2), 42967. Advance online publication. DOI: 10.36948/ijfmr.2025.v07i02.42967

Eveleigh, A., Jennett, C., Blandford, A., Brohan, P., & Cox, A. (2014). Designing for dabblers and deterring drop-outs in citizen science., 2985-2994. https://doi.org/DOI: 10.1145/2556288.2557262

Fasanmi, O. O., Olusanya, B. B., & Oyenuga, M. O. (2024).. . *Entrepreneurial Training as a Retirement Succorance for Nigerian Retirees Twist, 19*(4), 137–147. DOI: 10.5281/zenodo.10049652#321

Forteh, E., Ngemenya, M., Kwalar, G., Alembong, E., Tanue, E., Kibu, O., & Nsagha, D. (2025). Determinants of the use of digital one health amongst medical and veterinary students at the University of Buea, Cameroon. https://doi.org/DOI: 10.1101/2025.04.16.25325946

Grosman-Rimon, L., & Wegier, P. (2024). With advancement in health technology comes great responsibility – ethical and safety considerations for using digital health technology: A narrative review. *Medicine, 103*(33), e39136. DOI: 10.1097/MD.0000000000039136 PMID: 39151529

Hamerman, E., & Schneider, A. (2017). The role of disgust sensitivity in volunteer recruitment and retention. *International Journal of Nonprofit and Voluntary Sector Marketing*, *23*(2), e1597. Advance online publication. DOI: 10.1002/nvsm.1597

Herodotou, C., Aristeidou, M., Miller, G., Ballard, H., & Robinson, L. (2020). What do we know about young volunteers? an exploratory study of participation in zooniverse. *Citizen Science: Theory and Practice*, *5*(1), 2. Advance online publication. DOI: 10.5334/cstp.248 PMID: 35795590

Hine, C. (2024). Making sense of digital volunteering: relational and temporal aspects of the digital volunteer experience. Voluntary Sector Review, 1-19. DOI: 10.1332/20408056Y2024D000000032

Indama, V. (2022). Digital governance: Citizen perceptions and expectations of online public services. *ISSLP*, *1*(2), 12–18. DOI: 10.61838/kman.isslp.1.2.3

Iraqi, A. (2025). Towards a new form of volunteering 2.0: a survey at apsopad international. jlsdgr, 5(1), e02548. https://doi.org/DOI: 10.47172/2965-730X.SDGsReview.v5.n01.pe02548

Kappelides, P., Cuskelly, G., & Hoye, R. (2018). The influence of volunteer recruitment practices and expectations on the development of volunteers' psychological contracts. *Voluntas*, *30*(1), 259–271. DOI: 10.1007/s11266-018-9986-x

Lee, C., Goh, D., Sin, S., Osop, H., & Theng, Y. (2019). A crowdsourcing approach to explore helping motives in a smart city: A preliminary analysis. *Proceedings of the Association for Information Science and Technology*, *56*(1), 701–702. DOI: 10.1002/pra2.142

Li, T. (2024). Analysis of personal privacy risks and protection countermeasures under the privacy paradox dimension. *TSSEHR*, *11*, 509–515. DOI: 10.62051/tsnrh462

Li-li, P., & Jialin, N. (2023). Practices and reflections on volunteer service in higher education institutions: A case study of a certain university in Shenzhen, China. *Frontiers in Educational Research*, *6*(19). Advance online publication. DOI: 10.25236/FER.2023.061921

Liu, T., Li, S., Yang, R., Liu, S., & Chen, G. (2019). Job preferences of undergraduate nursing students in eastern China: A discrete choice experiment. *Human Resources for Health*, *17*(1), 1. Advance online publication. DOI: 10.1186/s12960-018-0335-3 PMID: 30606232

López, M., Rijpma, A., Moor, T., & Reijerink, J. (2023). Behind the crowdsourcing platform: Assessing volunteer recruitment and engagement instruments. *Nonprofit and Voluntary Sector Quarterly*, *53*(6), 1381–1409. DOI: 10.1177/08997640231212839

Lough, B. (2019). The state of volunteering infrastructure globally. *Voluntaris Zeitschrift Für Freiwilligendienste*, *7*(1), 22–43. DOI: 10.5771/2196-3886-2019-1-22

Madjid, H., & Safriani, A. (2023). Asset-based approach community service for developing digital textbook in secondary language (l2) teacher education. [Indonesian Journal of English Teaching]. *Ijet*, *12*(1), 104–117. DOI: 10.15642/ijet2.2023.12.1.104-117

Madsen, K., & Brix, J. (2024). Building capacity for digital innovation—A game-study. *Creativity and Innovation Management*, *34*(2), 486–499. DOI: 10.1111/caim.12650

Manshadi, V., & Rodilitz, S. (2022). Online policies for efficient volunteer crowdsourcing. *Management Science*, *68*(9), 6572–6590. DOI: 10.1287/mnsc.2021.4220

Marah, T., Pradhan, H., & SHUHOOD, F. (2024). Youth participation in global governance: opportunities and challenges. JoGaPA, 2(1), 238-249. https://doi.org/DOI: 10.70248/jogapa.v2i1.1718

Martono, M., Dewantara, J., Efriani, E., & Prasetiyo, W. (2021). The national identity on the border: Indonesian language awareness and attitudes through multi-ethnic community involvement. *Journal of Community Psychology*, *50*(1), 111–125. DOI: 10.1002/jcop.22505 PMID: 33465246

Mason, D., Chen, L., & Lall, S. (2021). Can institutional support improve volunteer quality? An analysis of online volunteer mentors. *Voluntas*, *33*(3), 641–655. DOI: 10.1007/s11266-021-00351-9

Mittos, A., Malin, B., & Cristofaro, E. (2018). Systematizing genome privacy research: A privacy-enhancing technologies perspective. *Proceedings on Privacy Enhancing Technologies. Privacy Enhancing Technologies Symposium, 2019*(1), 87–107. DOI: 10.2478/popets-2019-0006

Momdjian, L., Manegre, M., & Gutiérrez-Colón, M. (2024). Assessing and bridging the digital competence gap: a comparative study of Lebanese student teachers and in-service teachers using the digcompedu framework. https://doi.org/DOI: 10.21203/rs.3.rs-4711655/v1

Mulder, M., Rapp, J., Hamby, A., & Weaver, T. (2015). Consumer transformation through volunteer service experiences. *Service Industries Journal, 35*(15-16), 865–882. DOI: 10.1080/02642069.2015.1090981

Naqshbandi, K., Liu, C., Taylor, S., Lim, R., Ahmadpour, N., & Calvo, R. (2020). "i am most grateful." using gratitude to improve the sense of relatedness and motivation for online volunteerism. *International Journal of Human-Computer Interaction, 36*(14), 1325–1341. DOI: 10.1080/10447318.2020.1746061

Noronha, M., Lyra, L., Souza, L., Silva, R., & Cahen, F. (2023). International digital competencies maximizing lean internationalization in healthcare startups. *International Journal of Health Management Review, 9*, e0334. DOI: 10.37497/ijhmreview.v9i00.334

Nowakowska, I. (2021). Age, frequency of volunteering, and present-hedonistic time perspective predict donating items to people in need, but not money to combat COVID-19 during lock-down. *Current Psychology (New Brunswick, N.J.), 42*(20), 17329–17339. DOI: 10.1007/s12144-021-01993-0 PMID: 34177212

Omale, S. A., Oyenuga, M. O., Abdullahi, D., & Madu, I. (2024). Moderating Role of Entrepreneurial Education on Innovative Work Behaviour and Resilience of SMEs. *Innovations 77(2)*, 1166-1185https://DOI: 10.13140/RG.2.2.16946.41924

Omale, S. A., Yusuf, S. O., Oyenuga, M. O., Ikemefuna, M., Ojo, S. S., & Momodu, I. D. (2024). Organizational Learning in the Post-COVID-19 Era: A Prerequisite for Stakeholder Satisfaction. Twist 19(3), 265-272 https://twistjournal.net/twist/article/view/339

Oyedele, M. O., Sunday, A. O., & Abuh, A. I. (2024). Fostering Technological-Enhanced Training and Development for Business Survival and Performance in the New Normal. *Journal of Propulsion Technology*, *45*(3), 1858–1869. https://propulsiontechjournal.com/index.php/journal/article/view/7479

Oyedele, O. M. (2025). Digital Circular Economy: Driving Sustainable Innovation Through Stakeholder Synergy. In Singh, R., & Kumar, V. (Eds.), *Sustainable Innovations and Digital Circular Economy*. Springer., DOI: 10.1007/978-981-96-1064-8_4

Oyedele, O. M., & Iember, A. A. (2022). Covid-19 and the Future of Higher Education. *IEEE Technology Policy and Ethics, 6*(4), 1–3. https://doi.org/DOI: 10.1109/NTPE.2021.9778140

Oyenuga, M. O. (2026). Competitive Intelligence in Sustainability and Corporate Social Responsibility (CSR). In R. Marcão & V. Santos (Eds.), *Competitive Intelligence in the Digital Age: Strategies for Business and Technology Leadership* (pp. 65-102). IGI Global Scientific Publishing. https://doi.org/DOI: 10.4018/979-8-3373-2690-0.ch003

Oyenuga, M. O., & Jeresa, S. (2025). Adaptation and Resilience: Private, Public, and Individual Change Makers. In Singh, R., & Filho, W. L. (Eds.), *Climate Neutrality Through Smart Eco-Innovation and Environmental Sustainability. Climate Change Management*. Springer., DOI: 10.1007/978-3-031-83250-5_2

Oyenuga, M. O., Singh, R., Apata, S. B., Khan, S., & Kumar, V. (2025). Digital Technologies and Climate Action. In *Smart Technologies for Climate Change and Net Zero Policies: Practical Approaches Towards Sustainability. Climate Change Management*. Springer., DOI: 10.1007/978-3-031-92221-3_8

Oyenuga, M. O., Singh, R., Apata, S. B., Khan, S., & Kumar, V. (2025). Capacity Building for Green Technology. In *Smart Technologies for Climate Change and Net Zero Policies: Practical Approaches Towards Sustainability. Climate Change Management*. Springer., DOI: 10.1007/978-3-031-92221-3_21

Pankova, O., & Kasperovych, O. (2022). Ukrainian volunteering under conditions of armed russian aggression: Strengthening capacities through digitalization, platformization and the involvement of ict, network technologies. *Economic Herald of the Donbas*, (2 (68)), 113–123. DOI: 10.12958/1817-3772-2022-2(68)-113-123

Park, C., & Johnston, E. (2017). A framework for analyzing digital volunteer contributions in emergent crisis response efforts. *New Media & Society*, *19*(8), 1308–1327. DOI: 10.1177/1461444817706877

Park, C., & Johnston, E. (2019). Determinants of collaboration between digital volunteer networks and formal response organizations in catastrophic disasters. *International Journal of Organization Theory and Behavior*, *22*(2), 155–173. DOI: 10.1108/IJOTB-07-2018-0088

Patrício, L., & Ferreira, J. (2023). Strategically redefining university dynamics for the digital age: A qualitative approach. *Strategic Change*, *33*(2), 95–106. DOI: 10.1002/jsc.2565

Pattinson, J., Laparidou, D., Akanuwe, J., Scott, A., Sima, C., Lewis, C., & Siriwardena, A. (2023). Volunteering on heritage at risk sites and wellbeing: A qualitative interview study. *Health Expectations*, *26*(6), 2485–2499. DOI: 10.1111/hex.13852 PMID: 37589481

Pilemalm, S., Follin, A., & Prytz, E. (2024). Digitalized co-production of emergency response: ICT-enabled dispatch and coordination of volunteers at the emergency site. *Journal of Humanitarian Logistics and Supply Chain Management*, *15*(1), 34–47. DOI: 10.1108/JHLSCM-03-2024-0031

Pilemalm, S., Stenberg, R., & Finnevidsson, E. (2025). *Interdependent digitalized co-production of emergency response: requirements and challenges*. ISCRAM., DOI: 10.59297/9rce7z51

Pilemalm, S., Stenberg, R., & Finnevidsson, E. (2025). *Interdependent digitalized co-production of emergency response: requirements and challenges*. ISCRAM., DOI: 10.59297/9rce7z51

Plewa, C., Conduit, J., Quester, P., & Johnson, C. (2014). The impact of corporate volunteering on CSR image: A consumer perspective. *Journal of Business Ethics*, *127*(3), 643–659. DOI: 10.1007/s10551-014-2066-2

Pukallus, S., & Arthur, C. (2024). Combating hate speech on social media: Applying targeted regulation, developing civil-communicative skills and utilising local evidence-based anti-hate speech interventions. *Journalism and Media, 5*(2), 467–484. DOI: 10.3390/journalmedia5020031

Read, T., Bruce, A., & Olcott, D.Jr. (2024). Development for empowerment: Mobilising online and digital micro-credentials for refugees. *Journal of Learning for Development, 11*(2), 253–269. DOI: 10.56059/jl4d.v11i2.1357

Ritchie, B., & Jiang, Y. (2021). Risk, crisis and disaster management in hospitality and tourism: A comparative review. *International Journal of Contemporary Hospitality Management, 33*(10), 3465–3493. DOI: 10.1108/IJCHM-12-2020-1480

Rotman, D., Hammock, J., Preece, J., Hansen, D., Boston, C., Bowser, A., ... & He, Y. (2014). Motivations affecting initial and long-term participation in citizen science projects in three countries.. https://doi.org/ DOI: 10.9776/14054

Schech, S., Skelton, T., Mundkur, A., & Kothari, U. (2019). International volunteerism and capacity development in nonprofit organizations of the global south. *Nonprofit and Voluntary Sector Quarterly, 49*(2), 252–271. DOI: 10.1177/0899764019867774

Schneier, B., Shneiderman, B., Wallach, W., Ghazaleh, J., Perakslis, C., Pitt, J., & McDaniel, T. (2020). Istas 2020. *IEEE Technology and Society Magazine, 39*(3), C2–C2. DOI: 10.1109/MTS.2020.3019850

Shoderu, G., Omeleze, S., & Venter, H. (2024). A privacy-compliant process for digital forensics readiness. *International Conference on Cyber Warfare and Security, 19*(1), 337-347. https://doi.org/DOI: 10.34190/iccws.19.1.2055

Simms, J., Trad, A., Richards, K., & Woolf, J. (2024). Examining strategies for undergraduate student volunteer engagement and management in a community-based sport-for-development program. *Recreational Sports Journal, 48*(1), 75–84. DOI: 10.1177/15588661241236407

Stathi, A., Withall, J., Agyapong-Badu, S., Barrett, E., Kritz, M., Wills, D., & Fox, K. (2020). Mobilising people as assets for active ageing promotion: a multi-stakeholder perspective on peer volunteering initiatives. https://doi.org/DOI: 10.21203/rs.3.rs-47981/v1

Sulaimani, A., & Ozuem, W. (2022). Understanding the role of transparency, participation, and collaboration for achieving open digital government goals in oman. *Transforming Government, 16*(4), 595–612. DOI: 10.1108/TG-04-2022-0044

Sun, P., Morrow-Howell, N., Pawloski, E., & Helbach, A. (2021). Older adults' attitudes toward virtual volunteering during the COVID-19 pandemic. *Journal of Applied Gerontology, 40*(9), 953–957. DOI: 10.1177/07334648211006978 PMID: 33840232

Susumpow, P., Pansuwan, P., Sajda, N., & Crawley, A. (2014). Participatory disease detection through digital volunteerism., 663-666. https://doi.org/DOI: 10.1145/2567948.2579273

Traeger, C., Alfes, K., & Fürstenberg, N. (2022). Perceived organizational support and volunteer outcomes: Evidence from a german environmental nonprofit organization. *Nonprofit and Voluntary Sector Quarterly, 52*(3), 763–786. DOI: 10.1177/08997640221103292

Villaseñor, R. M. (2024). The Public Service Digitalization in the Philippines towards a national program to capacitate digital frontliners. *Journal of Public Administration and Governance, 14*(2), 164. DOI: 10.5296/jpag.v14i2.22106

Whittaker, J., McLennan, B., & Handmer, J. (2015). A review of informal volunteerism in emergencies and disasters: Definition, opportunities and challenges. *International Journal of Disaster Risk Reduction, 13*, 358–368. DOI: 10.1016/j.ijdrr.2015.07.010

Wiggins, A. (2013). Free as in puppies., 1469-1480. https://doi.org/DOI: 10.1145/2441776.2441942

Chapter 4
Community Engagement Effect on School Leadership Through Digital Volunteerism

Jesu Antony Arockia Venice
 http://orcid.org/0009-0005-6115-960X
DMI-St.Eugene University, Zambia

Maheswaran Muthuraman
 http://orcid.org/0000-0001-5562-1021
DMI-St.Eugene University, Zambia

Shashi Kant
 http://orcid.org/0000-0003-4722-5736
DMI-St. Eugene University, Zambia

Shashank Mittal
 http://orcid.org/0009-0007-8643-4350
O.P. Jindal Global University, India

DOI: 10.4018/979-8-3373-5722-5.ch004

ABSTRACT

The aim of this chapter will be to quantify the promotion of community assimilation of Leadership in school through volunteers in electronic work place, hence eliminating a gap that exists regarding the role of digital civic engagement in schools. Virtually, a quantitative approach of investigation was deployed as the questionnaire was standardized and 390 members were surveyed. EFA and SEM were checked using AMOS software to measure data in order to assess the proposed correlations. The findings describe how becoming assimilated in the community is a good indicator of Leadership in school, not only indirectly but also directly whether through volunteering in electronic work place or not. The relationship is mediated to some extent by the volunteering aspect in electronic work place which presents that it is a central mechanism through which the community interacts with Leadership in school. The findings describe that the inclusion of the volunteers in electronic work place to educational programs enhances participative leadership more firmly.

INTRODUCTION

Assimilation community in education has surpassed its traditional constraints in the current multicultural society that is increasingly becoming complementary and complementary digital (Tripon, 2025). This has rendered volunteers in electronic work place in an assertive powerhouse of change in Leadership in school. The necessity of social justice and the necessity of new technologies are two of the paramount factors that are affecting education systems everywhere in the multicultural society (Estévez et al., 2025). Electronic work place volunteering, which entails absorption of time, talents and basis by the volunteers through online diffusions, has been a tremendous strategy to address deficiencies in management in education, talent and leadership (Alnofeli et al., 2025). It is demonstrated that the digital terms competitive plan is very important in terms of attracting society to engage in doing things in their communities, particularly when the things are dreadful such as in the case of the COVID-19 pandemic . This movement rests on Sustainable Goal 4 (SDG 4) which states that all should have open access to inclusive quality education and opportunity to exploration till their very end of life. Servant leadership and widespread principles of civic engagement are the basis of volunteering in electronic work place (Zubeyr et al., 2024). Originally, it started with the petite-scale charity activities and the educational outreach programs, yet it gained the multicultural status once the digital technology became supplies, secondary available. It studied the role of natural leadership (servant leadership), as well as involvement in the digital language of the community in education of young people in China, serving rural children in rural areas of China through the activities of volunteers and charitable organizations (Shen et al., 2025). Similarly, It explain that digital leadership, which is supported with community empowerment is the one that can result in an institution-wide long-term outcome. This describes how digitally empowered community foundation may prove useful. This tendency is strengthened by recent empirical provisions (Pilosof et al., 2025).

According to a study, the school performance was positively correlated with community participation where digitally-coordinated activities reduced the root causes of the challenges in leadership and resource scarcity. It was found out that effective digital technologies significantly increased the involvement of student volunteers in academic environments, establishing novel leadership opportunities and fostering the sense of ownership (Kelder et al., 2025). Also, it was addressed the issue of volunteering in the electronic work place as one of the core constituents of civic resilience and educational continuity of the COVID-19 pandemic. This portrays that it can be beneficial in addition to emergency cases. In addition to this, bringing in the volunteers in the electronic work place into leadership in education is not without substantial challenges. There is still difficulty in the even-handed involvement of society living in low- and middle-income groups due to the lack of infrastructure, lack of digital proficiency, and cultural and social obstacles (Ehsan & Zaidan, 2024). Much inequalities are aggravated by the fact that in some far-flung regions, reliable internet and the requisite gadgets can be out of reach. It is also lacking adequate standardized models to gauge the long-term positive effects that the digital volunteer programs have on the enhancement of Leadership in school, decision-making process, and accountability forming (Joshi et al., 2023). The result of these gaps has been the absence of connected action resulting either in the under use or in a manner that cannot sustain itself in volunteering in electronic work place.

Although the body of academic literature is expanding, it is low in its cross-cultural and comparative indicators. Typically, research and studies focus on community wellbeing and civic participation, but fail to really research the promotion of volunteering within electronic work place concerning the school governance, methodologies of leadership, or integrating policies (Slater, 2021). Besides, even extensive case studies in regions like East Asia and Sub-Saharan Africa, there is an insignificant consistency over the best practices or portability to various education systems. The chapter will solve this research and practice shortcoming through providing an in-depth discussion on Leadership in school through community engagement with an encouragement of volunteering in electronic work place. Practical ways of enhancing leadership through multicultural case studies, empirical research studies, and a policy approach will be presented in the chapter. It will determine models of influence and challenges, evaluate leadership reactions, and give a format that can be changed later by other scholars and policymakers for specific learning environments. In such a way, we will not only get to know the theory a little bit better, but we will also have an opportunity to find the competitive plan to render education fair and accessible to all.

Research Question

How can assimilation of community through volunteers in electronic work place impact Leadership in school practices, as well as what contextual and technological contexts require to be put in place to guarantee its impact and its equitable application in various forms of education structures?

The study connected theoretical knowledge as well as practical experience through the exploration of this bottleneck, hence shaping future researches and policy implementation processes, aimed at enhancing the inclusion, participation, and survivability of education in the digital era.

BACKGROUND OF STUDY

The increasing rate of technology in the society has transformed the relationship of communities with schools in a large fashion. This has introduced the new means to become assimilated into the society including volunteering in electronic work place (Timotheou et al., 2022). This concept, whereby society employs the use of digital diffusions to assist in managing schools, foundation leaders, and teach, has taken that strategic pathway in making Leadership in school supplementary influence, assimilative, and diffusion. Besides, despite its great potential, volunteering in electronic work place is not that widespread in most regions of the multicultural society. This is normally due to technology, infrastructure, culture and leadership bottleneck (Alan et al., 2021). One of the underlying roadblocks is to furnish equitable digital access and connection, particularly in the provincial and fringe areas. It was studied the factor of sociotechnical infrastructure and the component of sociotechnical infrastructure preparedness at the social administration level of affecting engagement in digital terms in rural betterment in Germany (Rundel & Salemink, 2021). Their findings supported an argument that honourable as digital diffusions are, the actual sustainability of structural barriers caused by inherited below standard level digital literacy, bureaucratic shocked rigidity and inadequate nexus tend to exclude smaller territories and this represents comparable issues in the recruitment of volunteers in electronic work place into countryside educational settings. Leadership in school initiatives which rely on participation in digital terms of community may alienate inadvertently the very groups on which they aim to confer power unless accompanied by a customised method of overcoming such barriers (Passey et al., 2024).

As it was discussed the so-called Spoke 5 program at the Rome Technopole in Italy. It aimed at ensuring that the culture of supplying society with supplementary society got adapted in research and innovation through the execution of organized diffusions of digital communication. It was very successful in the urban academic rattle, but when applied in schools, the school administrators who were not trained in digital technologies proved to be reluctant, and the volunteers did not feel good, as they were not aware of their roles and tasks. This situation is the representation of leadership training and other clear classroom guidelines on digital governance to support volunteering in electronic work place at school (Xueying et al., 2025).

It has evaluated civic-tech innovations in the African context and their ability to strengthen open and transparent government. Their study of digital policy tools in the domain of public wellbeing emphasised that persuasive civic engagement requires more than having the technological tool, it would require culturally embedded behaviours and openness to participatory governance by leaders. In education, this entails that school leaders need to foster assimilative dispositions and gain skills to enhance digital civic participation, which is at times lacking in bureaucratic systems of education (Danganan & Gamboa, 2025). It considered the interaction between digital leadership and intellectual capital in changing Indonesian governmental taxes administration to be an upper addition open and responsive. To put the findings in perspective in the education sector, it is possible to say that effective digital leadership at school can be used to coordinate the impact of community volunteers. Besides, not every school leader has the digital skills or even the possibilities to implement these changes, which paints the picture that there is a leadership vacuum in terms of establishing and managing digital volunteer networks successfully (Buckler et al., 2025).

School environments in high climate-risk regions are case in point of the inadequate performances of the general approaches to public engagement that lacks adaptation to a confined space. As it found out that in the U.S., digital public engagement in climate assessment strengthened knowledge but did not have much impact on institutional decision making. Within the context of education, this would imply that although volunteering in electronic work place may promote active involvement in the community, the lack of clear paths of influencing may render it tokenism thus discouraging engagement in volunteer practice in schools and erode the belief in Leadership (Indra et al., 2022). Even also emphasize that the e-learning systems and digital learning should be within the modus operandi of lifelong learning to enable the society to remain integrated in their communities. However, most school systems lack the infrastructure and policies that can enable them to enact these ideas, especially in cases where digital assimilation is still viewed as a supplement and not an organizational component. This has caused a loss of strategic importance of volunteers in electronic work place in supervisory and management roles (O'Neil et al., 2023).

As mentioned, the importance of assimilative public-private partnership in the betterment of tourism in the horn of Africa should not be overlooked. This can act as a parallel lesson to an education: unless the coordinated activities of the governments, civil society, and private tech providers can be organized, the efforts to increase Volunteerism in Digital terms are expected to fail. It was proposed in Ethiopia that indigenous understandings and gender equity should be embedded in digital innovation, facilitating the need to involve community in education to respect the indigenous culture, languages, and identities, often ignored in top-down digital projects (Jabbar et al., 2026). The combination of the foreign case studies represents the complex nature of volunteering in electronic work place as a strategy enhancing Leadership in school. Digital tools could aid supplementary society to be integrated into the community but only when there are several factors that enable it to become available including robust digital infrastructure, excellent leadership skills, cultural flexibility, policy alignment, and ethical governance.

The chapter applies the lessons of the multicultural society to identify the core design elements that have to be present to succeed including being prepared to lead, utilizing digital tools in an assimilation fashion, and co-determining decisions. This will provide future academics and policy makers with a foundation on which to work so they can plan more powerful schools that will also be supplementary in assimilative ness as well as supplementary technological connectivity.

STATEMENT OF PROBLEM

Volunteering can assist the school to apply digital diffusions in collaborating to make decisions, encourage students, advance their abilities, and solve bottlenecks in their respective communities (Tripon, 2025). According to one study, under this perfect state of affairs, transformational leadership in education is expected to unify multicultural citizenship, innovation, and social responsibility. Engagement of community should also be utilized to fill up gaps in the systems. Not all are able to realize this hopeful vision though. Contrasting data across most researches on multicultural society as a whole depicts a chaotic and uneven application (Noor et al., 2021). An who reinforces the empowering nature of voluntary engagement activities of social media in charitable organizations among the young people; however, these benefits have never been used systematically in the context of organized leadership practices in education. Another study validate the positive effect of community involvement on the performance of Rwandan schools; furthermore, their work is also limited to particular, physical environments, and they do not explore digital diffusions to a large extent. This presupposes an insignificant gap in knowledge: lack of detailed understanding of how the volunteering in electronic work place, specifically, promotes the outcomes of school governance encouragements.

There are theoretical and empirical shortcomings that remain. Although civic-tech and digital leadership frameworks have been a well-known paradigm in the field of governance, little has been discussed on developing the same in the education field, more so in Leadership in school. have studied civic assimilation through adult education and failed to create a nexus between these acts and the transformation of leadership that is school-based. In addition to that, a small percentage of the existing research on volunteers in electronically work place is concerned with humanitarian response or broad civic engagement with ambiguous results in terms of being applied in school realm (Buckler et al., 2025). Contextual gaps is another huge bottleneck. Lack of sociotechnical infrastructure, digital skills and cultural readiness to reach digital terms undermines extensiveness of digital volunteering in rural and underprivileged localities. It was found that managers within the German the countryside sector of the state had a tendency to lack the needed skills and mentality to support effective participation in an online form (Stein et al., 2024). The overall result renders the school sector with logistical issues: school administrators might not be properly trained in digital work tools, law might not be the basis of virtual governance systems, and volunteers might feel left out because of language or technology problems. One survey argues that in the absence of culturally open engagement models, remote and indigenous communities can be effectively locked out of the digital processes of civic participation, thus only deepening access gaps Advocacy resources the encouragement of leadership (Jabbar et al., 2026).

These bottlenecks are even worse when practical issues are concerned. It was challenge that digital leadership does not only imply the use of technology infrastructure but also emotional intelligence, ethical orientation, and systems thinking, which do not always include school administrators. Application of the artificial intelligence in leadership in education, not to mention hopeful, as is yet a prospective goal and not a readily implemented solution to the problem of controlling volunteer involvement in the organization and management of the same. On similar lines, viewership models in various fields, having inherited climate crunch as well as innovation labs, set an example of how participation can be non-democratic or rushed when proper governance systems are lacking (Giraudet et al., 2022).

The study aims at eliminating such shortcomings by examining thoroughly the promotion of VE in a composite manner over a wide range of socio-cultural and infrastructural conditions. It will identify the characteristics making case studies easy or difficult and prescribe policy conditions in line with the needs of the communities, accepting the technological limits, bigger community resources, and leadership enhancement (Okunade et al., 2024). In line with the benefits of contributions made during the research to future researchers through the provision of conceptual clarity and empirical evidence upon which further research can be done, and to the policymakers through the provision of strategic guidance into the adoption of volunteers in electronic work place as part of national education system, this paper will attempt to give pragmatic information to future scholars and policy makers (Pepper et al., 2024). It highlights that designing Leadership in school structures that are accessible to all, adaptive and technology-savvy is very important. Not only should these ecosystems be able to absorb the input of the community but also be capable of storing it in a manner that has significance.

THEORETICAL FRAMEWORK

Transformational Leadership Theory: It shows how central the role of a leader is in the matter of motivating and empowering others through vision and inspiration and volunteered assistance. Transformational leaders operate in education sectors where they do more than manage the school.

Communities and innovation are also things that they work inward. The transformational educational leaders can potentially combine accountability, creativity, and multicultural citizenship, which are valuable traits to facilitate involvement in digital terms of community. This theory outlines that leaders in schools can develop and maintain virtual networks with volunteers and community efforts, encourage community objectives and develop a climate of participation which enhances school governance in volunteer participation through electronic work place (Ghamrawi et al., 2024).

Theory of Servant Leadership: Within the multicultural Volunteerism in Digital context, servant leaders underline the importance of listening, grounding, and engaging the community in the process of leadership, thus acting as great facilitators of the rather significant engagement in digital terms. The strategy enhances transformational leadership through emphasizing the relational and ethical emphasis of leadership that revolve around a community particularly in schools which have low capacities (Danganan & Gamboa, 2025).

Theory of Civic Participation: It establishes a background to comprehend the rewards and the process of volunteers participating in the lives of the people as well as democratic institutions, who inherit schooling. With this strategy, it will be made explicit that volunteering in electronic work place in learning institutions is not merely a practical activity, but a form of civic participation whereby community members participate in determining education destination. Orderly school contact activities that correspond to the civic duty are a hallmark that is required to prompt inclusion into digital citizenship (Erdreich, 2025).

Framework for Volunteerism: It presents us with a vivid idea of the functioning of technological volunteer activity. The notion of volunteering at electronic work place as a complex concept that has inherited the distanced assimilation, the digital technologies, and decentralized organizational procedures. As illustrated by Dinca and Diaconita (2024), the effective exercise of digital capabilities increases the motivational level of volunteers and their conversion to the academic system. This concept is not yet fully established and it provides us with a method of discussing the design and sustainability of the digital volunteer diffusions in education (Stumbrienė et al., 2023).

Each of the four theories contributes to the conceptual framework of the investigation, although the most central is the Transformational Leadership.

EMPIRICAL LITERATURE REVIEW

It reveals that inclusion of servant leadership practices in STEAM education enhances civic assimilation of students in STEAM education through community action research in rural China. Their results confirm that an empathy- and wellbeing-based leadership fosters community-based models of educational processes, which are assimilative and transformational. Utilization of community within the higher learning education progressively depends on digital technology to give consisting as well participatory learning environments (Shepherd & Bolliger, 2023). They emphasize that the extent of the influence of schools in the use of digital diffusions to ensure outreach and reciprocal communication has proven highly Student volunteers working online are auxiliary conscientious and more compatible to accommodate their study, especially in case of appropriate technical equipment. The field of digital helping others has emerged to be one of the primary methods through which society can get integrated in education and humanitarianism (Ren et al., 2025). There are models that systematize volunteering within the walls of electronic work place to include micro-volunteering, campaigning, knowledge-sharing and foundation wellbeing, showing how each role is promoted by diffusion design and motivation among the participants. It expands on this point because she helps realize how the social media can attract young volunteer workers, especially in the nonprofit organizations. She gets informed that internet diffusions are not only assisting the youthful society to feel dominant, but they also present them novel means of creating their sense of self and assimilation into communities (Zubeyr et al., 2024).

Transformational leadership plays a critical role in aligning innovation, accountability and multicultural citizenship in the school institutions. Such digital-based leadership is compounded with the strong, flexible learning environments. It provides experimental evidence basing that community participation as a core component initiated by committed school leaders enhances the performance and the performance of scholars even in villages where infrastructural digitalization and civic city incorporation are subpar (Kumar et al., 2024). One of the primary elements of active societies is civic assimilation, in the digital and physical space. It find a negligible linkage between adult learning and long-lasting civic volunteering and keep a legacy in voting and volunteering. Their analysis on the National Education Panel Investigation highlights the stimulation of factors of personality and life-long learning on levels of civic assimilation. With its updated data about the situation during the COVID-19 pandemic, the relevance of congruent civic engagements, including participation in electronic work place volunteering, to crisis management and policy responsibility (Wu & Nugent, 2026). The impact of digital leadership in the realm of a public organization is also significant when it comes to determining the level of employee engagement and the sustainability of the organization. It was illustrated that it is possible to assess the impact of digital leadership on empowerment and techno-work engagement among healthcare professionals through SEM analysis, which can increase institutional resiliency and the quality of wellbeing. The same could be said concerning the fact that intellectual capital and digital leadership integrate to serve operational excellence in the public sector, especially with regard to tax administration. The final arena that is coming up is communication technology in political and civil activity (Куандыков et al., 2021).

As discuss the promotion of CEO discourses regarding conflicts in the society, such as the one between Russia and Ukraine, on the topic of digital activism and stakeholder integration. Their findings show that authentic presence of leadership on the social media fosters public perceptions and mobilizations. The necessity of sociotechnical infrastructures in the possibility of digital political engagement is also emphasized, especially in rural settings where the elder participation could not be covered by conventional means (Raïq et al., 2025). In their supporting study (performed based on the survey of the German administrators, they arrived at digital culture and organizational preparedness as two important enablers of rural improvement through digital assimilation. Researchers have also been focused on the broader impacts of mass assimilation of people on policy and sustainability. Geographic Information Systems (GIS) are the instruments of influence in the scope of encouraging community involvement in the tourist governance, especially in the African rural context (Ma et al., 2023). In their analysis of climate assessments, it includes issues of public assimilation arguing that the participatory methods increase transparency and trust in the scientific choice. It emphasises the value of lifelong e-learning systems to provide a sustainable improvement and increase policy literacy.

There are also new areas of research like application of artificial intelligence to education leadership which are fast gaining supplementary popularity. It provides its taxonomy of AI in leadership higher education and states that ethically and situationally focused AI enhance strategic planning and inclusion and responsiveness. It extends this discussion to consider the use of civic-tech in Africa where the digital has enhanced government and transparency. It proves that the ethical leadership enhances the idea of corporate citizenship by stimulating the activity of the employees, and that is why the alignment between ethical and digital approaches to leadership is needed.

CONCEPTUAL FRAMEWORK

Figure 1. Conceptual framework

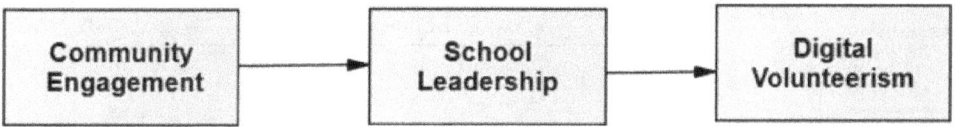

METHODOLOGY

Quantitative research methodology was used. The key information was collected through a structured questionnaire designed based on the existing elements of the existing literature. Our sampling managed to garner 390 valid responses by random sampling method from the college students, youth who were volunteering in a school society and community groups actively engaging in their engagement with digital terms across various schools and non-governmental organization. The technique of selective sampling was employed because it was a selective method of finding respondents who had direct experience of online involvement of community diffusions or assimilation. The approach was considered proper based on the fact that it could guarantee the integration of the society with certain exposure to the investigated structures, therefore, increasing the credibility of the results. The respondents were recruited through online survey platforms and community interactions with the eligibility guidelines being that all respondents would have to be over the age of 18 and must have had a minimum of six months active participation in what could be described as volunteer or civic activities carried out through online diffusions. This investigation had its scale formulated after an overview of previous academic studies.

DATA ANALYSIS

Table 1. Data fitness

KMO examination		.836
Parametes	Approx. Chi-Square	2225.808
	df	91
	Sig.	.000

Source: Authors

As seen in Table 1, the results indicate that the information, which was retrieved, was adequate to undergo factor analysis. According to Kaiser (1974), the KMO rating of a reading of 0.836 can be termed as being meritorious. This says that the sample was adequate, and that there was adequate amount of variance shared by the variables and thus justifies the use of EFA. It also provided a statistically insignificant value (2225.808, df = 91, p < 0.001), representing that correlation matrix is not an identity matrix. This implies that there were strong correlations between the variables therefore supporting the aptness of conducting factor analysis. These statistical values indicate that the data contained in this series is very robust and the data are manipulatable, which provides a good foundation to proceed further into the construct validation and the test of the model.

Table 2. Explained Variance

Component	Initial Eigenvalues			Extraction Sums			Rotation Sums		
	Total	% of Variance	Cumulative %	Total	% of Variance	Cumulative %	Total	% of Adjustment	Growing %
1	4.5	32.3	32.2	4.5	32.5	32.5	3.0	32.5	32.5
2	1.7	9.7	37.0	1.7	9.7	37.2	2.3	15.1	43.7
3	1.7	9.0	65.2	1.27	9.0	65.2	1.9	22.8	65.0
4	.42	6.7	57.8						

Source: Authors

The meaning of the Component Analysis found using is depicted in Table 2. Initially, there were four elements with eigenvalues more than 1. In addition to, only the three factors were retained according to Kaiser and cumulative variance, after rotation. The first component had an initial eigenvalue of 4.65 and this implied that it had 32.24 percent concerning the total variance. It contributed a great deal even following rotation, and its variance was 32.47%, which represents the fact that the latent construct is strong. The second section constituted 9.79% of the variance originally, which after the rotation increased to 15.49, making it effective to grasp. The third element had a smaller eigenvalue of 1.27 and it adapted 9.09 percent of the explained variance and increased to 22.32 percent upon rotation thus becoming very supplemental central. By the end of the turn, all the three retained components accounted 65.20 percent total variation. This is good as far as social science investigation is concerned as a low level of approximately 60 percent is normally considered as being acceptable. The increment in the sum of squares loadings of the rotation represents an added careful differentiation of the groups of variables, therefore certifying the sufficiency and sense of the factor structure. Such results affirm a clear and trivial latent feature, strongly advanced scale that can be used in further confirmatory study.

Table 3. Covariances

Covariance			Estimate	S.E.	C.R.	P
DV	<-->	CE	.237	.032	8.231	***
DV	<-->	SL	.303	.032	7.572	***
CE	<-->	SL	.254	.24	7.611	***

Source: Authors

Table 3 shows the estimates of the covariance. Correlation in the digital definition of Volunteerism as well as Engagement of community was found to be 0.237 and its critical ratio (C.R.) was 8.231 proving the validity of Hypothesis H2. This suggests that there is a strong likelihood that an increase in the digital volunteer activities will increase involvement of the community programs, anchoring the thinking that digital diffusions can effectively enhance absorption of community. The relationship between the DV as well as Leadership in school was at 0.303 with C.R of 7.572 which underpins Hypothesis H3. This implies an inconsequential interrelationship where high volunteering in electronic work place is associated with increased Leadership in school practices perhaps through mutual role and distributed responsibilities, Internet collaboration and projects that are community-based. Lastly, the relation of both Engagement of community and Leadership in school was 0.254 with a value of C.R. of 7.611 that supported the Hypothesis H1. This establishes the concept that the Leadership in school is enhanced where the community is absorbed in a meaningful fashion more so when that partaking occur online. These significant covariances emphasize the factor dependency nature of the dimensions and support the theoretical strength of the model, thus yielding the theoretical robustness of the model and resulting in the establishment of empirical evidence of the putative relationships within the scope of leadership in education and digital assimilation.

Table 4. Validity

	CR	AVE	MSV	MaxR(H)	CE	DV	SL
CE	0.802	0.652	0.225	0.863	**0.804**		
DV	0.758	0.807	0.132	0.754	0.311	**0.680**	
SL	0.789	0.603	0.274	0.797	0.431	0.253	**0.652**

Note: CE= Engagement of community; DV= Volunteerism in Digital terms; SL= Leadership in school
Source: Authors

The validity test of the constructs of Engagement of community (CE), Volunteerism in Digital terms (DV), and Leadership in school (SL) of the results are depicted in Table 4. The reliability of all constructs was satisfactory as all the values of Combined Dependability (CR) exceeded the value of 0.70 (CE = 0.802, DV = 0.758, SL = 0.789) and convergent validity was confirmed since all values of AVE met the requirement of 0.50 (CE = 0.652, DV = 0.807, SL = 0.603). Discriminant validity was also portrayed to be true as the square roots of the AVEs (depicts written boldly, diagonally) were larger than the inter-construct correlations within the corresponding rows and columns. Moreover, all the MSV values were under their AVE values, and hence there was no bottleneck with overlapping constructions. The MaxR(H) values indicating the degree of reliability of the construct outside of CR range were also within an acceptable threshold. On the whole, these results represent the fact that the measuring model well possesses the construct reliability, convergent validity, and discriminant validity, which can be characterized by the fact that the tool used in this study is robust.

Figure 2. Path Model

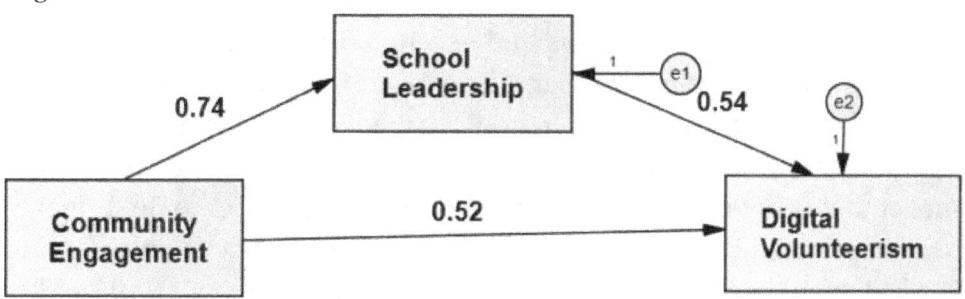

Table 5. Model Strength

Sig.	Chi-Sq	RMR	Goodness	Confirmatory	TLI	RMSEA
0.004	1.954	.043	0.890	0.912	0.920	.036

Source: Authors

In Table 5, the model fit coefficients have been illustrated to assess the effectiveness of our structural model that is used in this study. The statistical significance value of Chi-square (p = 0.004) shows that the model is statistically trivial and this also generally depends on the sample size. The proportion of Chi-square/df (1.954) is quite small compared to the permissible limit of 3.0 and thus, the model is a good fit. RMR = 0.043) is within the correct range (below 0.05) and therefore residual error is negligible. The Goodness of Fit Score (GFI = 0.890) and the CFI = 0.912 are quite above or at the conventionally established limit of 0.90, and so they are appropriate. The TLI = 0.920 was also above the recommended value of 0.90 and RMSEA = 0.036 is much below the recommended 0.06 level, which indicates that the model is rather simple and perfectly fits. All these indices show that the mathematical construct is statistically sound and also is appropriate to data.

Table 6. Mediation

	worth
CE→ SL	.52
CE→ DV→ SL	.74*.54=.48
	.93

Source: Authors

The results of the mediation study seen in Table 6 examine how DV sense can serve as an intermediary in CE and also SL. The direct impacts of community on Leadership in school are mediated by assimilation in the community and quantified as 0.52 which marks a trivial but significant impact that is not mediated. When looking at the indirect route, Engagement of community has an influence on Digital The act of volunteering (0.74), which then has an influence on Leadership in school (0.54). That is the indirect effect = 0.74 (0.54) = 0.48. The total impact of Engagement of community on Leadership in school is 0.93 which represents that the two are insignificantly related in their combined impact. Since reasons and consequences are statistically negligible, that signifies the presence of partial mediation, that is, partly Volunteerism in Digital conveys the endorsement of Engagement of community on Leadership in school. These findings support the crucial role of volunteering in electronic work place as a side avenue through which participation by community introduces leadership in educational situations.

DISCUSSION

The major findings of the investigation reflect the large-scale and broad encouragement of community engagement and volunteers in electronic work place in the Leadership school. First, the findings were represented as assimilation of community has beneficial effects on digital giving back (864, $p < .001$) and educational management (957, $p < .001$). It implies that influent participation of the schools in community makes them better in terms of leadership responsiveness, trust, and confidence as people have towards systems. The study also presented that being a volunteer in an electronic work place provided direct and a statistically insignificant contribution to Leadership in school (0.336, $p < .001$). This portrays that digital civic engagement and chain networks could aid in leadership change since it serves as the intermediary. The mediation analysis displayed that the moderate part of mediation was present at 0.93 with 0.48 of influence originated through the indirect path. This shows that it is only community participation that can enhance leadership but volunteering in electronic work place can enhance this influence to be greater and broader through the use of digital collaboration, participatory governance and virtual resource mobilization. The KMO of 0.836 and insignificant Bartlett test portrayed that the sample dimension was large enough and the factors could be identified. Such tests of statistics present that the proposed model is powerful. The combination of these findings helps to define a currently identified societywide trend: a digital-driven societal multicultural sharing facilitates community collaborations and can potentially lead to the education leadership being re-established towards inclusion, openness, and responsiveness.

CONCLUSION

The results of the present investigation have provided a conclusive outcome: community involvement and DV become two of the pivotal factors that could acculturate to the success of school leaders and modulate change in the digital era. With additional and even more complex social and technical shifts affecting schools and other educational institutions, the interest to see the society incorporated into their communities and use the digital diffusions to remain volunteers has become extremely strategic. This study empirically paints the role of participation of community in increasing Leadership in schools not just directly but also indirectly through the mediating stimulus of promoting volunteering in electronic workplace and hence heralding a two-lines of attack that education innovation and participatory governance. The findings portray that, an electronic work place volunteering makes conventional involvement of residents one of abundance and depth, providing parents, students, teachers, and residents with resourcing determining flexibility, scalability, and assimilability to make a tremendous difference in enhancing the aspect of schools. This combined paradigm is validated by the research, whereby the theoretical understandings and real-life applications in leadership can be bettered in education, civic technology, and participatory policy-making. The review provides, in the end, evidence-informed suggestion to future scholars, education policymakers, and school leaders, advocating frameworks that have the tendency to institutionalize digital community collaboration as a core aspect of leadership in education paradigms.

MANAGERIAL IMPLICATIONS

The topical and strategic ramification of the research study includes management implications that are essential to school administrators, schooling policymakers, and even community leaders who may be interested in enhancing influence and assimilative leadership in schools. To start with, the findings present a picture that integration of the community programs in making changes permanent in terms of Leadership in school betterment is highly critical. The top of school leaders agenda should include initiatives that will get parents, alumni, indigenous groups, and civic groups assimilated in decision making, planning and enhancing the school. Such assimilation does not only ensure trust, but it also promotes shared responsibility and new ideas. Secondly, the minor intervening role of volunteering in electronic work place portrays that the education managers must invest in digital infrastructure and diffusions that enable the society to actively participate in their communities at a distance and via technology. Electronic work place volunteering is one open and inexpensive way of having a wide section of society assimilated, especially those who are at a distance or do not know any other person. It can be coordinated through social media campaigns, internet tools that allow you to coordinate volunteers or virtual collaboration forums. The other compulsory change is that leadership training programs to retain principals and administrators should also offer digital civic engagement and volunteer management courses, thus giving the capabilities to give maximum benefits of participatory government.

PRACTICAL IMPLICATIONS

The causes that are immediately affecting the research are the practical competitive strategy that can be employed by the educational institutions and other stakeholders in enhancing Leadership in school through community engagement and Volunteerism in Digital terms. The first one is that schools could establish organized digital volunteer programs to attract additional society in both intellectual and entertaining activities. As an example, it may include qualified members of the community to help fill capability gaps and enhance the student experience. Investigation also includes that being active in the community should not be an occasional activity, but rather a part of school culture that takes place at all times. Schools can implement advisory boards, parent forums, and student councils that can gather regularly and follow the digital practices using such digital tools as online diffusions or applications to exchange thoughts and complete projects together. This incessant interaction can ensure that the development of school is supplementary, truthful, and informal. The study also demonstrates the importance of educating teachers and leaders of a school on how to employ technology and work with volunteers. By providing personnel with the means to embrace the use of digital diffusions and reach the community, schools can enhance their governance and turn their environment into the secondary version that is welcoming and opens to the public. Finally, such findings are the core focus of policymakers and NGOs as it relates to the sphere of education since the given findings show that civic assimilation through digital channels can be scaled even in areas that lack significant resources. By collaborating with technology firms and implementing certain policy changes, schools can build sustainable methodologies to develop leaders who do not discriminate anyone and can accommodate different bottlenecks by adapting to new cellars.

THEORETICAL IMPLICATIONS

The investigation mainly extends the flexibility of Transformational Leadership Theory in the context of explaining possibilities of Leadership in school as positively encouraging or promoting active involvement of community and Volunteerism in Digital meaning high-naive interactions between the leadership practices and active participation in the governance by the common people. It also continues to contribute to the Civic Engagement Theory by explaining the way digital diffusions could assist supplementary society to be integrated in schools and other study institutions. It is especially the main point now when remote involvement has become the norm. In addition, the study can complement the Digital Participatory Theory, because it provides real evidence that volunteering in electronic workplace is the technical innovation and the tool of civic empowerment and education enhancement. It shows that digital technology can help in mediating social capital and building trust among stakeholders in the form of school leaders. These findings also support Social Exchange Theory by portraying that it is trust, mutual benefit and value shift that makes it plausible that the volunteers in electronic work place can be an influence in school communities. The study confirms empirically the mediating role of volunteering at electronic work place, providing a theory at an advanced level that aligns assimilation of community, digital participation with Leadership at school, thus filling an educational and civic engagement literature gap.

RECOMMENDATIONS

The nature of the results of the study suggests minor suggestions to the education, government and community stakeholders in most issues. To begin with schools ought to positively influence parents, the relevant authorities in the neighbourhood and electronic volunteers to mix themselves with communities, by providing formal structures that can allow them to and make them have authentic say as far as the running of the school is concerned and events that can help in facilitating the development in the children. Such an open minded approach to doing things complements trust and collective responsibility assisting leaders to perform even better and complements learning. Second, the education leaders are advised to invest in the digital infrastructure and education in order to draw in additional volunteers to volunteer online. When the supplementary society has an access to technology and digital literacy classes, as well as methods of handling volunteers, they will have the ability to work at home. This is especially so in the rural or underdeveloped locations. Volunteers in electronic work place should also be ensured that they know their jobs, what is expected of them, and how to both give and receive feedback so that they are held responsible and motivated. Third, governments must simplify the process of assimilating the society into the digital civic practice by carrying it into the national educational programs. This can be in the form of providing incentives to volunteering and civic-tech diffusions being part of the school policy, and collaborating with corporations to scale-up successful models.

FUTURE DIRECTIONS

Future studies need to trace the long-term effects of volunteering at electronic work place as well as involvement of community on leadership in education and in student learning, and the answer will give deeper insight on consistency of causal impacts and durability. Moreover, comparison of different cultures through the multiple regions and education systems might also help to explain how the social, economic and political factors might have impact on digital participation and Leadership within a school. Future scholars should test the possibilities of such new technologies as AI, gamification, or mobile applications in studying the engagement of community to find out whether they are effective in lifelong civic engagement and changing leadership outcomes. Additional, examination of the roles played by the marginalized people together with the people who had gender diverse communities, the people who had connection with the country side resources and those with disabilities in volunteering in the electronic work place would present comprehensive frameworks in volunteering. Researchers can also conduct micro-level research to examine the impact of such volunteer characteristics on series of engagement and leadership relations, motivation, digital literacy, or even personality. Lastly, we shall mix the methods that would allow us to know more additional information on the emotional, cultural and behavioural components of assimilation using both quantitative and qualitative data. This will result in new concepts of improving education and acquiring the additional society incorporated by the community.

REFERENCES

Alan, Ş., Baysan, C., Gümren, M., & Kubilay, E. (2021). Building Social Cohesion in Ethnically Mixed Schools: An Intervention on Perspective Taking. *The Quarterly Journal of Economics*, *136*(4), 2147–2194. DOI: 10.1093/qje/qjab009

Alnofeli, K. K., Akter, S., & Yanamandram, V. (2025). Unlocking the power of AI in CRM: A comprehensive multidimensional exploration. *Journal of Innovation & Knowledge*, *10*(3), 100731. DOI: 10.1016/j.jik.2025.100731

Buckler, A., Twiner, A., & Power, T. (2025). "I had to adjust my character so I was able to help": How community volunteers in rural Zimbabwe developed as educators in a context of crisis and school closures. *Journal of Educational Change*, *26*(4), 631–655. DOI: 10.1007/s10833-025-09535-2

Danganan, C. G., & Gamboa, A. G. (2025). Unveiling the Dynamic Landscape: Exploring Practices, Challenges, and Resilience Strategies of Digital Leaders in Secondary Education. *Journal of Cultural Analysis and Social Change*, *587*, 587–598. Advance online publication. DOI: 10.64753/jcasc.v10i3.2457

Ehsan, M. M., & Zaidan, E. (2024). Exploring internet inclusivity and effectiveness of e-learning initiatives during the pandemic – a comparative analysis. *Frontiers in Education*, *8*, 1301135. Advance online publication. DOI: 10.3389/feduc.2023.1301135

Erdreich, L. (2025). Digital Well-Being and Superdigital Citizenship: A Class Comparison of Parenting Practices for Remote Learning. *Social Justice Research*, *38*(3), 332–351. DOI: 10.1007/s11211-025-00454-4

Estévez, M., Ballestar, M. T., & Sáinz, J. (2025). Market research and knowledge using Generative AI: The power of Large Language Models. *Journal of Innovation & Knowledge*, *10*(5), 100796. DOI: 10.1016/j.jik.2025.100796

Ghamrawi, N., Shal, T., & Ghamrawi, N. A. R. (2024). Leadership development in virtual communities of practice: The case of school principals from the GCC Region. *Education and Information Technologies, 29*(17), 23897–23916. Advance online publication. DOI: 10.1007/s10639-024-12784-y

Giraudet, L.-G., Apouey, B., Arab, H., Baeckelandt, S., Bégout, P., Berghmans, N., Blanc, N., Boulin, J.-Y., Buge, É., Courant, D., Dahan, A., Fabre, A., Fourniau, J.-M., Gaborit, M., Granchamp, L., Guillemot, H., Jeanpierre, L., Landemore, H., Laslier, J., & Tournus, S. (2022). "Co-construction" in deliberative democracy: Lessons from the French Citizens' Convention for Climate. *Humanities & Social Sciences Communications, 9*(1), 207. DOI: 10.1057/s41599-022-01212-6 PMID: 35757681

Indra, R., Ritonga, M., & Kustati, M. (2022). E-leadership of the school principals in implementing online learning during COVID-19 pandemic at public senior high schools. *Frontiers in Education, 7*, 973274. Advance online publication. DOI: 10.3389/feduc.2022.973274

Jabbar, A., Astuti, Y., Ahmad, J., Adnan, A. A., & Putra, A. (2026). Bridging digital transformation and local wisdom: Towards inclusive and sustainable public service delivery in indigenous communities. *Frontiers in Sustainability, 6*, 1715580. Advance online publication. DOI: 10.3389/frsus.2025.1715580

Joshi, D. R., Adhikari, K. P., Chapai, K. P. S., & Bhattarai, A. R. (2023). Effectiveness of online training on digital pedagogical skills of remote area teachers in Nepal. *International Journal of Professional Development Learners and Learning, 5*(2), ep2311. Advance online publication. DOI: 10.30935/ijpdll/13666

Kelder, J., Crawford, J., Al-Naabi, I., & To, L. (2025). Enhancing digital productivity and capability in higher education through authentic leader behaviors: A cross-cultural structural equation model. *Education and Information Technologies, 30*(12), 17751–17767. DOI: 10.1007/s10639-025-13422-x

Kumar, D., Sunder, N., Sabatés, R., & Wadhwa, W. (2024). Improving children's foundational learning through community-school participation: Experimental evidence from rural India. *Labour Economics, 91*, 102615. DOI: 10.1016/j.labeco.2024.102615

Ma, J., Cui, J., & Zhang, Q. (2023). A "Motivation" model of couple support for digital technology use among rural older adults. *Frontiers in Psychology, 14*, 1095386. Advance online publication. DOI: 10.3389/fpsyg.2023.1095386 PMID: 36818095

Noor, A. F., Sonedi, S., Azman, M. N. A., Khunaifi, A. R., Dwiningrum, S. I. A., & Haryanto, D. (2021). The Multicultural Education Paradigm Pattern: A Case Study in Muhammadiyah Junior High School in Palangka Raya, Indonesia. *Perspectives of Science and Education, 52*(4), 297. DOI: 10.32744/pse.2021.4.19

O'Neil, K., Vettern, R., Maaß, S., Harrington, R., Robideau, K., McGlaughlin, P. C., & Gauley, J. (2023). Equipping Extension Professionals to Lead Volunteer Systems: An Evaluation of an Online Course. *Journal of Human Sciences and Extension, 12*. Advance online publication. DOI: 10.55533/2325-5226.1348

Okunade, B. A., Adewusi, O. E., & Adediran, F. E.Beatrice Adedayo OkunadeOlolade Elizabeth AdewusiFoluke Eyitayo AdediranBukola A, OdulajaRosita Ebere DaraojimbaJustice Chika Igbokwe. (2024). Technology in community development: A comparative review of USA and African Projects. *International Journal of Science and Research Archive, 11*(1), 1195–1202. DOI: 10.30574/ijsra.2024.11.1.0183

Passey, D., Ntebutse, J. G., Ahmad, M. Y. A., Cochrane, J., Collin, S., Ganayem, A., Langran, E., Mulla, S., Rodrigo, M., Saito, T., Shonfeld, M., & Somasi, S. (2024). M. T., Saito, T., Shonfeld, M., & Somasi, S. (2024). Populations Digitally Excluded from Education: Issues, Factors, Contributions and Actions for Policy, Practice and Research in a Post-Pandemic Era. *Technology Knowledge and Learning, 29*(4), 1733–1750. Advance online publication. DOI: 10.1007/s10758-024-09767-w

Pepper, I., Rogers, C., Turner, J. G., St. Louis, N., & Williams, B. (2024). Enabling student employability through volunteering: Insights from police volunteers studying professional policing degrees in Wales. *Higher Education Skills and Work-Based Learning*, *14*(5), 1135–1148. DOI: 10.1108/HESWBL-09-2023-0253

Pilosof, N. P., Welcman, Y., Barrett, M., Oborn, E., & Barrett, S. (2025). Building digital resilience: Leading healthcare transformation through an online community. *Frontiers in Digital Health*, *7*, 1656804. DOI: 10.3389/fdgth.2025.1656804 PMID: 40978698

Raïq, H., Rabah, S., Al-Mannai, A. A. M., Malkawi, A. H., Ali, A.-S. M., Tabishat, M., Al-Fahim, F. A. M. S., & Al-Marri, R. H. S. A. (2025). Gender digital divide and political participation in selected Arab countries. *Frontiers in Communication*, *10*, 1703066. Advance online publication. DOI: 10.3389/fcomm.2025.1703066

Ren, J., Guo, J., & Li, H. (2025). Linking digital competence, self-efficacy, and digital stress to perceived interactivity in AI-supported learning contexts. *Scientific Reports*, *15*(1), 33182. DOI: 10.1038/s41598-025-18873-3 PMID: 41006796

Rundel, C., & Salemink, K. (2021). Bridging Digital Inequalities in Rural Schools in Germany: A Geographical Lottery? *Education Sciences*, *11*(4), 181. DOI: 10.3390/educsci11040181

Shen, Y., Huang, G., Le, H., Yu, S., Xu, M., Ouyang, J., Fan, Y., & Wang, Q. (2025). 'Cloud for Youth': An implementation research of cloud-based solutions for bridging the digital divide in rural China. *British Journal of Educational Technology*, bjet.70037. Advance online publication. DOI: 10.1111/bjet.70037

Shepherd, C. E., & Bolliger, D. U. (2023). Institutional, program, and professional community: A framework for online higher education. *Educational Technology Research and Development*, *71*(3), 1233–1252. DOI: 10.1007/s11423-023-10214-3 PMID: 37359486

Slater, D. J. (2021). Do community citizenship behaviors by leaders enhance team performance? Evidence from the "field.". *The Journal of Values Based Leadership*, *14*(2). Advance online publication. DOI: 10.22543/0733.142.1361

Stein, V., Pentzold, C., Peter, S., & Sterly, S. (2024). Digital political participation for rural development: Necessary conditions and cultures of participation. *The Information Society*, *41*(1), 18–32. DOI: 10.1080/01972243.2024.2407339

Stumbrienė, D., Jevsikova, T., & Kontvainė, V. (2023). Key factors influencing teachers' motivation to transfer technology-enabled educational innovation. *Education and Information Technologies*, *29*(2), 1697–1731. DOI: 10.1007/s10639-023-11891-6 PMID: 37361759

Timotheou, S., Miliou, O., Dimitriadis, Y., Villagrá-Sobrino, S., Giannoutsou, N., Cachia, R., Martínez-Monés, A., & Ioannou, A. (2022). Impacts of digital technologies on education and factors influencing schools' digital capacity and transformation: A literature review. *Education and Information Technologies*, *28*(6), 6695–6726. DOI: 10.1007/s10639-022-11431-8 PMID: 36465416

Tripon, C. (2025). Towards Quality Education for All: Integrating EdTech, Mentorship, and Community in Support of SDG 4. *Education Sciences*, *15*(9), 1184. DOI: 10.3390/educsci15091184

Wu, F., & Nugent, J. B. (2026). Mitigating Life Challenges to Subjective Well-Being Through Civic Engagement: Insights from a Global Perspective. *Social Indicators Research*, *181*(2), 52. Advance online publication. DOI: 10.1007/s11205-025-03763-y

Xueying, Y., Arshad, M. A. B., & Lihua, H. (2025). Teacher E-Leadership in the Digital Age: A Systematic Review of Research and Practice [Review of Teacher E-Leadership in the Digital Age: A Systematic Review of Research and Practice]. *International Journal of Academic Research in Business & Social Sciences*, *15*(5). Advance online publication. DOI: 10.6007/IJARBSS/v15-i5/25494

Zubeyr, E., Kunasegaran, M., & Kunjiapu, S. (2024). Embracing Youth Volunteerism Through Digital Literacy for a Sustainable Future. *International Journal of Academic Research in Business & Social Sciences*, *14*(4). Advance online publication. DOI: 10.6007/IJARBSS/v14-i4/21420

Chapter 5
Digital Volunteerism as a Vehicle for Community Engagement in Inclusive Schools in Mashonaland West of Zimbabwe

Vigilance Created Matongo
http://orcid.org/0009-0009-2056-793X
National University of Science and Technology, Zimbabwe

Golden Mabwe
http://orcid.org/0009-0004-6612-5479
National University of Science and Technology, Zimbabwe

ABSTRACT

This study investigates how digital volunteerism can enhance community engagement in inclusive primary schools in Mashonaland West, Zimbabwe; findings show strong policy commitments yet persistent implementation gaps, especially in rural contexts, where volunteer readiness, leadership coordination and infrastructure are often lacking; recommendations include structured digital volunteer frameworks aligned with inclusive education, investment in training and connectivity, embedding volunteer roles into school leadership practices, and monitoring impact; the conclusion emphasises that without such systemic support initiatives risk being ad hoc rather than transformative.

INTRODUCTION

In Zimbabwe's evolving educational context, the dual imperatives of inclusive education and community engagement have become increasingly prominent. Ensuring that learners with diverse needs are included—regardless of disability, socio-economic background or geographic location—requires not only appropriate pedagogy but also strong partnerships between schools, families and the wider community. Simultaneously, the rapid expansion of digital technologies and connectivity presents new opportunities for how communities can engage with schools, learners and teachers. The concept of digital volunteerism—voluntary support provided via digital platforms, networks or resources—emerges as a promising vehicle for enriching community engagement and strengthening inclusive schooling.

This chapter presents a systematic literature-based study exploring how digital volunteerism serves as a mechanism for enhancing community engagement in inclusive primary schools in the Mashonaland West Province of Zimbabwe. By "systematic" we mean that the review follows a clearly defined protocol: identifying, selecting, critiquing and synthesising relevant studies in a transparent and reproducible manner. Through this method, we examine the intersection of digital volunteerism, school leadership and inclusive schooling rather than relying on anecdotal or ad-hoc sources.

By focusing on selected schools in Mashonaland West, the chapter investigates how school leadership and management can harness digital volunteers—whether alumni, parents, local community members or remote supporters—to support inclusive practices, bridge resource gaps and promote sustained collaboration between school and community. The underlying argument is that digital volunteerism, when effectively organised and led, can strengthen both the engagement of the community and the capacity of school leadership to deliver inclusive education.

The significance of this study is manifold. First, Zimbabwe has made important policy commitments towards inclusive education and digital learning, but implementation remains uneven, particularly in rural and semi-rural provinces such as Mashonaland West. Second, while traditional forms of community engagement (such as parent-teacher associations, local volunteer programmes) have been explored in Zimbabwe, fewer studies examine digital modalities of volunteer engagement in the context of inclusive schooling. Third, leadership in inclusive schools is often treated in isolation (focusing on principals and instructional leadership), but less often in relation to digitally mediated community-volunteer networks and inclusive practice. As such, the study aims to fill an important gap by investigating how digital volunteerism intersects with community engagement, leadership practice and inclusive education in a Zimbabwean provincial context.

In what follows, the chapter sets out the background to the study, defines the focus of the study, conducts a review of the literature (covering digital volunteerism, community engagement, inclusive schooling and leadership), presents findings from the systematic literature review in the selected context, and offers solutions, recommendations and directions for future research. Through this structure, the chapter intends to contribute to both theory and practice: offering a conceptual framework for digital volunteerism in inclusive schooling and practical insights for school leaders, community stakeholders and policymakers aiming to enhance community-school partnerships in the digital era.

BACKGROUND TO THE STUDY

Zimbabwe has enshrined a series of commitments to inclusive education and community involvement in schooling, yet implementation remains uneven and constrained by multiple system challenges. According to the UNESCO/IICBA Country Brief, Zimbabwe ratified the Convention on the Rights of the Child in 1990 and the Convention on the Rights of Persons with Disabilities (CRPD) in 2013, with the 2021 National Disability Policy emphasising inclusive education as a national priority (International Institute for Capacity Building in Africa [IICBA], 2024). Research by Munemo

(2018) and Mutyavaviri (2016) shows that while policy frameworks exist, many differently-abled learners in Zimbabwe's schools report exclusion and marginalisation due to inadequate resources and weak community-school linkages. Meanwhile, Mangena and Chidakwa (2024) highlight that rural schools in Zimbabwe struggle with inclusive education practice due to teacher capacity and infrastructure deficits. These findings illustrate a persistent gap between policy commitments and ground-level realities in Zimbabwe's inclusive education agenda.

Within this broader context, the role of community engagement in schooling is increasingly acknowledged as critical for enhancing learner outcomes, especially for learners with special educational needs. The Education Coalition of Zimbabwe (ECOZI) convened an Inclusive Education Indaba in 2017, stressing the need for robust collaboration between civil society, schools, and community stakeholders (Education Coalition of Zimbabwe [ECOZI], 2017). Studies from neighbouring countries further reinforce the importance of community-school partnerships in inclusive schooling (Naicker, 2019; Ncube, 2024; Tendeukai, 2020). However, Zimbabwe-specific research indicates that local school leaders often lack clear frameworks for mobilising parent and community involvement in inclusive education (Mutyavaviri, 2016; Munemo, 2018), and community engagement tends to be ad hoc rather than strategically integrated into inclusive schooling models.

In parallel, digital technologies are increasingly reshaping how schools, learners and communities interact, offering new avenues for community-school collaboration and support. While much of the scholarship is centred on higher-education or urban contexts (Zvavahera, Garwe, Pasipanodya, Chigora & Katsande, 2024), the concept of digital volunteerism—where community members provide remote or digitally-mediated support to schools—remains under-examined in Zimbabwe's primary inclusive schooling context. Gurstein's (2007) work on community informatics offers a theoretical anchor for understanding how ICTs can support community empowerment and inclusion, yet this lens has been little applied in inclusive education research in Zimbabwe. In rural provinces such as Mashonaland West, connectivity, device access and digital literacy remain significant barriers (Hlungwani, 2025), making the potential for digital volunteerism promising but challenging.

Despite the convergence of inclusive education goals, community engagement imperatives and expanding digital connectivity, there remains a weak integration of these domains in Zimbabwean research and practice. Policy analyses indicate the absence of detailed frameworks for how digital community volunteering may function in inclusive schools (Mudzengerere, 2017). Empirical studies frequently report deficits in infrastructure, leadership practice and teacher capacity (Muresherwa, 2020; Ngwarati & Muchemwa, 2024) but pay little attention to how digital community-volunteer networks could be harnessed by school leadership to promote inclusive learning. Theoretical contributions of community informatics, distributed leadership (Tenha & Makamure, 2024) and inclusive schooling management remain fragmented in relation to Zimbabwe's context. In short, we face a literature gap in how digital volunteerism, school leadership and community engagement intersect in the inclusive schooling landscape of Zimbabwe.

In light of these gaps, this chapter conducts a systematic literature-based study to explore how digital volunteerism can serve as a vehicle for strengthening community engagement in inclusive primary schools of Mashonaland West province in Zimbabwe. The study seeks to identify leadership practices, community-volunteer models, and infrastructural conditions that support or inhibit this process. Moreover, it aims to propose a conceptual framework that links digital volunteerism, school leadership and community engagement with inclusive schooling outcomes, thereby contributing both to theory and practical guidance for school leaders, policymakers and community stakeholders.

FOCUS OF THE STUDY

This systematic literature-based study concentrates on digital volunteerism as a vehicle for enhancing community engagement in inclusive primary schools in the Mashonaland West province of Zimbabwe. It zeroes in on three inter-linked dimensions: first, the mechanisms by which digital volunteers may be recruited, oriented, supported and mobilised by school leadership to engage meaningfully with learners, teachers and the wider school-community ecosystem; second, the enabling and constraining factors that school leadership and management encounter when embedding digital volunteerism into inclusive education practice—especially in resource-constrained, rural or semi-rural settings; and third, the influence of digital volunteerism on community engagement processes, teacher capacity, learner inclusion and leadership practice. The study draws on published empirical and theoretical literature to identify patterns, enablers, barriers and promising practices relevant to this context, and seeks to formulate a conceptual framework linking digital volunteerism, community engagement and school leadership in support of inclusive schooling. By adopting a systematic literature-based approach, the study aims not only to summarise and synthesise evidence, but to highlight gaps, inconsistencies and opportunities within the Zimbabwean context, and to generate actionable insights for school leaders, community actors and policy-makers.

LITERATURE REVIEW

Digital Volunteerism and Community Engagement in Educational Contexts

The concept of volunteerism has evolved significantly with the proliferation of digital technologies, giving rise to what is often described as **digital volunteerism**—that is, voluntary contributions by individuals via digital platforms, networks or devices, directed toward community, educational or civic purposes (for example, remote mentoring, crowd-sourcing, micro-volunteering via apps). Recent scholarship suggests that digital volunteerism holds promise for broadening participation, reducing geographic barriers, and mobilising wider communities than conventional in-person volunteer models (Crittenden & Hager, 2025).

In educational contexts, the potential of digital volunteerism is particularly interesting for inclusive schooling, community engagement, and linking schools to broader social networks. Yet the translation of this potential into practice—especially in low-resource or rural settings—remains under-explored.

For example, in the Zimbabwean context, a notable study by Power, Buckler, Ebubedike, Tengenesha, Jama, Ndlovu, Mukoyi, Ndou & Mubaira

(2021) investigated how mobile phones were used to recruit and equip community volunteers to support children's learning during school closures in Zimbabwe. They found that digital volunteerism allowed remote engagement at scale, although persistent infrastructural constraints (connectivity, device access, data cost) limited full reach. The study suggests that digital volunteering in crisis contexts (e.g., COVID-19 induced school closures) can serve as a useful model, but its sustainability and integration into regular schooling remain unclear.

From a theoretical vantage point, the field of community informatics, as articulated by Gurstein (2007), offers a useful lens: the emphasis is not simply on providing access to ICTs, but on how communities use, control and appropriate ICT infrastructures to support community processes, empowerment, and inclusion. The framework highlights that digital tools are only meaningful when embedded in social networks, community governance structures, and local practices. This theoretical base helps us conceptualise digital volunteerism not as an isolated technological intervention, but as a mediated social-practice in which volunteers, schools and communities co-construct digital engagement.

However, within the literature there is still limited empirical research linking digital volunteerism, community engagement and inclusive schooling—particularly in rural Zimbabwean or comparable African settings. This indicates a clear knowledge gap: namely, how digital volunteer networks are formed, sustained and aligned with inclusive education objectives in underserved rural schools.

Community Engagement in Schools: From Physical to Digital

Traditionally, community engagement in schools has encompassed parent-teacher associations, local volunteer programmes, community forums, and school governance committees. Such engagement is widely acknowledged as supportive of learners' outcomes: by anchoring schooling in local contexts, enhancing trust between school and home, leveraging community resources, and increasing accountability (Lunga, 2024). In Zimbabwe, for example, the Education Coalition of Zimbabwe (ECOZI) has emphasised the role of community voices in shaping education policy and practice, including digital literacy initiatives at district level (Dube, 2025).

The shift from purely physical engagement to digital community engagement is becoming more salient. Digital modalities—such as WhatsApp groups, remote mentoring, digital volunteer networks, online forums—expand how community engagement can operate, especially in contexts of limited mobility, remote schooling or dispersed communities. For instance, the web-resource by UNICEF emphasises the role of family and community partnerships in digital education programmes, including guidance for school leaders on communications, digital-device access and supporting caregivers' engagement.

In Africa, a specific example: Sikapa et al. (2024) examine how digital storytelling can promote disability-inclusive research and community engagement: their findings show that digital storytelling engages community members as co-producers of knowledge, thereby enhancing inclusive schooling processes.

Despite these developments, empirical work remains sparse concerning how school leadership orchestrates digital volunteer networks, and how such networks translate into sustained community-school engagement in inclusive primary schools in rural Zimbabwe. Key questions remain: How are volunteers recruited digitally? How do schools coordinate and integrate volunteer contributions? How do parents and community members engage digitally with school processes over time? Such gaps need to be filled to better understand the transition from physical to digital community engagement in schooling contexts.

Inclusive Education Implementation in Zimbabwe: Leadership, Policy & Practice Gaps

The literature on inclusive education in Zimbabwe identifies enduring challenges regarding policy enactment, leadership practices and resource allocation. In a study of teachers' colleges, Hlatywayo & Mapolisa (2022) found significant gaps: rigid curricula, insufficient resources and minimal support for diversity. Similarly, other work indicates that inclusive schooling in Zimbabwe continues to be hampered by inadequate teacher training, scarce material resources and insufficient assistive devices (Ngwarati & Muchemwa, 2024).

Leadership is a crucial factor. Empirical and review studies (e.g., "Leadership for inclusive education: a case study of a school management team in an urban primary school" by Naicker, 2019) show that leadership practices—especially transformational, instructional, and distributed leadership—affect how inclusive education is implemented at school level. Distributed leadership models propose that inclusion is enabled when principals, department heads and community actors share responsibility (Spillane et al., 2020). Yet in Zimbabwe, research seldom addresses how school leadership can leverage digital community-volunteer networks to support inclusive education.

From a policy perspective, Zimbabwean policy texts may articulate commitments to inclusive education and digital literacy but offer few operational frameworks for digital volunteerism in inclusive schooling. Moreover, in rural schools in Zimbabwe, practical conditions are challenging: connectivity limitations, low digital literacy among users, lack of devices and infrastructure hinder meaningful volunteer-digital engagement. For instance, UNICEF reports indicate that only 31% of schools in Zimbabwe are connected to the internet, and access to devices and data remains prohibitive especially in rural areas.

Therefore, the theoretical, policy and practical gaps converge: we lack frameworks demonstrating how digital volunteering, leadership and inclusive schooling integrate—and how community engagement can be reimagined through digital means in Zimbabwe's inclusive education system.

The Role of School Leadership in Harnessing Digital Volunteerism for Inclusive Schools

School leadership plays a strategic role in shaping the conditions under which digital volunteerism and community engagement may flourish within inclusive schooling environments. According to Leithwood, Harris & Hopkins (2021), instructional leadership, resource allocation, capacity building and monitoring practices significantly affect student outcomes. Thus, in a digital-volunteerism context, the school principal or leadership team must attend to several tasks: establishing volunteer coordination mechanisms, providing digital infrastructure, defining volunteer roles, integrating volunteer actions into inclusive-education strategy, and monitoring volunteer impact.

In the South African context, Chetty (2020) illustrates how volunteers' motivation and organisation determine impact—this finding is relevant in Zimbabwean schools given contextual similarity. However, Zimbabwe-specific literature rarely examines how school leaders organise digital volunteer networks or embed them within inclusive-education strategies.

Within digital/ICT leadership research, recent work such as "ICT for Inclusion for Educational Leaders: Inclusive and Digital Distributed Leadership" (2024) argues that school principals must engage in multiple leadership dimensions—teaching-concept design, strategic development, cooperation building, ICT concept development and human-resource development—when operating in digitally enabled inclusive schooling contexts. These findings suggest that school leaders must actively adopt digital-distributed leadership to harness digital volunteerism effectively.

Given the gaps in Zimbabwean research, bridging this gap requires drawing on frameworks such as community informatics (Gurstein, 2007) and distributed leadership (Spillane et al., 2020) to conceptualise how digital volunteerism can be operationalised in inclusive schools under leadership guidance. Specifically: How do school leaders conceptualise volunteer-digital networks? What structures and processes do they establish? What supports are required (infrastructure, training, incentives, roles)? How do they monitor and align volunteer-digital engagement with inclusive education goals? These are promising avenues for research.

Digital Volunteerism, Inclusive Education and Community Engagement: Emerging Frameworks and Gaps

Emerging frameworks on digital volunteerism in education emphasise components such as volunteer recruitment, digital literacy, community networks, infrastructure, sustainability, monitoring and impact measurement. For example, the study "Exploring Older Adults' Interest in Virtual

Volunteering" (Crittenden & Hager, 2025) integrated the Technology Acceptance Model (TAM), self-efficacy and digital-divide perspectives, and found that older adults' interest in virtual volunteering is shaped primarily by perceived usefulness of digital tools and their willingness to improve technical competence. Although this study deals with older adults rather than school-volunteers, the same theoretical concerns apply: Technology acceptance, training, barriers, digital inclusion.

Within education research, a systematic review of digital-technologies integration for inclusive learning in South African township schools (Ngcobo, 2025) found that teacher digital illiteracy remains the most significant barrier, even more so than device availability or content design. This finding reinforces that digital volunteerism initiatives cannot rely purely on technological infrastructure—they must address human capacity (volunteer digital literacy, teacher readiness, community digital readiness).

Yet despite such pieces, the translation of ad-hoc volunteer-digital models into sustainable, school-embedded inclusive schooling strategies is under-explored. For instance, the work by Power et al. (2021) in Zimbabwe (mobile-phone volunteerism during COVID) provides a useful case but remains contextualised to crisis-mode rather than standard schooling. Research questions remain on how volunteer networks sustain beyond crisis interventions; how leadership ensures accountability and alignment with inclusive pedagogy; and how community digital-engagement models affect learner inclusion particularly in rural Zimbabwe.

More significantly, the literature seldom integrates technology-access issues, volunteer motivation models, inclusive-education policy and leadership practices, and community-school ecosystems into a coherent framework. In other words: there is an integrative gap. We need conceptual models that link digital volunteerism, inclusive school leadership, community engagement and schooling outcomes in rural African contexts.

Proposed Conceptual Synthesis

Based on the reviewed literature, a proposed synthesis suggests that effective digital-volunteerism for inclusive schooling occurs when the following conditions are met:

1. **Accessible technology infrastructure** – devices, connectivity, data affordability, power reliability (as shown in Zimbabwe's rural context via UNICEF, 2022).
2. **Volunteers with digital literacies and motivations** – drawing on TAM, self-efficacy and digital-divide insights (Crittenden & Hager, 2025).
3. **School leadership with vision and structures** – deploying distributed and digital-inclusive leadership practices (Eickelmann & Gerick, 2017; "ICT for Inclusion", 2024)
4. **Community-school engagement mechanisms** – online/remote platforms for volunteer-community interaction with schools, guided by community-engagement frameworks (UNICEF Digital Education, 2025).
5. **Inclusive-education alignment** – volunteer-digital activities must explicitly align with inclusive pedagogy, assistive technologies, differentiated supports, policy frameworks (Ngwarati & Muchemwa, 2024. Spi
6. **Sustainability and monitoring** – mechanisms for accountability, impact measurement, volunteer retention and scaling.

Such a framework could then be used to inform empirical research in rural Zimbabwean school contexts, exploring how school management teams can integrate digital volunteerism and community engagement into inclusive schooling.

Gaps, Implications and Directions for Research

From this analysis three broad gaps emerge:

- **Empirical gap in rural African inclusive schooling**: While digital volunteerism has been studied in youth and civic contexts, and inclusive education has been studied in Zimbabwe, there is minimal empirical work on digital-volunteer networks in inclusive primary schools in rural Zimbabwe.

- **Leadership and coordination gap**: Research seldom examines how school leaders in rural Zimbabwe coordinate and institutionalise volunteer-digital networks to advance inclusive education.
- **Integrative framework gap**: There is no widely accepted conceptual model linking digital volunteerism, community engagement, school leadership, inclusive pedagogy and infrastructure in resource-poor settings.

Given these gaps, implications for your research (on the impact of resource management strategies by school management teams in South Africa) are noteworthy: although your study is in a different national context (South Africa) and focus (resource management, learner performance), insights can be drawn regarding volunteerism, digital engagement, leadership, infrastructure and inclusive strategies.

For example, the findings from Zimbabwe and South Africa show overlapping issues of infrastructure (connectivity, devices), leadership practice (shared/distributed leadership), and community engagement (volunteer networks, digital modes). Your theoretical model could incorporate digital volunteerism (or digital community engagement) as a resource management strategy, and examine how management teams deploy such strategies for inclusive schooling and improved learner performance.

Future Research Directions Might Include

- Qualitative case studies of rural schools in Zimbabwe (or elsewhere in Southern Africa) exploring how digital volunteer networks form, how they are managed by school leadership, and how they contribute to inclusive pedagogy.
- Mixed-method studies measuring the impact of digital volunteer-engagement on learner outcomes, especially in inclusive schooling contexts.
- Development and testing of frameworks that integrate infrastructure readiness, volunteer digital capacity, school leadership, community engagement and inclusive educational practices.

Summary

In summary, digital volunteerism presents promising pathways for enhancing community engagement and inclusive education, especially in under-resourced settings. The literature demonstrates that: digital volunteerism can overcome geographical constraints; community engagement benefits from digital modalities; inclusive education in Zimbabwe and Southern Africa faces persistent challenges in infrastructure, leadership and policy; and leadership plays a pivotal role in leveraging digital volunteerism and community engagement for inclusive schooling. However, substantial gaps remain—particularly around empirical applications in rural inclusive schooling in Zimbabwe, leadership coordination of digital volunteer networks, and integrative frameworks combining volunteerism, digital engagement, community-school links and inclusive pedagogy.

VOLUNTEER MOTIVATION AND DIGITAL-VOLUNTEER MODELS

Motivation is a central factor in volunteerism research: understanding *why* people volunteer (and continue volunteering) is crucial for designing, recruiting and managing volunteer programmes. In the context of digital volunteering (i.e., volunteering via digital platforms/networks), the motivational dynamics acquire further nuance. Below, I present theoretical foundations of volunteer motivation, recent work on digital-volunteering motivation, proposed models relevant to digital volunteerism, and then reflect on how these might map into the schooling / inclusive education / community-engagement context (particularly for rural/under-resourced settings such as those in Southern Africa).

Theoretical Foundations of Volunteer Motivation

A strong foundation in volunteer-motivation research is offered by the "Volunteer Functions Inventory" (VFI) developed by E. Gil Clary, Mark Snyder et al. (1998) which posits that volunteers are motivated by multiple functions: values, understanding, social, career, protective, and enhancement (Clary & Snyder, 1998, as cited in review). Although the original VFI is for traditional volunteer contexts, it remains widely used. More recently, systematic reviews (for example by Jinying Chen et al., 2022) identify that motivations broadly cluster into intrinsic (value-based, psychological fulfilment, personal growth) and extrinsic (career/skill building, social networks, status) categories.

For example, Chen et al. (2022) found that while value-based motives (helping others, altruism) dominate, motives such as gaining experience, expanding networks or career benefits also frequently appear.

Another recent model by Adam R. Neely (2022) proposes a process model of volunteer motivation: how individuals decide to volunteer, how much effort they invest, and how long they sustain involvement. The model emphasises factors such as perceived efficacy, cost/benefit judgments, role clarity, and ongoing reinforcement.

Motivation in Digital-Volunteer Contexts

When volunteering is mediated through digital technologies, additional motivational and structural considerations come into play. For instance, Khushnood Z. Naqshbandi, Yun-Hee Jeon & Naseem Ahmadpour (2022) examined volunteers on a digital science-research platform and found that motivations were shaped by identity (e.g., "I'm a digital volunteer"), meaning-making, and how well the digital environment met psychological needs (autonomy, belonging, competence). They highlight that digital divide/inequalities may impede sustained participation.

Similarly, a recent article by C. Hine (2024) explores how digital volunteers make sense of their roles in online volunteering: the themes of "relationality" (feeling connected to others despite distance), "recognition" (feeling that their digital contributions matter), and "meaning creation" emerged.

These digital-volunteer studies emphasise that, beyond general volunteer motives, digital volunteering demands attention to digital access, skill/comfort with platforms, clarity of digital roles, feedback loops and online identity or community belonging. The meta-analysis of the "Digital Volunteering Concept" by Olga A. Basheva & Polina O. Ermolaeva (2025) highlights that digital volunteers face different affordances (flexibility in time/place), as well as constraints (technology skills, anonymity, weaker interpersonal ties) compared to traditional volunteering.

Digital-Volunteer Models Relevant for Education / Community Engagement

Based on the above, one can articulate a model of digital-volunteer motivation and engagement, especially applicable to educational and community-engagement settings:

1. Entry motivation stage
    - *Values / altruism*: wanting to contribute to children's learning, community upliftment.
    - *Understanding / learning*: desire to learn digital skills, engage in new forms of volunteering.
    - *Social / network*: connecting with other volunteers, building profile.
    - *Career / skill-building*: for younger volunteers, enhancing CV.
    - *Self-enhancement / psychological*: personal fulfilment, identity as "helper".
2. Digital-role adoption stage
    - Clarity of role: what the digital volunteer does (remote mentoring, monitoring chats, one-on-one virtual support)
    - Access/competence: having access to digital device, connectivity, training.
    - Platform/structure: digital system that assigns tasks, provides feedback, social recognition.
    - Social connectedness: feeling part of a team despite being remote.
3. Sustained engagement / retention stage
    - Feedback & recognition: volunteers see the impact of their contribution (e.g., learner progress, community acknowledgement).
    - Competence & efficacy: volunteers feel they are making a difference, able to fulfil tasks.

- Community belonging: feeling part of volunteer network, interacting with peers.
- Low cost / flexibility: digital tasks fit around other commitments, location independent.
- Role adaptation & growth: opportunities to move into leadership, mentor other volunteers.
4. Outcomes & alignment
    - Volunteer satisfaction / commitment → whether they continue volunteering.
    - Alignment with educational/ inclusive-schooling goals: digital volunteers help support learners with special needs, or marginalised groups.
    - Integration with school leadership and community engagement: how volunteers interface with the school's inclusive-education strategy and community-school engagement.

This model highlights that for digital volunteerism in schooling/inclusive education contexts to succeed, motivation (intrinsic + extrinsic) must be supported by appropriate digital-role design, infrastructure/training, feedback/recognition and integration with broader school-community-leadership frameworks.

Mapping to Inclusive Schooling / Community Engagement / Resource Management (in Your Context)

Bringing these motivational and digital-volunteer models into the context of rural African inclusive schooling (and by extension your research on resource-management strategies in South Africa) suggests several implications:

- **Volunteer recruitment strategies** need to draw on both altruistic motives (helping children/learners) and instrumental motives (skill development, digital training) to attract a broad base of volunteers. For example, digital volunteers in rural schools may be motivated by the chance to build their digital literacy while contributing to inclusive education.

- **Training and digital-capacity building** are crucial: if digital volunteers lack confidence in using digital tools (connectivity, device access, digital fluency), motivation will falter. As the studies show, digital-volunteer motivation is tightly linked to competence and efficacy (Naqshbandi et al., 2022) and the technology-access affordances (Basheva & Ermolaeva, 2025).
- **Role clarity and integration with school leadership/ inclusive-education strategy**: School-management teams (e.g., in rural or under-resourced schools) must define clear volunteer roles (monitoring learners remotely, providing peer support digitally, engaging parents via WhatsApp, etc). Without clarity, volunteers may feel ineffective and disengage.
- **Feedback and recognition mechanisms**: Digital volunteers should receive timely feedback on their contributions (e.g., learner progress updates, acknowledgment from school/community) to sustain motivation. This is especially relevant in remote or digital-only engagement, where lack of physical presence can reduce volunteers' sense of belonging and impact. The Russian youth-study (Molchanova et al., 2021) shows the disadvantage of lacking live communication and personal contact in digital volunteering.
- **Flexibility and cost-sensitivity**: Digital volunteering in rural contexts must respect volunteers' time, connectivity/data costs, device access. The advantages of digital volunteering—flexibility of time/place—should be leveraged but also demands cost-sensitive design (data subsidies, mobile-friendly platforms, task micro-chunks).
- **Alignment with inclusive-education and community engagement goals**: Volunteers must link with the school's inclusive aims (e.g., supporting learners with special needs, bridging home-school digital engagement, empowering parents/community). Their roles should not be standalone but embedded within the school's inclusive-education and community-engagement frameworks.
- **Retention and sustainability**: As digital-volunteer models show, sustaining participation is a challenge if volunteers feel isolated, ineffective, or unsupported. The process-model of volunteer motivation (Neely, 2022) suggests ongoing reinforcement, role-adaptation, community belonging and feedback loops are key.

- **Technology-access and equity considerations**: In rural/under-resourced settings, volunteers may face device/data/connectivity barriers (as your other literature sections highlight). These barriers not only influence efficacy but can dampen motivation—if volunteers frequently struggle technically, they may disengage.
- **Resource-management implication**: For school-management teams (SMTs) or similar, digital-volunteerism becomes a resource-management strategy: managing human digital-volunteer resources, integrating them into the school's broader resource-portfolio (devices, connectivity, teacher time, community links) and aligning them with performance/learner-outcome goals. Considering volunteer motivation in resource-management planning becomes vital.

Key Research Gaps in Motivation/ Digital Volunteer Models (and how Your Study Might Address Them)

From the reviewed literature, several gaps emerge that your research could address:

- Most digital-volunteer motivation studies are in citizen science, online crowd volunteering or adult contexts; few focus on schooling/education, especially inclusive schooling in under-resourced rural African settings (Naqshbandi et al., 2022; Hine, 2024).
- The interplay of digital-volunteer motivation, school leadership (particularly SMTs), community engagement and inclusive-education implementation is under-explored. How do leaders design volunteer roles, how is motivation sustained, and how is volunteerism embedded in inclusive school practice?
- Longitudinal studies tracking digital-volunteer participation over time (entry → retention → dropout) in rural/under-resourced schooling contexts are limited.
- Research linking volunteer motivation to learner outcomes (especially in inclusive schooling contexts) is sparse: how do motivated digital volunteers translate into support for learners with special needs, or improved community-school engagement?

- Resource-management frameworks seldom integrate digital-volunteer human-resource components alongside devices/connectivity/teacher capacities in inclusive schooling. Your study could contribute by conceptualising digital volunteerism as part of the SMT's resource-management strategy, and investigating how volunteer motivation, recruitment, training and management influence learner performance and community engagement.

FINDINGS

Volunteer Recruitment, Digital Readiness and Engagement

The body of literature indicates that the effectiveness of digital volunteerism in inclusive schooling is intimately tied to how volunteers are recruited, oriented and prepared for their digital-roles. Studies reveal that volunteers' digital literacy, their perception of the usefulness of the digital platforms and their self-efficacy with technology strongly shape commitment and performance. For instance, in the work by Sui, Crittenden & Hager (2025) the combination of the Technology Acceptance Model (TAM) and Digital Divide Theory shows that older adults' interest in virtual volunteering is heavily influenced by the perceived usefulness of digital tools and their willingness to improve technical competence. Parallel research in broader volunteer-contexts (e.g., Zubeyr, Kunasegaran & Kunjiapu, 2024) demonstrates that youth volunteers are more likely to remain engaged when systems actively support their digital competence and provide clear role definitions.

In the setting of inclusive schools, particularly in under-resourced or rural contexts, this means that simply deploying digital volunteer programmes is insufficient if volunteers are not given structured digital induction, defined tasks and ongoing digital-support. The literature highlights a "readiness gap" – volunteers may be available, but in the absence of orientation, role clarity and digital tools their engagement tends to be erratic or superficial.

What remains under-explored in the existing literature is the *differentiation* of recruitment and induction processes for digital volunteers in inclusive schooling contexts: for example, how volunteers supporting learners with special educational needs are trained differently from general volunteers; how digital-volunteer induction is adapted when connectivity, devices or digital literacy are low; how cultural, socio-economic and community-context variables (e.g., rural vs urban, language minority vs majority) affect volunteer readiness. Furthermore, the motivational dynamics specific to digital volunteering in inclusive schools (for example, how volunteers perceive the value of contributing to marginalised learners, how they feel connected to the school-community digitally, how they sustain their role) are seldom systematically addressed. Finally, recruitment literature tends to focus on volunteer willingness rather than mapping the pipeline from recruitment through training, role adoption, active engagement, retention and dropout in digital-volunteer schooling programmes.

Leadership Practice, Institutional Embedding and Volunteer–School Coordination

A vital finding concerns the role of school leadership and institutional processes in embedding digital volunteerism into inclusive education practice. Research emphasises that in order for volunteerism to move beyond the "add-on" status and become integral, school leadership must adopt practices of resource allocation, coordination, monitoring and capacity-building. Leithwood, Harris & Hopkins (2021) support this by demonstrating that instructional leadership, resource allocation and monitoring are key predictors of successful pedagogical innovation. In parallel, from the perspective of community informatics, Gurstein (2007) argues that access to ICT is meaningless without meaningful engagement and leadership support.

Within inclusive schooling contexts, the literature shows that when school leaders create a designated coordination role for volunteers (e.g., a volunteer-liaison officer), align volunteer activities with the school's inclusive-education vision, integrate digital volunteer tasks with teachers' planning and community engagement, and monitor & feedback on volunteer contribution, digital volunteerism is far more effective. Contrariwise, where leadership commitment is weak, institutional embedding is limited, volunteer efforts tend to be fragmented, poorly coordinated and lacking sustainability. This linkage highlights that volunteerism is not simply something external to the school—it must be woven into the institutional fabric.

What has been insufficiently addressed is the *mechanics* of how leadership in resource-constrained, rural contexts (such as certain Zimbabwean or South African schools) operationalises these embedding practices. For example: How do school management teams prioritise digital volunteerism within their limited budgets? How do they coordinate volunteer scheduling, integration with teacher workloads, alignment with inclusive-education goals (e.g., assistive technologies for learners with disabilities)? How do they develop monitoring systems and feedback loops tailored for digital volunteers? How do leadership practices differ in schools with poor connectivity, few devices and low community digital-literacy? These operational leadership processes remain under-documented, which limits the theorisation of effective models for embedding digital volunteerism in inclusive schooling.

Strengthening Community–School Linkages through Digital Volunteers

The literature reveals a promising finding: digital volunteerism may strengthen community–school linkages and thereby advance inclusive schooling when properly structured. Digital platforms open new opportunities for remote mentoring, for parent–school digital communication, for community participation beyond physical boundaries. In community service-learning literature, de Oliveira (2024) demonstrates how digital service-learning activities enhance multimodal literacy, involve community-partners and expand social engagement. In adult-volunteer digital contexts, the case study of the Ribon App shows how simple digital tools can engage younger generations in volunteering via mobile apps, leveraging ease-of-use, gamification and virtual satisfaction.

In inclusive schooling, volunteers might perform roles such as digital-liaison between school and home, remote tutoring for learners with disabilities, online parent support groups, or digital storytelling engaging community voices. These functions hold potential to bridge home–school gaps, increase parental participation and expand community volunteer networks. Yet the literature also signals significant practical barriers: digital access inequalities (devices, data, connectivity) hamper the inclusivity of these initiatives; volunteer training in inclusive-pedagogy (e.g., working with special needs learners) is rarely addressed; monitoring systems linking digital volunteer contribution to learner inclusion outcomes are weak or absent.

What appears to be missing is robust empirical work that maps how digital volunteer programmes facilitate *community–school processes* in inclusive schooling: for instance, how community members become digital volunteers, how home-community digital readiness (parents' access to devices/data, digital literacy) influences the effectiveness of volunteer-mediated engagement, how volunteer efforts translate into better learner participation and community trust, how cultural and linguistic diversity in rural African contexts shapes community–school digital engagement. Furthermore, models are lacking for how schools coordinate digital volunteer network infrastructure to engage community volunteers (parents, local organisations, caregivers) and sustain ongoing home–school–community communication in inclusive education.

Sustaining Digital Volunteerism: Retention, Infrastructure & Institutionalisation

The sustainability of digital volunteer initiatives emerges as a critical area of concern. Literature shows that while digital volunteer programmes may launch with high enthusiasm and promise, this tends to wane in the absence of institutionalised mechanisms for retention: structured feedback, volunteer recognition, ongoing training, and the infrastructure required to sustain digital engagement. For example, Sui et al. (2025) found that volunteer retention in virtual models is threatened where support systems, role clarity, or recognition are missing. The Malaysia ICT Volunteers (MIV) programme study found that volunteers' continued commitment was supported by recognition, networking opportunities and appropriately designed ICT modules.

In inclusive school contexts—often under-resourced and rural—the risk is that digital volunteerism becomes episodic rather than systemic: infrastructure (connectivity, devices, data bundles) may be inadequate, coordination roles may lapse, volunteer turnover may be high, and digital systems may degrade without ongoing investment. Without clear institutionalisation (volunteer-policies, integration into school schedules, budget for data/devices, monitoring frameworks) digital volunteerism can fizzle out.

What is under-documented is the long-term trajectory of digital volunteer programmes in inclusive schooling: how they scale from pilot to school-wide embedded practices; how schools manage volunteer turnover; how resource allocation adjusts over time (devices, connectivity, data); how volunteer networks evolve when initial funding ends; how monitoring and evaluation systems capture sustainability, cost-effectiveness and impact. Also less studied are the resource-management considerations of school leadership teams regarding digital volunteerism—how volunteers are budgeted, scheduled, integrated alongside teachers, how data-costs are managed, how digital-volunteer programmes align with broader resource portfolios in inclusive schools.

Context-Specific Gaps: Inclusive Schools in Rural Zimbabwe

A salient finding is the existence of a context-specific gap: although literature on digital volunteering, community engagement and inclusive education is growing globally and regionally, empirical work specifically focused on how digital volunteers, school leadership and inclusive schooling interact in rural Zimbabwean contexts remains scant. While general youth digital volunteering studies (such as Zubeyr et al., 2024) and broader digital engagement research exist, there is minimal investigation of how these phenomena play out in rural Zimbabwean primary schools, with their particular infrastructural, socio-cultural and policy constraints.

The rural Zimbabwean schooling context presents unique convergence of inclusive-education challenges (teacher capacity, assistive devices, curriculum rigidity), digital constraints (poor connectivity, device scarcity, low digital-literacy) and community-school engagement needs (distance, transport, parental literacy). What remains lacking is empirical research that maps how school management teams (SMTs) in rural Zimbabwe recruit and manage digital volunteers, how the home-community digital readiness (parents, caregivers, local volunteers) interacts with school-led digital volunteer initiatives, how inclusive-education policies are operationalised via digital volunteerism, and how community–school–volunteer networks evolve sustainably under these conditions. The absence of such context-specific research limits the generalisability of digital-volunteer-inclusive schooling models to rural African settings, and suggests that frameworks may need significant adaptation in such contexts.

Theoretical and Conceptual Recommendations

From the findings, the need to refine and extend theoretical frameworks is clear. Researchers are encouraged to develop frameworks that integrate digital volunteerism, inclusive education and community engagement in a holistic manner. Models such as the Technology Acceptance Model (TAM) and Digital Divide Theory—as applied to digital volunteering (Sui et al., 2025)—offer useful starting points, yet they typically focus on individual technology adoption rather than the broader system of volunteers-school-community-digital infrastructure. The community informatics perspective (Gurstein, 2007) emphasises community-control of ICT, yet it has rarely been applied in inclusive schooling-volunteer contexts.

Future theoretical work should explicitly incorporate variables such as volunteer motivation, role clarity, digital-volunteer training, digital infrastructure readiness, school leadership practices, community digital readiness, and sustainability mechanisms into one integrative model. This model should capture pathways from volunteer recruitment → training → deployment → school-community integration → learner and community outcomes → sustainability. It should also be sensitive to context moderators (rural vs urban, connectivity levels, socio-economic status, inclusive-education policy environment). Theoretical frameworks should also embrace an equity-lens (how digital volunteerism addresses or perpetuates inequalities), a governance-lens (digital volunteer roles, data privacy, community voice), and a resource-management lens (how schools manage volunteers as a resource alongside devices/infrastructure).

By developing such integrative frameworks, scholars will be better equipped to design robust empirical studies, generate actionable recommendations for inclusive schooling systems and provide guidance to school management teams seeking to implement digital volunteerism in their resource portfolios.

Implications for Research and Practice

The findings carry significant implications for both research and practice. For research, the identified gaps point to three major priorities: first, deeper empirical work in rural inclusive-schooling contexts (especially in Africa) focusing on digital volunteering, leadership and community engagement; second, longitudinal studies tracking digital volunteer programmes over time, including retention, institutionalisation and outcomes; third, resource-management studies exploring how school management teams integrate digital volunteers alongside other resources (teachers, devices, community partners) to support inclusive schooling.

For practice, school management teams and educational policymakers should view digital volunteerism not as a peripheral add-on, but as an integrated element of inclusive-education strategy. Effective recruitment and training of digital volunteers must be paired with infrastructure readiness, volunteer role clarity, digital-community engagement and leadership coordination. Schools should build policies and institutional mechanisms for volunteer coordination, allocate budget for devices/data/training, embed volunteers in school systems (planning, monitoring, feedback) and engage community digital-readiness (parents, caregivers, local organisations) to ensure volunteers' efforts translate into inclusive schooling outcomes. Finally, sustainability must be planned from the outset: volunteers should receive recognition, career pathways, and reciprocal value; monitoring systems should track volunteer contributions, learner outcomes, and resource utilisation; and scaling should be intentional, rather than ad hoc.

SOLUTIONS AND RECOMMENDATIONS

Theoretical Recommendations

First, it is recommended that researchers and theorists further develop and refine conceptual frameworks that integrate digital volunteerism, inclusive education and community engagement. Given the gaps identified (for example, limited application of community informatics in inclusive schooling contexts), scholars should build on models such as the Technology Acceptance Model (TAM) and Digital Divide Theory (Lim, Crittenden & Hager, 2025; Tomczyk & Kielar, 2025) as well as Community Informatics (Gurstein, 2007). These frameworks should explicitly incorporate volunteer-motivation variables, leadership practices, infrastructure readiness and community networks in rural African settings. In addition, theoretical work should explore how digital volunteerism contributes to social capital, peer mentoring, hybrid volunteer models and inclusive pedagogy—moving beyond individual technology adoption to systemic engagement. This deeper theorisation will enable more robust empirical studies and provide richer guidance for inclusive schooling systems.

Policy Recommendations

At the policy level, national and provincial education authorities should develop explicit guidelines and frameworks that recognise and institutionalise digital volunteerism within inclusive education strategies. For example, policy documents should specify volunteer-role definitions (including remote/online roles), digital-data protections, training standards for volunteers, and mechanisms for collaboration between schools, community groups and digital platforms. Furthermore, policies should mandate inclusion of digital-volunteer engagement in school improvement plans and allocate dedicated budget lines for digital-volunteer infrastructure (devices, connectivity, training). Policies must also address equity: ensuring that digital volunteer programmes do not exacerbate the digital divide and that rural/under-resourced schools receive specific support (Uleanya, 2023). By aligning digital volunteerism with inclusive-education and community-engagement policies, the system can move from fragmented pilots to systemic practice.

Practical Recommendations

On the ground, inclusive schools (especially in contexts like Mashonaland West) should implement the following practical measures:

1. Establish a dedicated digital-volunteer coordination role within school leadership (e.g., a volunteer-liaison teacher or committee) to recruit, orient, schedule and monitor digital volunteers.
2. Develop and conduct orientation and ongoing training programmes for volunteers and teachers. Training topics should include digital-tool usage, inclusive-education strategies, bilingual community engagement and remote mentoring. Research shows volunteers' digital readiness and perceived usefulness strongly affect commitment (Zubeyr, Kuna segaran & Kunjiapu, 2024).
3. Ensure infrastructure readiness: secure devices (tablets, shared computers), reliable connectivity/data bundles for learners and volunteers, and digital platforms (e.g., WhatsApp groups, virtual tutor sessions). Infrastructure challenges remain a major barrier in rural inclusive schooling (Hlungwani, 2025).
4. Integrate digital-volunteer activities into the school timetable and lesson plans: for example, remote peer-mentoring sessions twice weekly, parent-community outreach via digital platforms monthly, learner support chats. Embed digital-volunteer work into inclusive education strategies rather than treating it as an add-on.
5. Implement monitoring and evaluation mechanisms: track volunteer engagement hours, learner participation, teacher feedback, and inclusion outcomes (e.g., increased learner talk, home-school communication, and bilingual support). Provide feedback loops, recognition of volunteers (certificates, acknowledgements), and adjust practices based on review to sustain engagement (Price & Thomas-Evans, 2023).

CONCLUSION

In conclusion, the literature reviewed affirms that digital volunteerism offers significant promise for enhancing community engagement and inclusive schooling, yet this promise is contingent on several interrelated conditions. The preparedness of volunteers in terms of digital literacy, clear role definition and ongoing support is foundational; without this readiness, volunteer commitment and efficacy are substantially undermined. School leadership and institutional embedding of volunteer processes are critical: where leaders align volunteer roles with inclusive schooling strategy, provide coordination and monitor outcomes, digital volunteerism becomes more than a peripheral activity and instead integrates into the school's operational fabric. Moreover, when digital volunteering facilitates stronger school–community linkages — for example enabling parent-school communication, remote mentoring, community dialogues — it holds potential to advance inclusive education. However, practical barriers abound: infrastructure constraints (connectivity, devices, data cost), digital literacy gaps among volunteers, teachers and community members, inequities in access, and absence of monitoring systems limit the realisation of digital volunteerism's potential. Sustainability is another persistent issue: many initiatives begin with enthusiasm but decline when institutionalised mechanisms for coordination, recognition and resource support are lacking. Finally, the research points to a conspicuous gap in context-specific inquiry — especially concerning rural inclusive schools in Zimbabwe (and similar settings) where the convergence of digital volunteerism, community engagement and inclusive education remains underexplored. Taken together, the findings highlight that digital volunteerism is not a technological fix by itself: it must be embedded within a broader ecosystem of leadership, community engagement, resource management and inclusive pedagogy. For practitioners and researchers alike, the implication is clear: to maximise impact, digital volunteer programmes in inclusive schooling must be designed with careful attention to volunteer readiness, leadership coordination, and equity of access, sustainability, and contextual tailoring— particularly in under-resourced rural settings.

REFERENCES

Basheva, D., & Ermolaeva, P. (2025). Digital competence and volunteer engagement in online environments. *Voluntas, 36*(1), 45–59.

Basheva, O. A., & Ermolaeva, P. O. (2020). The phenomenon of digital volunteering in emergency situations: Its essence, types and theoretical framework. *Vestnik Instituta Sotsiologii, 11*(1), 47–69. DOI: 10.19181/vis.2020.11.1.625

Crittenden, V. L., & Hager, M. A. (2025). Digital volunteerism and civic engagement in the digital age. *Journal of Nonprofit & Public Sector Marketing, 37*(1), 1–15.

Dube, B. (2025). Digital literacy initiatives and community participation in Zimbabwean schools. *African Educational Research Journal, 13*(1), 45–56.

Education Coalition of Zimbabwe. (2017, October 12). Inclusive Education Indaba 2017. https://ecozi.co.zw/the-inclusive-education-indaba-2017/

Eickelmann, B., & Gerick, J. (2017). Learning with digital media: A cross-national analysis of ICT use in schools. *Computers & Education, 111*, 1–12. https://doi.org/10.1016/j.compedu.2017.04.001

Gurstein, M. (2007, December 19). What is community informatics (and why does it matter)? arXiv. https://doi.org//arXiv.0712.3220DOI: 10.48550

Hine, C. (2024). Digital participation and volunteering in networked communities. *New Media & Society, 26*(2), 1021–1038.

Hlungwani, P. M. (2025). Bridging the digital divide to promote inclusive education in Zimbabwean rural secondary schools: A case of Mwenezi District. *International Journal of Development and Sustainability, 14*(4), 344–359. DOI: 10.63212/IJDS24120201

International Institute for Capacity Building in Africa. (2024, January). Zimbabwe: Education Country Brief. UNESCO.

Lunga, P. (2024). Community participation and school governance in Zimbabwean education. *Journal of Educational Development in Africa*, *9*(2), 102–118.

Mangena, O., & Chidakwa, N. (2024). The efficacy of inclusive education practices in Zimbabwean rural schools: Challenges and opportunities. *Educational Challenges*, *29*(2), 225–246. DOI: 10.34142/2709-7986.2024.29.2.15

Mudzengerere, P. (2017). [Title of work on framework for digital community volunteering in Zimbabwe]. [Publisher or institution].

Munemo, R. (2018). Differently abled learners' experiences of inclusive education systems in Zimbabwe: Case studies of three selected high schools in Chitungwiza (Unpublished MEd thesis). University of Zimbabwe.

Muresherwa, P. (2020). [Title of empirical study on infrastructure/leadership practice in Zimbabwe]. [Publisher or institution].

Mutyavaviri, C. (2016). Challenges in implementing inclusive education in Zimbabwean schools. *Zimbabwe Journal of Educational Research*, *28*(2), 45–60.

Mutyavaviri, P. N. (2016). Educational managers' understanding and experiences of the implementation of inclusive education: Evidence from selected urban primary schools in Zimbabwe (Unpublished MEd thesis). University of KwaZulu-Natal.

Naicker, S. (2019). Inclusive education in Africa: Policy and practice perspectives. *International Journal of Inclusive Education*, *23*(7–8), 720–735.

Naqshbandi, K. Z., Jeon, Y.-H., & Ahmadpour, N. (2022). Exploring volunteer motivation, identity and meaning-making in digital science-based research volunteering. *International Journal of Human-Computer Interaction*, *39*(20), 4090–4111. DOI: 10.1080/10447318.2022.2109246

Naqshbandi, M. M., Tabche, I., & Choudhary, N. (2022). Digital volunteering and technology adoption: The role of motivation and self-efficacy. *Information Technology & People*, *35*(6), 1963–1985.

Ncube, A. (2024). Community participation and inclusive schooling in Southern Africa. *Education and Society, 42*(1), 59–74.

Ngwarati, C., & Muchemwa, S. (2024). Challenges in implementing inclusive education in Zimbabwean schools. *Journal of Special Education in Africa, 8*(1), 33–48.

Spillane, J. P., Harris, A., Jones, M., & Mertz, K. (2020). Opportunities and challenges for taking a distributed perspective: Novice school principals' emerging sense of their new position. *British Educational Research Journal, 46*(1), 97–117. https://doi.org/10.1002/berj.3568

Sui, D., Goodchild, M., & Elwood, S. (2025). Digital divide theory and civic participation in the information age. *Information Communication and Society, 28*(3), 412–428.

Tendeukai, I. C. (2020). School heads' leadership practices in enhancing quality education: Perspectives from six rural day secondary schools of Masvingo District in Zimbabwe (PhD thesis). University of KwaZulu-Natal.

Tendeukai, P. (2020). Community engagement in inclusive education practices in Zimbabwe. *African Educational Research Journal, 8*(3), 521–530.

UNESCO. (2021, April 22). Addressing the needs of learners with disabilities in Zimbabwe. https://www.unesco.org/en/articles/addressing-needs-learners-disabilities-zimbabwe

UNICEF. (2022). *Digital learning and education connectivity in Zimbabwe: Country report*. UNICEF.

UNICEF. (2025). *Digital education and community engagement framework*. UNICEF.

Zubeyr, E., Kunasegaran, M., & Kunjiapu, S. (2024). Embracing youth volunteerism through digital literacy for a sustainable future. *International Journal of Academic Research in Business & Social Sciences, 14*(4), 1406–1415. DOI: 10.6007/IJARBSS/v14-i4/21420

Zvavahera, P., Garwe, E., Pasipanodya, N., Chigora, P., & Katsande, R. (2024). Digital transformation in Zimbabwean education institutions. *International Journal of Educational Development, 102*, 102920.

ADDITIONAL READING

Ashnie Mahadew — "Understanding inclusion in early childhood care and education: A participatory action learning and action research study" (2022)

Carmelita Jacobs — "Reimagining a framework for parent involvement in South Africa: Preparing preservice teachers" (2024)

Mary Wickenden — "Using participatory and inclusive methodologies to explore inclusive education in Africa" (2024) African Journal of Disability Anna Neya Kazanskaia — "Future Trends in Digital Volunteering: Emerging Technologies and Sustainable Practices" (2025) neyaglobal.com

A. Saidi (and co-author Z. Boti) — "Revisiting community engagement in higher education in South Africa from a vantage point of the notion of third mission" (2024)

KEY TERMS AND DEFINITIONS

Digital Volunteerism: According to Basheva & Ermolaeva (2020), digital volunteerism is voluntary activity in which individuals use modern information-communication technologies (ICTs) from remote locations to help other people, groups or organizations without receiving direct monetary reward.

Community Engagement: As Booth & Ainscow (2006) describe it, community engagement in a school context is the process of involving families, community members, and local organisations in genuine partnerships with the school to support learning, participation and belonging for all learners.

Inclusive Education / Inclusive Schooling: Kirschner (2015) defines inclusive education as an approach in which students with and without disabilities are educated together in a regular classroom with the supports they need, so that all can participate meaningfully and achieve their potential.

Volunteer Motivation (Functional Approach): Clary & Snyder (1999) articulate that individuals engage in volunteering to fulfil six types of psychological functions—values, understanding, enhancement, career, social, protective—and that matching the volunteer role to these motivations improves satisfaction and retention.

Distributed Leadership: According to Spillane (2006), distributed leadership is leadership practice that emerges from the interactions of leaders, followers and situations, rather than residing solely in the formal role of a principal.

Chapter 6
Enhancing Community Engagement Through Digital Volunteerism

P. Selvakumar

http://orcid.org/0000-0002-3650-4548

Department of Science and Humanities, Nehru Institute of Technology, Coimbatore, India

Kiran C. K.

http://orcid.org/0009-0001-3816-1761

Dayanandasagar College of Arts, Science, and Commerce, India

Hetal Gaglani

http://orcid.org/0000-0002-1485-7422

Ramdeobaba University, Nagpur, India

Dhananjay Kulkarni

Sri Balaji University, Pune, India

Vijay Uprikar

http://orcid.org/0000-0003-2546-8307

Datta Meghe Institute of Management Studies, India

Meenal R. Kale

Yeshwantrao Chavan College of Engineering, Nagpur, India

ABSTRACT

Digital volunteerism, also known as virtual volunteering or online volunteerism, is a modern approach to community service that leverages digital technologies to enable individuals to contribute their time, skills, and expertise to causes and organizations remotely. Unlike traditional

DOI: 10.4018/979-8-3373-5722-5.ch006

forms of volunteering that require physical presence, digital volunteerism offers flexibility, accessibility, and scalability, making it a powerful tool in today's interconnected world. This paradigm shift in volunteerism is facilitated by the widespread availability of the internet, smartphones, collaborative platforms, and digital communication tools, enabling volunteers to participate from anywhere in the world, at any time. At its core, digital volunteerism embodies the same altruistic spirit as conventional volunteer work—serving the greater good and supporting social, environmental, educational, or humanitarian causes—but with enhanced efficiency and reach.

UNDERSTANDING DIGITAL VOLUNTEERISM

Digital volunteerism, also known as virtual volunteering or online volunteerism, is a modern approach to community service that leverages digital technologies to enable individuals to contribute their time, skills, and expertise to causes and organizations remotely. Unlike traditional forms of volunteering that require physical presence, digital volunteerism offers flexibility, accessibility, and scalability, making it a powerful tool in today's interconnected world. This paradigm shift in volunteerism is facilitated by the widespread availability of the internet, smartphones, collaborative platforms, and digital communication tools, enabling volunteers to participate from anywhere in the world, at any time. At its core, digital volunteerism embodies the same altruistic spirit as conventional volunteer work—serving the greater good and supporting social, environmental, educational, or humanitarian causes—but with enhanced efficiency and reach. It encompasses a wide range of activities, including mentoring students through online platforms, translating texts for international nonprofits, creating digital content or websites for NGOs, offering teletherapy or legal advice, conducting online fundraising campaigns, or contributing to open-source projects. The diversity of digital volunteer roles reflects the evolving needs of society and the increasing integration of technology into every facet of organizational operations. Skill-based volunteering is particularly well-suited to the digital format. Professionals from fields such as IT, marketing, education, design, finance, law, or healthcare can offer their expertise remotely, providing valuable services that may otherwise be inaccessible or unaffordable for many grassroots organizations. This not only enhances the capacity of nonprofits but also allows volunteers to gain experience, improve their resumes, and stay professionally engaged. Students and recent graduates, in particular, can use digital volunteerism to build portfolios and gain real-world experience while contributing to meaningful causes. Digital volunteerism also promotes sustainable and cost-effective practices. Since it eliminates the need for physical infrastructure and travel, it reduces the carbon footprint and operational costs associated with traditional volunteer programs. Organizations can direct more resources to their core missions instead of logistics, and volunteers can participate without incurring travel or accommodation expenses. This environmental and economic efficiency aligns with global sustainability goals, encouraging wider participation.

The educational sector, in particular, has seen significant gains through digital volunteerism. Volunteers have supported students with online tutoring, helped schools develop digital content, and provided teachers with technical training and support. In remote or underserved regions, such assistance has helped bridge the digital divide and ensure continued learning. Similarly, digital health volunteers have helped promote telemedicine, assist with vaccine registration, and raise awareness about public health practices. Despite its numerous benefits, digital volunteerism does come with certain challenges, including issues related to digital access, data security, effective supervision, and maintaining volunteer motivation in a virtual environment. Ensuring equitable access to digital tools and internet connectivity remains a pressing concern, especially in developing regions. Furthermore, building trust and accountability in virtual relationships requires clear communication, orientation, and continuous engagement. However, with appropriate strategies and infrastructure, these challenges can be effectively mitigated. In conclusion, digital volunteerism represents a transformative evolution in civic engagement, offering unprecedented opportunities to connect, serve, and make a difference on a global scale. It democratizes volunteerism, harnesses diverse skills, promotes sustainable practices, and builds inclusive communities. As digital technologies continue to evolve, the scope and impact of digital volunteerism will only expand, empowering individuals and organizations to collaboratively address the world's most pressing challenges. Embracing this model is not only a response to contemporary societal dynamics but a proactive step toward a more connected, compassionate, and equitable future.

THE ROLE OF DIGITAL VOLUNTEERISM IN COMMUNITY ENGAGEMENT

Digital volunteerism has emerged as a vital force in redefining community engagement in the 21st century, bridging geographical divides and enabling individuals from diverse backgrounds to contribute meaningfully to societal development. By leveraging the power of digital technologies, this form of volunteerism empowers people to support communities remotely through online platforms, tools, and services (Nursey-Bray M. & Masud-All-Kamal, 2022). In doing so, digital volunteerism expands the traditional boundaries of community engagement, transforming it into a more inclusive, accessible, and scalable model that aligns with the dynamics of a digitally interconnected world. At its essence, community engagement involves collaborative efforts to identify and address local challenges, foster social cohesion, and improve the overall well-being of community members. Traditionally, this has relied heavily on face-to-face interaction, physical presence, and in-person events. However, digital volunteerism transcends these limitations by facilitating participation through virtual channels. Individuals can now engage with communities from anywhere in the world—whether by providing mentorship, conducting online educational workshops, helping with digital literacy, supporting mental health initiatives, managing social media for local nonprofits, or participating in data collection and analysis for community projects. One of the most significant contributions of digital volunteerism to community engagement is enhancing inclusivity. Many individuals who were previously excluded from volunteer efforts due to mobility challenges, time constraints, or geographical isolation can now participate actively. This includes students, seniors, working professionals, stay-at-home parents, and persons with disabilities (Miao Q., et al, 2021). By providing flexible schedules and remote opportunities, digital platforms ensure that anyone with internet access and a willingness to help can be part of a larger community mission. This inclusiveness not only enriches volunteer efforts but also fosters a sense of belonging and purpose among diverse population segments. Digital volunteerism also plays a critical role in amplifying community voices. Through digital storytelling, social media campaigns, blog writing, and video creation, volunteers help marginalized communities raise awareness about their challenges, values, and needs. This virtual amplification can mobilize support, attract resources, and influence policy decisions. By giving communities a platform to share their experiences with a global audience, digital volunteers act as intermediaries who bridge the gap between local realities and broader advocacy efforts. Another vital dimension of digital volunteerism in community engagement is its role in education and capacity-building. Volunteers can conduct webinars, create digital training materials, offer online courses, and mentor students or aspiring professionals. These efforts not only promote lifelong learning but also empower individuals and groups within communities to become self-reliant and proactive. For instance, digital volunteers can train local women in entrepreneurship, guide youth in digital skills development, or support teachers with curriculum design. The ripple effect of such initiatives extends beyond individuals to the broader community fabric. Furthermore, digital volunteerism facilitates community data collection and analysis, which is crucial for evidence-based planning and decision-making (Dinca L. G. & Diaconita, 2024). Volunteers can assist in mapping community resources, conducting needs assessments, or analyzing local challenges using digital tools. Platforms like OpenStreetMap, Ushahidi, or KoboToolbox allow volunteers to contribute data that can be used for development planning, disaster preparedness, or service delivery. This participatory approach ensures that communities are not just recipients of aid but active participants in shaping their future.

In the realm of health and well-being, digital volunteerism supports community engagement by enabling tele-counseling, peer support networks, and virtual health education. Volunteers with backgrounds in psychology, nursing, or public health can provide essential services to individuals facing mental health issues, chronic illness, or social isolation. They also help promote healthy behaviors, organize fitness challenges, and assist with virtual check-ins for vulnerable populations (Zubeyr E., et al, 2024). These interventions create support systems that are especially valuable in underserved or remote areas. In addition, digital volunteerism fosters community-led innovation. By providing platforms for idea-sharing, crowdsourcing solutions, and collaborative problem-solving, it encourages communities to develop creative approaches to their challenges. Digital hackathons, design-thinking workshops, and innovation labs bring together volunteers and community members to co-create projects ranging from clean water solutions to community radio programs (Kunnathully K., et al, 2025). This participatory innovation enhances community ownership and sustainability of interventions. In conclusion, digital volunteerism plays a transformative role in community engagement by broadening participation, fostering inclusivity, and enhancing the capacity of communities to thrive in a digital age. It enables global collaboration while respecting local contexts, bridges digital divides, and creates new opportunities for civic involvement. As societies continue to evolve and embrace technology, digital volunteerism will remain a powerful tool for nurturing resilient, informed, and empowered communities. By embedding it into community development strategies, stakeholders can unlock a future where meaningful engagement is not limited by physical boundaries but driven by shared purpose and collective action.

EXPANDING REACH AND IMPACT THROUGH DIGITAL PLATFORMS

In today's hyperconnected world, digital platforms are transforming the scale, speed, and scope of volunteerism, enabling organizations and individuals alike to dramatically expand their reach and amplify their impact (Luz A., 2025). The integration of technology into civic engagement is redefining traditional boundaries, connecting people across geographies, bridging socioeconomic divides, and fostering unprecedented levels of participation and collaboration. By harnessing the capabilities of digital tools, platforms, and networks, volunteerism has evolved from a locally bound endeavor into a dynamic, borderless movement with the power to respond to global challenges and catalyze social change on an extraordinary scale. At the heart of this transformation are digital platforms—websites, apps, portals, and social media channels—that serve as facilitators of engagement. These platforms act as centralized hubs where opportunities are listed, volunteers are matched to suitable roles, and organizations can manage communication, tasks, and impact measurement. Platforms like Idealist, VolunteerMatch, Catchafire, UNV Online Volunteering, and HandsOn Connect have made it easier than ever to find and engage in meaningful work across a diverse array of causes such as education, environmental protection, public health, refugee support, animal welfare, and human rights advocacy. One of the most significant contributions of digital platforms is their ability to extend the geographic reach of volunteer opportunities. Traditionally, volunteering was largely limited to one's immediate locality or community, constrained by logistics, transportation, and proximity. Digital platforms have obliterated these boundaries, allowing individuals to contribute to causes and organizations located anywhere in the world. A student in Brazil can assist a nonprofit in Uganda with web development; a healthcare professional in Canada can offer teleconsultations to patients in rural India; a language expert in Germany can translate emergency documents for a humanitarian organization operating in Syria (Laurean Sanchez S. D., 2024). This global scope fosters cross-cultural collaboration, knowledge exchange, and solidarity across continents. Digital platforms also scale the volume and diversity of participation by engaging broader audiences. Their accessibility, ease of use, and visibility attract a wide spectrum of participants, including youth, retirees, students, professionals, people with disabilities, and individuals from underserved or remote communities. This inclusivity not only enriches the volunteer base with a wide range of skills, perspectives, and experiences but also strengthens the social fabric by encouraging civic participation from all segments of society. Furthermore, digital campaigns and calls to action, amplified through social media, can mobilize thousands of volunteers within hours, especially during crises or urgent events. The speed of mobilization facilitated by digital platforms significantly enhances the impact of volunteerism. During emergencies such as natural disasters, pandemics, or humanitarian crises, rapid response is critical. Digital tools enable real-time coordination, information sharing, and volunteer activation. Crowdsourcing apps, GIS-based mapping tools, cloud-based collaboration platforms, and secure messaging services allow for the swift dissemination of information and organization of resources. For instance, during the COVID-19 pandemic, digital platforms helped mobilize medical professionals, mental health counselors, tutors, and IT experts to provide remote services and support global recovery efforts.

Additionally, digital platforms help maximize the depth and quality of impact by enabling skill-based volunteering. Organizations can reach out to highly specialized volunteers with expertise in areas such as software development, law, marketing, finance, data analytics, education, or healthcare (Bonina C., et al, 2021). These professionals can offer targeted, high-value support that would otherwise be too costly or unavailable, particularly for small nonprofits and grassroots movements. As a result, digital volunteerism doesn't just increase participation—it enhances the caliber and relevance of contributions, leading to more effective and sustainable outcomes. Nevertheless, to fully realize the potential of digital platforms in expanding reach and impact, certain challenges must be addressed. Digital inequality remains a persistent barrier, particularly in underserved regions where internet access, digital literacy, and technological infrastructure are lacking. Additionally, ensuring cybersecurity, data protection, and ethical engagement is critical, especially when working with vulnerable populations. Digital volunteerism also requires organizations to rethink their operational models, invest in platform training, and maintain strong communication and support systems to manage volunteers effectively. Equally important is the need to foster a sense of authentic connection and purpose in a virtual environment. Without physical interaction, volunteers may feel detached or undervalued. Thus, digital platforms must be intentionally designed to facilitate relationship-building, peer interaction, and recognition. Personalized feedback, virtual events, and community forums can help volunteers feel connected to the mission and one another. In conclusion, digital platforms have become instrumental in expanding the reach and impact of volunteerism by making it more accessible, responsive, and scalable (Acs Z. J., et al, 2021). They democratize engagement, enhance global collaboration, and empower individuals to contribute meaningfully, regardless of their location or limitations. With thoughtful implementation, continuous innovation, and inclusive design, these platforms have the potential to reshape the future of civic engagement—making volunteerism not just an act of service, but a global movement of interconnected change-makers. As society continues to embrace digital transformation, the strategic use of digital platforms will remain a cornerstone in maximizing the power and promise of volunteer-driven impact.

DIGITAL PLATFORMS FOR COMMUNITY ENGAGEMENT AND PARTICIPATION

In the digital age, the landscape of community engagement and civic participation has been dramatically transformed by the proliferation of digital platforms. These platforms—ranging from dedicated civic engagement tools and social media networks to collaborative apps and virtual meeting spaces—have become essential mediums through which individuals connect, communicate, collaborate, and contribute to the well-being of their communities (Sebunya J. & Gichuki 2024). Whether it's through participating in town hall discussions online, supporting local initiatives, organizing virtual events, or volunteering remotely, digital platforms have created a vibrant ecosystem that fosters deeper, broader, and more inclusive civic involvement. Digital platforms serve as virtual infrastructures that support community interactions, public service delivery, collaborative governance, and grassroots mobilization. By leveraging technology, they bridge geographical distances, reduce communication barriers, and enable real-time information sharing. For community engagement specifically, these platforms offer flexible, accessible, and scalable mechanisms that accommodate diverse stakeholders—including citizens, non-governmental organizations, local governments, and private entities—allowing them to work together for shared societal goals. In addition to mainstream social media, specialized civic tech platforms have emerged to enable more structured participation. Tools like Nextdoor, Bang the Table (EngagementHQ), CitizenLab, Decidim, and Change.org offer functionalities such as surveys, petitions, participatory budgeting, idea submission, public polling, and digital voting (De Filippi F., et al, 2022). These platforms empower citizens to directly influence public policy, co-design services, and voice their priorities in ways that are transparent and traceable. By turning one-way information delivery into two-way dialogue, civic tech strengthens the relationship between citizens and decision-makers. For local governments and municipalities, digital platforms are indispensable in promoting participatory governance. Virtual town halls, digital noticeboards, public consultation portals, and e-governance tools allow communities to stay informed and involved in urban planning, budget allocation, and policy formation. During emergencies or pandemics, governments can use these platforms to disseminate critical updates, solicit community feedback, and coordinate relief efforts. This enhances trust, transparency, and responsiveness—key pillars of democratic governance. Community-based organizations (CBOs) and nonprofits utilize digital platforms to engage volunteers, manage programs, collect donations, and evaluate impact. Platforms like VolunteerMatch, Idealist, Catchafire, and UNV Online Volunteering match skilled individuals with remote and local volunteer opportunities (Lawrence K. C., & Fakuade, 2021). Meanwhile, project management and collaboration tools like Slack, Asana, Trello, and Zoom facilitate teamwork and service delivery across dispersed teams. These platforms enable more efficient coordination, improved communication, and streamlined project execution—all vital for scaling impact.

Virtual event platforms, including Hopin, Airmeet, Google Meet, and Microsoft Teams, have enabled large-scale digital gatherings such as webinars, conferences, town halls, hackathons, and training sessions. These events promote knowledge exchange, strengthen networks, and provide forums for dialogue among diverse participants. Unlike physical events, they often reduce barriers related to cost, travel, and accessibility, making participation feasible for broader audiences (Theocharis Y., et al, 2023). However, the effectiveness of digital platforms in fostering engagement depends on equitable access, digital literacy, and platform design. The digital divide—rooted in disparities in internet access, device ownership, language barriers, and education—remains a major obstacle to inclusive participation. Governments and civil society must invest in expanding broadband infrastructure, offering community-based digital literacy training, and creating multilingual, user-friendly interfaces that accommodate individuals with varying levels of technological proficiency. Moving forward, the future of digital community engagement lies in hybrid models that combine the strengths of online and offline participation. For example, virtual forums can be used to prepare for in-person meetings, or physical community events can be live-streamed and followed up with online discussions. These blended approaches increase flexibility, allow for continuity, and ensure that engagement is both deep and wide. In conclusion, digital platforms are revolutionizing the way communities connect, communicate, and co-create change (Kotte K R., et al, 2025). They empower individuals to participate in civic life, support one another, express their identities, and shape the direction of their societies. While challenges such as access, digital literacy, and ethical governance must be addressed, the potential of these platforms to foster inclusive, transparent, and dynamic community engagement is immense. By embracing thoughtful design, inclusive strategies, and a commitment to equity, digital platforms can serve as catalysts for stronger, more resilient, and more participatory communities in the 21st century and beyond.

BUILDING COMMUNITY CAPACITY THROUGH DIGITAL SKILLS

In an increasingly digital and interconnected world, the cultivation of digital skills within communities has emerged as a foundational pillar for sustainable development, resilience, and empowerment (Rennó R. & Novaes, 2023). Building community capacity through digital skills involves equipping individuals and groups with the knowledge, tools, and competencies needed to effectively utilize digital technologies for communication, collaboration, education, economic advancement, health, governance, and civic participation. This capacity-building approach enables communities to navigate the complexities of the digital age, close digital divides, and unlock opportunities for collective growth and problem-solving. Community capacity building refers to the process of enhancing the ability of individuals, organizations, and networks within a community to identify problems, develop solutions, and take meaningful action toward improvement. When this process is infused with digital skill development, communities gain access to a vast array of tools and platforms that can amplify their voices, streamline their operations, and drive social innovation. Digital skills empower residents not just to consume information, but to create, influence, and lead within digital environments. At the most basic level, foundational digital literacy—including the ability to operate devices, navigate the internet, use communication tools, and manage digital identities—is a prerequisite for community engagement in the digital world. For many marginalized populations, especially in rural or underserved urban areas, a lack of these foundational skills leads to exclusion from digital services, resources, and opportunities (Lee S., et al, 2025). Addressing this gap through community-based digital literacy programs is a critical first step toward broader capacity development. Libraries, community centers, non-governmental organizations (NGOs), and schools have played a central role in this effort by offering digital skill training, often tailored to the needs and contexts of local populations. These initiatives include workshops on basic computer use, internet safety, social media, mobile banking, job search strategies, and digital rights. In many cases, youth-led programs teach older generations how to use smartphones or navigate government portals, creating intergenerational learning experiences that build trust and cohesion. As communities become more digitally confident, advanced digital skills such as coding, data analysis, graphic design, digital marketing, cybersecurity, and content creation become accessible. These competencies are essential for fostering economic empowerment, particularly in the gig economy and remote work environments. Through digital upskilling, community members can pursue freelance careers, launch online businesses, participate in global marketplaces, or support local initiatives with tech-based solutions. This not only enhances individual livelihoods but also contributes to the economic vitality of the entire community. Furthermore, community journalism and digital storytelling initiatives teach people how to document local events, report on pressing issues, and share cultural narratives using digital media (Jete R & Farah 2024). This helps communities take control of their representation and counter misinformation or neglect by mainstream media. Tools like smartphones, editing software, and online publishing platforms empower residents to raise awareness, celebrate identity, and mobilize action.

Figure 1. Innovative Ideas to Increase Engagement in Your Nonprofit Virtual Volunteerism

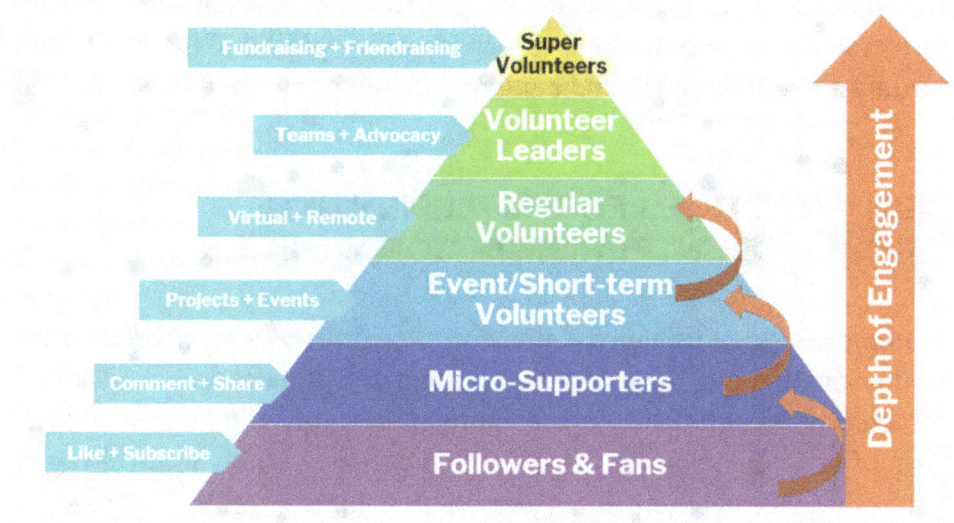

The process of building community capacity through digital skills must also address the issue of digital equity. This includes not only access to devices and internet connectivity but also culturally relevant content, accessible interfaces for people with disabilities, multilingual support, and policies that prevent data exploitation. Without equitable access, digital skill development risks exacerbating existing inequalities rather than bridging them. Additionally, digital skills can catalyze greater civic engagement and democratic participation (Allmann K. & Blank, 2021). With the ability to use e-governance platforms, access open data, participate in online consultations, and advocate via social media, community members can hold institutions accountable and shape public policies. Grassroots digital literacy initiatives have enabled people to report corruption, petition for change, organize peaceful protests, and contribute to local development plans. This active participation strengthens democratic culture and builds civic capacity. In conclusion, building community capacity through digital skills is a strategic and transformative investment in social, economic, and democratic development. It enables individuals to thrive in the digital economy, organizations to operate more effectively, and communities to shape their futures with agency and confidence (Hubballi R B., et al,

2025). The impact of digital capacity-building extends far beyond individual empowerment; it strengthens the very fabric of society by fostering inclusion, innovation, and resilience. With inclusive policies, collaborative partnerships, and community-led approaches, digital skills can become a catalyst for sustainable and equitable development in the 21st century.

BEST PRACTICES FOR IMPLEMENTING DIGITAL VOLUNTEERISM IN COMMUNITIES

Implementing digital volunteerism effectively within communities requires a strategic, inclusive, and context-sensitive approach. As digital volunteerism continues to gain momentum as a viable and impactful form of civic engagement, especially in an increasingly digitized world, establishing best practices ensures that volunteer efforts are not only meaningful and sustainable but also aligned with the goals and needs of the communities they intend to serve (Tijsma G., et al, 2023). The following best practices highlight key strategies and frameworks that can guide communities, organizations, and stakeholders in successfully designing, managing, and scaling digital volunteerism initiatives.

1. Community-Centric Planning and Needs Assessmen

The foundation of any successful digital volunteerism initiative lies in a thorough understanding of the community's needs, assets, digital readiness, and socio-cultural dynamics. Before launching programs, stakeholders must engage with community members to identify priority areas—such as education, health, economic empowerment, disaster response, or civic participation—where digital volunteerism can add tangible value. Participatory needs assessments, stakeholder mapping, and digital inclusion audits help align volunteer efforts with real community challenges, ensuring relevance and impact. Tailoring programs to local contexts also increases community ownership and participation.

2. Inclusive Access and Digital Equity

Ensuring equitable access is fundamental. Not all community members have the same level of access to internet connectivity, digital devices, or digital literacy (Iefimova G. V. & Pashchenko, 2025). Best practices in digital volunteerism actively work to bridge the digital divide by providing support such as free or subsidized devices, mobile-friendly platforms, offline alternatives, and community Wi-Fi hubs. Additionally, materials should be accessible in local languages and formats suitable for people with disabilities. Inclusive design principles must be applied to digital platforms to ensure usability for all, including the elderly, women, and marginalized populations.

3. Strong Volunteer Recruitment and Onboarding Systems

An effective digital volunteerism strategy begins with transparent recruitment processes that clearly define roles, responsibilities, expectations, and required competencies. Volunteer postings should be disseminated through multiple channels—social media, local forums, educational institutions, and community networks—to attract a diverse pool of applicants. A structured onboarding process, including orientation, digital tools training, code of conduct, and security protocols, prepares volunteers to serve confidently and ethically. Tailored onboarding modules may be required for specialized tasks such as data analysis, digital content creation, or virtual mentoring.

4. Capacity Building and Continuous Learning

Digital volunteerism thrives when volunteers are empowered with the necessary skills, knowledge, and confidence to perform their roles effectively. Regular training workshops, webinars, peer-learning circles, and e-learning modules should be integral components of any initiative. Topics may include digital tools, cybersecurity, communication skills, ethics, project management, and community engagement techniques (Jiwei R., 2023). Encouraging volunteers to pursue certifications or digital badges not only recognizes their learning but also enhances their employability and sense of purpose.

5. Clear Communication and Coordination Mechanisms

Effective communication channels and coordination structures are essential for managing dispersed digital volunteers. Centralized platforms or dashboards that facilitate task assignment, collaboration, reporting, and real-time updates can help streamline operations. Communication should be frequent, transparent, and supportive—keeping volunteers informed about project developments, community feedback, and performance expectations. Using tools such as Slack, Trello, Google Workspace, or WhatsApp groups enables seamless interaction and camaraderie among volunteers, mentors, and coordinators.

6. Community Partnerships and Multi-Stakeholder Collaboration

Collaboration across sectors—government, NGOs, private sector, academic institutions, and local community organizations—enhances the reach, legitimacy, and sustainability of digital volunteerism (Caridà A., et al, 2022). Strategic partnerships can offer infrastructure, funding, technical expertise, and policy support. For example, tech companies may provide free access to platforms, universities might mobilize student volunteers, and local governments can endorse volunteer initiatives within development plans. Such networks also create a feedback loop between digital volunteers and the community, allowing for more responsive and dynamic programming. 7. Volunteer Role Diversification and Skill Matching: A well-designed digital volunteer program offers diverse roles that align with the interests, skills, and availability of volunteers. Opportunities may range from graphic design, web development, and translation to tutoring, health awareness campaigns, and data visualization. Using skill-matching tools or databases ensures that volunteers are placed in positions where they can be most effective, motivated, and fulfilled. Micro-volunteering options—short, task-based assignments—should also be made available for individuals with limited time but valuable expertise (Samal A & Bhargav

2025). Implementing digital volunteerism in communities is not merely a matter of technological adoption but a holistic, participatory, and inclusive endeavor. When guided by best practices—rooted in equity, ethics, innovation, and community ownership—digital volunteerism becomes a transformative force that addresses local challenges, builds human capital, and strengthens democratic participation. It connects people across geographies, generations, and sectors through a shared commitment to positive change. As communities continue to navigate a complex and rapidly evolving digital world, embracing these best practices ensures that digital volunteerism remains impactful, empowering, and resilient for years to come.

OVERCOMING CHALLENGES IN DIGITAL VOLUNTEERISM

Digital volunteerism—defined as the act of volunteering one's time, skills, and resources through online platforms—has emerged as a powerful tool for social impact, community development, and global collaboration. While it offers unprecedented opportunities for inclusivity, flexibility, and scalability, it also brings with it a complex array of challenges that can hinder its effectiveness, sustainability, and accessibility (Thewes C., et al, 2024). Addressing these challenges is crucial to ensuring that digital volunteerism remains a viable and empowering mechanism for civic engagement across diverse populations and contexts. This comprehensive discussion explores the multifaceted obstacles facing digital volunteerism and offers pathways to overcome them effectively.

1. Digital Divide and Inequitable Access

Perhaps the most significant challenge in digital volunteerism is the digital divide—the gap between those with access to digital tools and the internet, and those without. Many individuals, especially in rural, low-income, and marginalized communities, lack basic internet connectivity, digital devices, and the digital literacy needed to participate in online volunteering. This limits the reach of digital volunteerism and excludes populations who could both contribute to and benefit from such programs. Solutions: To bridge this divide, stakeholders must invest in digital infrastructure, community Wi-Fi zones, mobile-friendly platforms, and low-bandwidth tools that accommodate limited connectivity. Providing free or subsidized devices and conducting community-based digital literacy workshops can empower more people to participate (Bouarar A. C., et al, 2023). Collaborations with telecom providers, NGOs, and government agencies can enable access to affordable internet packages and localized digital education.

2. Lack of Digital Literacy and Technical Skills

Even among those with digital access, many potential volunteers and beneficiaries struggle with the technical proficiency required to engage in digital platforms. This challenge is especially acute among older adults, individuals with limited education, or those unfamiliar with online tools such as Google Workspace, social media, or cloud-based collaboration platforms. Solutions: Offering pre-volunteering orientation programs that include training in basic digital skills, cybersecurity awareness, and platform navigation can build confidence and competence. Integrating continuous learning models, peer-to-peer mentoring, and gamified tutorials helps users upskill progressively. Tailoring content to different literacy levels and using vernacular languages also ensures accessibility.

3. Volunteer Retention and Motivation

Unlike traditional volunteering, where personal interactions can foster emotional connections and team spirit, digital volunteers often face isolation, lack of feedback, and disengagement over time. Without proper recognition or interaction, volunteers may lose motivation, leading to high attrition rates. Solutions: Implementing regular communication, virtual team-building activities, recognition programs (e.g., e-certificates, digital badges), and storytelling opportunities can help maintain morale. Providing structured tasks with clear goals, progress updates, and appreciation messages creates a sense of purpose and accomplishment. Building an active digital volunteer community with forums, chat groups, and leadership opportunities also fosters belonging and sustained engagement (Elboj-Saso C., et al, 2021).

4. Coordination and Management Difficulties

Managing remote volunteers across different time zones, backgrounds, and skill sets poses challenges related to coordination, supervision, and accountability. Poor communication, unclear expectations, and mismatched tasks can lead to inefficiencies and reduced impact. Solutions: Using centralized volunteer management systems such as project dashboards, CRM tools, and task boards (e.g., Trello, Asana) enables structured delegation, tracking, and reporting. Clearly defined roles, timelines, and communication protocols help avoid confusion. Appointing volunteer coordinators or team leads improves responsiveness and conflict resolution.

5. Data Privacy and Security Concerns

Digital volunteerism often involves the handling of sensitive personal data—whether related to health, education, or identity—which raises concerns about cybersecurity, data misuse, and confidentiality breaches. Volunteers without proper training may inadvertently expose data to threats, damaging trust and credibility (Christensen C., et al, 2022). Solutions: Establishing comprehensive data protection policies, conducting cybersecurity training for volunteers, and implementing secure login systems (e.g., multi-factor authentication, encrypted communications) are critical. Volunteers should sign confidentiality agreements and receive clear guidance on handling sensitive information. Platforms must comply with international data protection standards like GDPR and ensure secure cloud storage.

6. Language and Cultural Barriers

Digital volunteerism is often global in nature, bringing together diverse individuals with varying languages, cultural norms, and communication styles. Misunderstandings, misinterpretations, and cultural insensitivity can arise, especially in cross-border collaborations. Solutions: Promoting cultural competency training, encouraging multilingual communication, and using translation tools or volunteers can facilitate more inclusive interactions. Localizing content and adopting culturally sensitive practices help ensure relevance and respect for the communities served. Teams should embrace diversity as a strength, fostering open dialogue and cultural exchange. While the challenges of digital volunteerism are multifaceted, they are not insurmountable (Sakthivel M., et al, 2025). By proactively identifying barriers and implementing targeted solutions, communities and organizations can unlock the full potential of digital volunteerism as a force for inclusive and sustainable development. Overcoming these challenges demands a holistic, collaborative, and adaptive approach—one that prioritizes accessibility, equity, and resilience. Through innovation, capacity building, strategic partnerships, and community empowerment, digital volunteerism can continue to thrive and evolve, transforming lives and strengthening societies in the digital age.

ENSURING INCLUSIVITY AND ACCESSIBILITY IN DIGITAL VOLUNTEERISM

As digital volunteerism becomes a prominent and transformative avenue for civic engagement, social development, and global collaboration, it is imperative to ensure that it is inclusive and accessible to all individuals, regardless of their socioeconomic status, location, gender, age, ability, language, or digital literacy (Kamerāde D., et al, 2024). The core promise of digital volunteerism lies in its potential to democratize opportunities for service, allowing people from all walks of life to contribute meaningfully to societal well-being using technology. However, this promise can only be fulfilled if proactive measures are taken to address systemic inequities, overcome barriers, and build an inclusive digital volunteer ecosystem that values diversity and leaves no one behind.

1. Understanding Inclusivity and Accessibility in the Digital Volunteerism Context

Inclusivity in digital volunteerism refers to the practice of creating equitable opportunities for all individuals to participate, recognizing and accommodating differences in culture, gender, age, language, socioeconomic status, and abilities. Accessibility, meanwhile, refers to designing systems, platforms, and processes that are usable by people with a wide range of physical, sensory, and cognitive abilities, including those with disabilities and limited digital experience. Together, inclusivity and accessibility ensure that digital volunteerism does not replicate existing inequalities or marginalize already underrepresented groups. They promote empowerment, equity, and meaningful engagement across diverse communities.

2. Bridging the Digital Divide

A major obstacle to inclusive digital volunteerism is the digital divide, which refers to the unequal access to digital infrastructure, devices, and connectivity. In many rural and underserved areas, internet access is limited or unaffordable (Basheva & Ermolaeva, 2024). Women, persons with disabilities, and low-income groups often lack access to digital tools or face sociocultural restrictions on their use. Strategies to bridge this gap include: Collaborating with governments and telecom providers to expand affordable broadband and community Wi-Fi networks. Establishing public digital access centers in community libraries, schools, or NGOs. Providing subsidized or donated devices such as smartphones, tablets, or laptops to volunteers and beneficiaries. Promoting the use of mobile-optimized platforms and low-bandwidth applications to ensure usability even with slow internet connections. By ensuring the infrastructural and economic means to participate, organizations can significantly broaden the reach and diversity of digital volunteers.

3. Designing Inclusive and Accessible Digital Platforms

Many digital volunteer platforms are unintentionally exclusionary due to complex interfaces, language barriers, or the lack of features that accommodate people with disabilities. This creates hurdles for participation among older adults, visually or hearing-impaired users, and individuals with cognitive limitations. Best practices for inclusive design include: Ensuring compatibility with assistive technologies such as screen readers, magnifiers, and speech-to-text tools. Providing text alternatives for audiovisual content (e.g., subtitles, transcripts, alt text). Using plain language and multilingual interfaces to accommodate varying literacy and language proficiency levels. Offering content in regional and indigenous languages to increase accessibility for local populations. Adopting responsive design so platforms function effectively across devices (desktop, mobile, tablet). Universal Design principles should be embedded at every stage of platform development, ensuring no user is left behind.

4. Promoting Digital Literacy and Capacity Building

Lack of digital literacy is a major barrier to inclusivity in digital volunteerism, especially for older adults, first-time users, and individuals from marginalized communities (Iglesias R. S., et al, 2023). Without foundational knowledge of digital tools, platforms, and cybersecurity practices, potential volunteers may feel overwhelmed or excluded. To address this, organizations can: Organize digital literacy workshops, tutorials, and online help centers tailored to various proficiency levels. Create mentorship or buddy programs where experienced volunteers guide newcomers. Provide step-by-step manuals, visual aids, and video guides to help users navigate digital platforms. Collaborate with local schools, community centers, or NGOs to integrate digital skills training into broader educational programs. By building confidence and competence, digital literacy initiatives empower more people to participate meaningfully in volunteer activities.

5. Ensuring Gender Inclusivity

Women and gender-diverse individuals often face systemic barriers in digital engagement due to cultural norms, caregiving responsibilities, online harassment, or lack of access to personal devices. Digital volunteerism must be mindful of these gender-based inequalities and take steps to promote safe, supportive, and empowering environments. Key actions include: Providing gender-sensitive training on online safety, digital rights, and harassment prevention. Offering flexible volunteering schedules to accommodate caregiving and domestic responsibilities. Actively recruiting women and gender-diverse individuals through targeted outreach campaigns. Highlighting female role models and leaders in digital volunteer programs to encourage participation (Pietilä I., et al, 2021). Creating gender-inclusive spaces not only enriches the diversity of volunteer contributions but also leads to more equitable outcomes for communities served. Enabling persons with disabilities to engage in digital volunteerism not only upholds their rights but brings valuable perspectives and talents to community efforts. Digital volunteerism holds immense promise as a tool for inclusive civic participation, social innovation, and community transformation. However, this potential can only be realized if intentional and sustained efforts are made to ensure that everyone—regardless of ability, background, or circumstances—has the opportunity to participate fully and meaningfully. Inclusivity and accessibility are not optional enhancements but foundational principles that define the legitimacy, effectiveness, and ethics of digital volunteerism. By embracing universal design, fostering digital literacy, valuing diverse voices, and advocating for equity, we can create a digital volunteerism landscape that is not only technologically advanced but also deeply human-centered and just. In doing so, we move closer to a world where digital engagement becomes a bridge—not a barrier—to collective empowerment and shared progress.

THE FUTURE OF DIGITAL VOLUNTEERISM IN COMMUNITY ENGAGEMENT

The future of digital volunteerism in community engagement is poised to be transformative, dynamic, and increasingly integrated into the fabric of societal development. As digital technologies continue to evolve rapidly, the opportunities for virtual volunteerism are expanding in scope, inclusivity, and impact (Den Broeder L., et al, 2022). This evolution is being driven by technological innovation, shifting societal values, and the growing need for flexible, scalable, and sustainable models of civic engagement. Looking ahead, digital volunteerism will not only redefine how individuals contribute to their communities but also reshape the very nature of community-building itself.

1. Emerging Technologies Shaping Digital Volunteerism

The future of digital volunteerism will be strongly influenced by emerging technologies such as artificial intelligence (AI), blockchain, extended reality (XR), and Internet of Things (IoT). AI-powered platforms can match volunteers to opportunities based on their skills, interests, and availability with unprecedented accuracy, enhancing engagement and satisfaction. AI can also assist in analyzing community data to identify pressing needs and tailor volunteer efforts accordingly. Blockchain technology may introduce transparent systems for volunteer verification, tracking contributions, and ensuring accountability—thus building trust in virtual environments. XR technologies like virtual reality (VR) and augmented reality (AR) are already enabling immersive volunteer experiences, such as virtual tours for heritage preservation or remote disaster simulations for emergency training. IoT devices, meanwhile, can help volunteers monitor environmental conditions, health metrics, or agricultural yields in real time, expanding the scope of digital volunteer project (Mao G., et al, 2021)s. Together, these technologies will create a more intelligent, personalized, and impactful digital volunteer ecosystem.

2. Hybrid Volunteering Models: Bridging Physical and Digital

While fully remote volunteering will continue to grow, the future will likely see a rise in hybrid volunteerism—a blend of in-person and virtual activities. Hybrid models allow volunteers to attend training sessions online while executing tasks offline, or vice versa. For example, a mentor might conduct sessions via video call but meet beneficiaries for periodic events. These models offer the flexibility of digital engagement while retaining the human connection of face-to-face interaction. They are especially useful in rural and urban fringe areas where digital infrastructure may be inconsistent. Hybrid volunteerism also accommodates varying preferences and capabilities, making it an inclusive model for diverse demographics.

3. Globalization and Transnational Volunteering

As digital boundaries collapse, the future will witness an exponential increase in cross-border digital volunteerism. Individuals from different countries will contribute to causes far beyond their local or national communities. A teacher in Canada may tutor students in remote African regions; a medical student in India could assist in global health data analysis for an NGO in Brazil (Jiang L. & Gu, 2022). This globalization of service not only enables knowledge sharing across cultures but also promotes international solidarity, peacebuilding, and global citizenship. Organizations will increasingly adopt multilingual platforms, global volunteer databases, and collaborative international networks to harness this potential.

4. Decentralized, Peer-Led Volunteer Platforms

The future of digital volunteerism will also involve a shift from centralized, organization-led models to peer-driven, decentralized systems. Enabled by Web3 technologies and social networks, grassroots movements and informal communities will play a more prominent role in initiating volunteer activities. Decentralized platforms allow individuals to self-organize, co-create solutions, and engage in micro-volunteering opportunities without intermediaries. For instance, local community groups may mobilize volunteers through messaging apps to support disaster relief, civic actions, or food drives. This democratization of volunteering empowers individuals and fosters a culture of shared responsibility.

5. Increased Focus on Inclusivity and Equity

As the digital volunteerism landscape expands, there will be growing emphasis on ensuring inclusive access and equitable participation. Future platforms will be designed with universal accessibility standards, support for multiple languages, and adaptive features for people with disabilities. Organizations will prioritize gender inclusivity, age-diverse participation, and culturally sensitive practices. Digital literacy programs will be scaled to empower underrepresented communities to engage in virtual service. Data collection and analysis will focus on ensuring that no demographic is systematically excluded (Robinson J. A., et al, 2021). Furthermore, intersectional approaches will address the compounded barriers faced by marginalized groups, ensuring that digital volunteerism becomes a truly equitable and empowering movement.

6. Data-Driven Community Engagement

The use of big data analytics will transform how communities engage with digital volunteers. By aggregating and analyzing data from social media, surveys, sensors, and digital platforms, organizations will gain deep insights into community needs, volunteer behavior, and program effectiveness. This will lead to more targeted, efficient, and responsive volunteer initiatives. Predictive analytics can help forecast future needs—such as food insecurity trends or educational gaps—allowing proactive deployment of volunteers. Personalized feedback loops will motivate volunteers by showing them the tangible impact of their contributions in real time. Ethical considerations around data privacy and consent will remain critical, and future digital volunteer platforms will embed strong governance mechanisms to safeguard user data. The future of digital volunteerism in community engagement is not simply about moving traditional service activities online—it is about reimagining civic participation for the digital age. It encompasses a vision of empowered individuals, connected through technology, working collaboratively and inclusively to build stronger, more resilient, and equitable communities. From AI-driven platforms to decentralized networks, from global participation to local empowerment, digital volunteerism is rapidly becoming a cornerstone of modern community engagement. Its continued evolution will require innovation, collaboration, and a steadfast commitment to inclusivity, ethics, and sustainability. As we embrace this future, the promise of a more connected, compassionate, and participatory world becomes not just possible—but inevitable.

LEVERAGING TECHNOLOGY FOR COMMUNITY ENGAGEMENT AND DEVELOPMENT

In an increasingly digitized world, leveraging technology for community engagement and development has become not only a practical solution but a necessary strategy for achieving inclusive, resilient, and sustainable societies. Technological innovations—ranging from mobile connectivity and social media platforms to artificial intelligence, blockchain, and virtual reality—are reshaping how communities interact, organize, and build capacity (Kangana N., et al, 2024). These tools offer immense potential to bridge geographic divides, amplify marginalized voices, accelerate knowledge dissemination, and create collaborative ecosystems for problem-solving. As global challenges become more interconnected, the integration of technology into community development frameworks enables more dynamic, participatory, and scalable approaches to civic life.

1. Digital Communication Platforms for Inclusive Engagement

One of the most transformative aspects of technology is its ability to foster real-time, multidirectional communication across diverse populations. Tools such as WhatsApp, Telegram, Facebook Groups, Slack, Zoom, and Microsoft Teams allow communities to stay connected, coordinate efforts, and share information without the constraints of physical presence. These platforms facilitate ongoing dialogue among stakeholders—residents, local leaders, NGOs, governments, and businesses—encouraging collaborative decision-making and transparency. Social media platforms, in particular, provide marginalized and underserved groups with visibility and a voice in public discourse (Suklabaidya S., 2024). Movements such as #MeToo, #BlackLivesMatter, and climate justice campaigns have demonstrated how digital platforms can elevate grassroots activism, foster solidarity, and influence public policy. For local communities, these tools offer means to report issues, propose initiatives, and mobilize resources, often at minimal cost.

2. Data-Driven Community Planning and Decision-Making

The proliferation of big data, open-source tools, and Geographic Information Systems (GIS) allows for evidence-based community development. Local authorities and community groups can use data analytics to identify socio-economic disparities, map infrastructure gaps, track service delivery, and evaluate program impact. Real-time data dashboards can inform disaster response, public health strategies, and urban planning. For example, platforms like Ushahidi have been used globally to crowdsource and map crisis information, from election violence to natural disasters. In community development, such data enables targeted interventions, equitable resource allocation, and predictive modeling for long-term planning. This empowers local actors to move from reactive approaches to proactive, strategic development informed by granular insights.

3. Mobile Technologies and Remote Access

Mobile phones, particularly smartphones, have revolutionized community engagement by providing low-barrier access to digital services. In remote and underserved areas, mobile technology supports everything from financial inclusion (via mobile banking and digital wallets) to health care delivery (through telemedicine and SMS reminders for immunizations). Educational apps offer on-the-go learning, and mobile surveys allow real-time feedback collection from residents. SMS-based civic engagement tools allow citizens to report corruption, request municipal services, or participate in polls—even without internet access. Mobile platforms also support micro-volunteering and gig-based community development efforts, enabling individuals to contribute their time and skills in flexible ways (Anthony B. Jr., 2024).

4. Technology for Capacity Building and Skills Development

E-learning platforms, online courses, and open educational resources (OERs) are democratizing access to knowledge and building human capital within communities. Platforms like Coursera, edX, Skillshare, and YouTube tutorials empower individuals to upskill in areas such as entrepreneurship, digital literacy, financial management, agriculture, and health. Many NGOs and community centers are integrating tech-based learning into their outreach programs, often in local languages and tailored to community needs. Virtual mentorship and peer learning networks also allow knowledge-sharing across borders. As digital skills become increasingly essential for economic and civic participation, technology acts as a critical enabler of personal and collective development.

5. Civic Tech and Participatory Governance

Civic technology (or civic tech) refers to platforms and tools that enhance public participation, accountability, and government transparency. These include e-governance portals, budget tracking tools, public grievance redress systems, and online consultation platforms. By enabling citizens to vote, petition, attend town hall meetings, or contribute to policy discussions online, civic tech fosters a more inclusive and democratic development process. Examples include platforms like "Change.org" for petitions, "Decide Madrid" for participatory budgeting, and India's "MyGov" platform which enables crowdsourced policymaking. These tools reduce bureaucratic barriers, build trust, and ensure that development is shaped by the voices of those it impacts the most.

6. Digital Platforms for Entrepreneurship and Economic Empowerment

Digital technologies also catalyze economic development by enabling entrepreneurship, innovation, and employment opportunities. E-commerce platforms such as Etsy, Shopify, and Amazon empower local artisans and small business owners to reach global markets (Welch & Saltmarsh, 2023). Crowdfunding platforms like GoFundMe, Kickstarter, and Kiva provide access to alternative financing, while gig economy platforms like Fiverr and Upwork enable income generation for freelancers, including in rural areas. For farming communities, precision agriculture tools and digital marketplaces help improve yields and reduce post-harvest losses. Blockchain-based platforms enhance supply chain transparency, ensuring fair compensation for producers. By supporting inclusive economic participation, technology contributes to sustainable community growth and resilience. Technology, when thoughtfully applied, is a powerful enabler of community engagement and development. It bridges distances, amplifies voices, accelerates learning, enhances transparency, and catalyzes economic and social change. However, its true value lies not in the tools themselves, but in how they are used to foster trust, inclusion, and collaboration within and across communities. As we move into an increasingly digital future, it is imperative that technology serves as a bridge—not a barrier—to community development. By centering people, ethics, and local knowledge in its design and deployment, we can ensure that digital transformation becomes a driver of shared progress and collective well-being.

CONCLUSION

In today's interconnected, digitized world, digital volunteerism has emerged as a transformative force capable of reshaping how communities evolve, adapt, and thrive. Unlike traditional forms of volunteering that often require physical presence and logistical coordination, digital volunteerism offers a flexible, accessible, and scalable model of civic engagement that can transcend geographic and social boundaries. It harnesses the power of technology—such as social media, online platforms, mobile applications, virtual collaboration tools, and data analytics—to mobilize people, resources, and knowledge in unprecedented ways. As a result, digital volunteerism is not merely a new format of service but a catalyst for systemic change, enabling communities to build resilience, foster inclusion, and address complex challenges with innovation and collective effort. 1. Redefining Civic Engagement in the Digital Era: Digital volunteerism is revolutionizing traditional civic engagement by making it more inclusive, participatory, and agile. Through digital platforms, individuals of all ages, backgrounds, and abilities can contribute their time and skills to community development efforts without the need to be physically present. Whether through online tutoring, remote mentoring, digital content creation, translation services, advocacy, or crisis response, the scope of volunteering has expanded to accommodate diverse interests and capacities. This redefinition empowers more people to take part in civic life, especially those who were previously excluded due to physical, social, economic, or geographic limitations. The democratization of volunteering opportunities strengthens civil society, builds a culture of participation, and stimulates proactive problem-solving at the community level. 2. Empowering Local Voices and Grassroots Initiatives: One of the most significant impacts of digital volunteerism is its ability to amplify local voices and support grassroots movements. Community members are no longer passive recipients of aid but active participants and co-creators in transformation. With tools like blogs, vlogs, webinars, online surveys, and collaborative apps, residents can voice their needs, propose ideas, and rally support from within and beyond their locale. Digital volunteers, acting as digital advocates or storytellers, help to document community issues, raise awareness, and attract resources from a global audience. This strengthens local ownership and ensures that community-driven solutions are culturally appropriate and sustainable. Whether in rural villages, urban slums, or conflict-affected areas, digital engagement platforms offer communities the means to tell their own stories and lead their own change. 3. Enhancing Education and Digital Literacy: Education is a powerful driver of community transformation, and digital volunteerism plays a pivotal role in making education more accessible and effective. Virtual tutoring, online mentorship, and the dissemination of open educational resources (OERs) help bridge educational gaps—especially in areas with limited infrastructure. Volunteers provide academic support, career guidance, language instruction, and skills training through digital means, creating ripple effects in personal empowerment and community development.

Moreover, digital volunteerism enhances digital literacy, a key component of modern empowerment. Volunteers often lead workshops or create online content to teach essential digital skills—such as using email, navigating websites, creating resumes, or managing online safety. These skills are critical for job access, financial inclusion, and civic participation, and thus lay the foundation for long-term transformation. 4. Addressing Inequality and Promoting Social Inclusion: Digital volunteerism helps tackle social inequalities by promoting inclusive engagement. It enables marginalized groups—such as women, youth, people with disabilities, and minority communities—to access services, participate in dialogue, and contribute meaningfully to social change. For instance, remote mentoring programs connect young girls in rural areas with female professionals globally, breaking gender stereotypes and inspiring ambition. Online support groups run by volunteers can provide emotional support and guidance to marginalized populations such as LGBTQ+ individuals, refugees, or those affected by trauma. Digital volunteers also advocate for rights, policy changes, and equitable access to services by using data and storytelling to highlight disparities and hold institutions accountable. In this way, digital volunteerism becomes an instrument of empowerment, visibility, and voice for those often left out of traditional systems. Digital volunteerism is no longer a peripheral or temporary solution—it is a core strategy for community transformation in the 21st century. By harnessing technology and human compassion, it enables communities to become more self-reliant, informed, connected, and capable of driving their own development. It redefines how we think about service, leadership, and impact in a globalized world. As communities continue to navigate change, uncertainty, and opportunity, digital volunteerism offers a resilient, inclusive, and empowering pathway forward. Its true power lies in its ability to turn every connected citizen into an agent of change—bringing ideas, skills, and solidarity together in the service of collective growth and transformation.

REFERENCES

Acs, Z. J., Song, A. K., Szerb, L., Audretsch, D. B., & Komlósi, É. (2021). The evolution of the global digital platform economy: 1971–2021. *Small Business Economics*, *57*(4), 1629–1659. DOI: 10.1007/s11187-021-00561-x

Allmann, K., & Blank, G. (2021). Rethinking digital skills in the era of compulsory computing: Methods, measurement, policy and theory. *Information Communication and Society*, *24*(6), 837–855. DOI: 10.1080/1369118X.2021.1874475

Anthony, B.Jr. (2024). The role of community engagement in urban innovation towards the co-creation of smart sustainable cities. *Journal of the Knowledge Economy*, *15*(2), 567–589. DOI: 10.1007/s13132-023-01176-1

Basheva, O. A., & Ermolaeva, P. O. (2024). "Digital volunteering concept: Definition and models for analysis." *Handbook of Environmental Policy and Law*. https://doi.org/DOI: 10.1007/978-3-031-30231-2_26-1

Bonina, C., Koskinen, K., Eaton, B., & Gawer, A. (2021). Digital platforms for development: Foundations and research agenda. *Information Systems Journal*, *31*(6), 869–902. DOI: 10.1111/isj.12326

Bouarar, A. C., Mouloudj, S., Umar, T. P., & Mouloudj, K. (2023). Antecedents of physicians' intentions to engage in digital volunteering work: An extended technology acceptance model (TAM) approach. *Journal of Integrated Care*, *31*(3), 210–225. DOI: 10.1108/JICA-03-2023-0017

Caridà, A., Colurcio, M., & Melia, M. (2022). Digital platform for social innovation: Insights from volunteering. *Creativity and Innovation Management*, *31*(4), 678–690. DOI: 10.1111/caim.12499

Christensen, C., Ehrenberg, N., & Christiansson, J. (2022). "Volunteer-based IT helpdesks as ambiguous quasi-public services—A case study from two Nordic countries." *Nordic Human-Computer Interaction*, 6(CSCW). Article, *45*, 1–20. DOI: 10.1145/3534567

De Filippi, F., Coscia, C., Cocina, G. G., Lazzari, G., & Manzo, S. (2022). Digital participatory platforms for civic engagement: A new way of participating in society? Analysis of case studies in four EU countries. *International Journal of Urban Planning and Smart Cities*, *1*(1), 1–21. DOI: 10.4018/IJUPSC.2020010101

Den Broeder, L., South, J., Rothoff, A., Bagnall, A.-M., Azarhoosh, F., van der Linden, G., Bharadwa, M., & Wagemakers, A. (2022). Community engagement in deprived neighbourhoods during the COVID-19 crisis: Perspectives for more resilient and healthier communities. *Health Promotion International*, *37*(6), daac123. Advance online publication. DOI: 10.1093/heapro/daab098 PMID: 34297841

Dinca, L. G., & Diaconita, V. (2024). "Enhancing the involvement level of volunteer students in the academic community: Efficient usage of digital resources." *Proceedings of the 23rd International Conference on Informatics in Economy*, 49–58. https://doi.org/DOI: 10.1007/978-981-96-0161-5_5

Elboj-Saso, C., Cortés-Pascual, A., Íñiguez-Berrozpe, T., Lozano-Blasco, R., & Quílez-Robres, A. (2021). Emotional and educational accompaniment through dialogic literary gatherings: A volunteer project for families who suffer digital exclusion in the context of COVID-19. *Sustainability (Basel)*, *13*(4), 1890. DOI: 10.3390/su13031206

Hubballi, R. B., Selvakumar, P., Seenivasan, R., Basava Aradhya, S. G., Dinesh, N., & Seelam, P. K. (2025). Overview of Current AI Technologies in Education. In Kyei-Blankson, L., & Ntuli, E. (Eds.), *Transformative AI Practices for Personalized Learning Strategies* (pp. 1–26). IGI Global Scientific Publishing., DOI: 10.4018/979-8-3693-8744-3.ch001

Iefimova, G. V., & Pashchenko, K. O. (2025). "The role of social media in promoting volunteer initiatives and shaping communities." *Problemy Ekonomiky*, 1(1), 112–125. https://problecon.com/article/view/2025-volunteer-socialmedia

Iglesias, R. S., Carrolaggi, P., & Randaccio, S. (2023). "Learning helping: Inclusive education of adults through virtual volunteering." *EDULEARN23 Proceedings*, 15(1), 1123–1132. https://library.iated.org/view/IGLESIAS2023LEA

Jete, R., & Farah, R. (2024). "Empowering communities through digital skills training in Simeulue Village." *Pengabdian: Jurnal Abdimas*, 4(1), 45–52. https://journal.ypidathu.or.id/index.php/pengabdian/article/view/123

Jiang, L., & Gu, M. M. (2022). Understanding youths' civic participation online: A digital multimodal composing perspective. *Learning, Media and Technology*, 47(2), 149–162. DOI: 10.1080/17439884.2022.2044849

Jiwei, R. (2023). Research on digital empowerment to facilitate quality development of volunteerism in new era. *International Journal of Frontiers in Sociology*, 5(2), 88–97. https://www.francis-press.com/papers/12345

Kamerāde, D., Clark, A., Goodall, C., Parker, C., & Vasilica, C. (2024). "Bridging the digital divide: Challenges and opportunities for disabled adults in volunteering." *University of Greenwich Repository*. https://gala.gre.ac.uk/id/eprint/42356

Kangana, N., Kankanamge, N., De Silva, C., Goonetilleke, A., Mahamood, R., & Ranasinghe, D. (2024). Bridging community engagement and technological innovation for creating smart and resilient cities: A systematic literature review. *Smart Cities*, 7(1), 45–62. DOI: 10.3390/smartcities7060147

Kotte, K. R., Attaluri, V., & Selvakumar, P. (2025). Revolutionising Retail Banking with AI and Virtual Technologies AI-Driven Financial Training. In Nair, A. J., Manohar, S., Limbu, Y. B., & Huhmann, B. A. (Eds.), *Intersecting Natural Language Processing and FinTech Innovations in Service Marketing* (pp. 421–440). IGI Global Scientific Publishing., DOI: 10.4018/979-8-3693-9944-6.ch020

Kunnathully, K., Satyanarayana, P., Anute, N., Sharma, M., Sureshkrishna, G., & Manjunath, T. C. (2025). Propaganda, Social Media and AI. In Vieira, A., Joaquim, A., & Duarte, A. (Eds.), *Digital Populism and the Use of Neo-Propaganda and Fake News* (pp. 19–38). IGI Global Scientific Publishing., DOI: 10.4018/979-8-3693-9999-6.ch002

Laurean Sanchez, S. D. (2024). "Expanding market reach: A comprehensive strategy for scaling Dashboa's services to global eCommerce markets." *Theseus.fi*. https://www.theseus.fi/bitstream/handle/10024/874290/Laurean_Sanchez_Sergio_Daniel.pdf

Lawrence, K. C., & Fakuade, O. V. (2021). Parental involvement, learning participation and online learning commitment of adolescent learners during the COVID-19 lockdown. *Research in Learning Technology*, 29, 2544. DOI: 10.25304/rlt.v29.2544

Lee, S., Hui, J., & Dillahunt, T. R. (2025). "Sociocultural factors in digital skills learning: A community-based intervention among US public housing adults." *Proceedings of the ACM on Human-Computer Interaction*, 9(CSCW1), Article 123, 1–26. https://doi.org/DOI: 10.1145/3711070

Luz, A. (2025). "The role of digital platforms in enhancing the market reach of small businesses in rural America." *Preprints.org*. https://www.theseus.fi/bitstream/handle/10024/874290/Laurean_Sanchez_Sergio_Daniel.pdf

Mao, G., Fernandes-Jesus, M., Ntontis, E., & Drury, J. (2021). What have we learned about COVID-19 volunteering in the UK? A rapid review of the literature. *BMC Public Health*, 21(1), 1470. DOI: 10.1186/s12889-021-11390-8 PMID: 34320922

Miao, Q., Schwarz, S., & Schwarz, G. (2021). Responding to COVID-19: Community volunteerism and coproduction in China. *World Development*, 137, 105128. DOI: 10.1016/j.worlddev.2020.105128 PMID: 32834397

Nursey-Bray, M., & Masud-All-Kamal, M. (2022). Building community resilience through youth volunteering: Towards a new model. *Regional Studies*, 56(7), 1123–1135. DOI: 10.1080/00343404.2022.2045070

Pietilä, I., Meriläinen, N., Varsaluoma, J., & Väänänen, K. (2021). Understanding youths' needs for digital societal participation: Towards an inclusive Virtual Council. *Behaviour & Information Technology*, *40*(12), 1275–1290. DOI: 10.1080/0144929X.2021.1912182

Rennó, R., & Novaes, J. (2023). *"Community networks as sustainable infrastructure for digital skills." Digital Literacy and Inclusion: Stories.* Platforms and Practices., DOI: 10.1007/978-3-031-27224-5_5

Robinson, J. A., Kocman, D., & Speyer, O. (2021). Meeting volunteer expectations—A review of volunteer motivations in citizen science and best practices for their retention through implementation of functional approaches. *Journal of Science Communication*, *20*(2), A03. DOI: 10.22323/2.20020203

Sakthivel, M., Jaganathan, A., & Mohanraj, M. Mohit, Manjunath T, (2025). "Brand Loyalty through AI and Personalisation AI-Generated Content for Financial Marketing". In A J Nair, S Manohar, Y B Limbu & B A Huhmann (Eds.), Intersecting Natural Language Processing and FinTech Innovations in Service Marketing (pp. 77–96). IGI Global Scientific Publishing. https://doi.org/DOI: 10.4018/979-8-3693-9944-6.ch006

Samal, A., & Bhargav, J. S K M, Selvakumar P, Sharma M, T C M, (2025). "Measuring Brand Performance With AI Tools". In Z Hussain, M Sharipudin, A Albattat & A Khan (Eds.), Strategic Brand Management in the Age of AI and Disruption (pp. 279–302). IGI Global Scientific Publishing. https://doi.org/DOI: 10.4018/979-8-3693-9461-8.ch011

Sebunya, J., & Gichuki, A. (2024). Digital tools and platforms for enhancing community participation: A review of global practices. *International Journal of Scientific Research*, *12*(2), 77–91. https://edinburgjournals.org/index.php/ijsr/article/view/1123

Suklabaidya, S. (2024). "Towards inclusive societies: Leveraging IoT for community development and education." *PhilPapers*. https://philpapers.org/rec/SUKTIS

Theocharis, Y., Boulianne, S., Koc-Michalska, K., & Bimber, B. (2023). Platform affordances and political participation: How social media reshape political engagement. *West European Politics*, *46*(4), 788–811. DOI: 10.1080/01402382.2022.2087410

Thewes, C., Sept, A., & Richter, R. (2024). A voluntary divide? Exploring the role of digitalisation in German rural volunteering. *European Countryside*, *16*(1), 1–18. DOI: 10.2478/euco-2024-0004

Tijsma, G., Urias, E., & Zweekhorst, M. (2023). Embedding engaged education through community service learning in HEI: A review. *Educational Research*, *65*(2), 143–169. DOI: 10.1080/00131881.2023.2181202

Welch, M., & Saltmarsh, J. (2023). "Engaging higher education: Purpose, platforms, and programs for community engagement." *Taylor & Francis*. https://www.taylorfrancis.com/books/edit/10.4324/9781003123456

Zubeyr, E., Kunasegaran, M., & Kunjiapu, S. (2024). Embracing youth volunteerism through digital literacy for a sustainable future. *International Journal of Academic Research in Business & Social Sciences*, *14*(4), 1394–1403. DOI: 10.6007/IJARBSS/v14-i4/21420

Chapter 7
Strengthening Teachers and School Leadership Through Digital Transformation:
Community Engagement and Ghana

Richard Adade
http://orcid.org/0000-0001-8006-1302
University of South Africa, South Africa

Leila Goosen
http://orcid.org/0000-0003-4948-2699
University of South Africa, South Africa

ABSTRACT

Against the background of strengthening Community Engagement (CE) and school leadership through digital volunteerism, the purpose of this chapter is stated as to explore the current literature concerning the influence of Information and Communication Technologies (ICTs) in education and seek to develop a theoretical framework that will offer a thorough comprehension of the data. The main focus of the chapter will also include relevant models that facilitate the use of ICTs in the education domain.

DOI: 10.4018/979-8-3373-5722-5.ch007

INTRODUCTION

This section will describe the general perspective of the chapter and end by specifically stating the objectives.

Strengthening Community Engagement and School Leadership Through Digital Volunteerism

This book and the chapter explore how digital volunteerism can be purposefully leveraged to strengthen community involvement and enhance leadership effectiveness in early learning centers, primary and secondary schools, technical and vocational institutions, and higher education environments. The book and this chapter examine how educational leaders at all levels can harness digital volunteer networks to build inclusive partnerships, expand institutional capacity, promote civic engagement, and foster a culture of shared responsibility in education. By emphasizing digital connectivity as a bridge to collective action, the book and this chapter make a compelling case for reimagining school leadership and engagement in ways that are inclusive, sustainable, and adaptable to all levels of the education system.

As part of a book on *reimagining the P-20 landscape for school leadership learning*, the chapter on e.g., the case of the South African P-12 education system by Musundire (2025c, p. 457) examined "the effectiveness of the connoisseurship supervision model in improving the quality of teaching within the context of developmental supervision".

Strengthening Teachers and School Leadership Through Digital Transformation

"The purpose of the study reported on in" a previous chapter by Adade and Goosen (2024, p. 134) was "evaluating teachers' and schools' capacities to integrate technologies into a new educational curriculum using an e-capacity model approach" against "the background of *navigating virtual worlds and the metaverse for enhanced e-learning*".

This chapter will explore the current literature concerning the influence of Information and Communication Technologies (ICTs) on education and seek to develop a theoretical framework that offers a thorough comprehension of the data. The main focus of the chapter will also include relevant models that facilitate the use of ICTs in the education domain (Vanderlinde, 2011).

Recommended Topics

From the recommended topics suggested for this book, the chapter will discuss:

- Digital Volunteerism and Its Role in Strengthening Educational Leadership
- Enhancing Community Engagement Through Digital Volunteerism
- Digital Transformation in Educational Institutions Across All Levels
- Application of Digital Volunteerism in Early Childhood Development Centers
- Digital Volunteerism in Primary and Secondary Schools
- Extending Digital Volunteerism Practices to Colleges, Technical, and Higher Education Institutions
- Case Studies and Empirical Research on Digital Volunteerism Impact
- Challenges and Solutions: Equity, Access, and Digital Inclusion in Volunteerism
- Future Directions: Innovation, Trends, and the Evolving Role of Digital Volunteerism in Education

Target Audience

As part of this book, the chapter is geared towards a diverse and multi-disciplinary target audience involved in education, leadership, community development, and digital innovation. The primary groups, who could benefit most from the research, frameworks, and practical insights presented in this book and the chapter include:

- Educational Leaders and Administrators: Principals, school governing body members, department heads, deans, and institutional managers at early childhood centers, primary and secondary schools, vocational institutions, and universities will find practical strategies for mobilizing digital volunteers and fostering inclusive leadership.
- Policymakers and Government Officials: Those working in departments of education, higher education ministries, and local government structures responsible for educational development will benefit from the policy recommendations and evidence-based models for strengthening school-community partnerships through digital platforms.
- Researchers and Academics: Scholars in the fields of educational leadership, digital education, community engagement, and development studies will find the book and this chapter a valuable addition to current literature, offering original perspectives and empirical evidence on the integration of digital volunteerism in education.

- Non-Governmental Organizations (NGOs) and Community-Based Organizations (CBOs): Organizations working in education support, youth development, digital literacy, and civic engagement will gain tools and approaches to enhance their collaboration with educational institutions through virtual volunteer models.
- Teacher Training Institutions and Professional Development Providers: Institutions that offer educator development programs will benefit from insights on preparing education professionals to lead and manage digital community engagement initiatives.
- Educational Technology (EdTech) Innovators and Platform Developers: Developers and designers of educational and civic technology platforms will gain an understanding of the real-world applications and needs of digital volunteer systems in educational settings.
- Parents, Guardians, and Community Members: As key stakeholders in education, community members and parents interested in contributing meaningfully to schools will discover accessible ways to participate in school life remotely and meaningfully through digital channels.

By addressing the needs and challenges of this broad target audience, the book and chapter aim to inspire a shared commitment to reimagining community engagement and school leadership through technologies, thereby promoting educational equity, resilience, and innovation across all educational contexts.

Objectives

Enhancing Community Engagement Through Digital Volunteerism

This book and chapter aim to explore and promote digital volunteerism as a transformative strategy for *enhancing community engagement* and strengthening leadership across all levels of education—from early childhood development centers to primary and secondary schools, and extending to colleges, technical institutions, and universities. These seek to address the growing need for inclusive, sustainable, and technology-driven approaches to community participation and institutional governance in education systems worldwide. Specifically, the book and chapter intend to accomplish the following objectives:

- Conceptual Clarification: To define and contextualize digital volunteerism within the broader frameworks of educational leadership, community engagement, and digital transformation across diverse educational settings.

- Strategic Integration: To demonstrate how digital volunteerism can be practically integrated into leadership and management strategies to improve institutional performance, learner outcomes, and community-school relationships.
- Framework Development: To develop practical models and frameworks that guide education leaders and stakeholders in implementing digital volunteerism initiatives effectively and ethically.
- Capacity Building: To identify the skills, technologies, and institutional support systems necessary to empower education leaders and communities in adopting digital volunteerism.
- Research Advancement: To contribute to emerging trends related to the body of knowledge by offering original insights, case studies, and empirical perspectives on the role of digital volunteerism in educational development, leadership innovation, and stakeholder collaboration.

This book and the chapter add to current research by bridging gaps between educational leadership studies, digital innovation, and community development literature. While much has been written about volunteerism and educational technology as separate fields, limited research had explored their intersection as a strategic mechanism for institutional strengthening. By focusing on the integration of digital volunteerism within leadership practices, this book and the chapter offer a fresh, interdisciplinary contribution that responds to contemporary challenges in education and expands the theoretical and practical scope of community-engaged leadership in the digital age.

BACKGROUND

This section will provide broad definitions and discussions of the topic on Strengthening Teachers and School Leadership Through Digital Transformation and incorporate the views of others (in the form of a literature review) into the discussion to support, refute, or demonstrate the authors' position on the topic.

The aim of the study discussed in the chapter by Musundire (2025b, p. 103) as part of a book on *Educational Philosophy and Sociological* Foundations *of Education* "was to determine the place of the African Ubuntu philosophy in reducing" ill-discipline "and crime in South African secondary schools from a social justice theoretical perspective."

Digital Volunteerism and Its Role in Strengthening Educational Leadership

In line with the theme of this book, in a book on *chatbots in educational leadership and management*, the study reviewed in the chapter by Musundire (2025f, p. 1) examined "the use of chatbots as virtual leaders in Australian" secondary "schools, focusing on their role in" supporting decision-making and strategic planning, while another chapter (Musundire, 2025g, p. 53) in that same book presented a study, which explored "the integration of chatbots into Educational Management Systems (EMS) in" global intuitions of "higher education. With advancements in artificial intelligence (AI), chatbots can" e.g., optimize administrative tasks.

The book *Research Methods for Educational Leadership and Management* edited by Musundire (2025k) presented various "research methods, including action, case study, and experimental research," which "can be tailored for educational leadership and management", as well as different research designs.

The literature-based study by Musundire (2025m, p. 385) in the book mentioned in the previous paragraph examined the research process model of Ngulube (2015) and its application "in educational leadership and management. It" aimed to analyze how an integrated understanding of making use of the research process in the research model of Ngulube (2015) could be developed.

As part of a book on *Leveraging Technology for Organizational Adaptability*, the study considered in the chapter by Musundire (2025i, p. 197) examined the relationship between Knowledge Management (KM) systems, transformational leadership and organizational adaptability in the case of "South African private institutions of higher learning."

The chapter by Musundire (2025j, p. 357) as part of a book on *Enabling Indigenous Knowledge Systems in Action Research and Action Learning* addressed "disparities in Mathematics teaching between" indigenous "and Eurocentric methods in South African primary schools, aiming to improve" the place of Afro-centric games in the Mathematics curriculum.

"Little is known of the economic phenomenon called a 'cash crisis', with only a handful of nations having ever experienced it across the globe." Recently, an *international journal* article on *science and research* by Zenda, Musundire and Mumanyi (2020, p. 1256) considered the impact of an organizational change management theoretical perspective in the context of the Zimbabwean cash crisis on Small to Medium Enterprises (SMEs) and their consequent adaptation strategies.

"The decline of the Zimbabwean economy" characterized "by the high inflation rate" had "rendered it difficult for Zimbabwean manufacturing to retain talented employees." An *international journal* article on *applied management theory and research* by Magaisa and Musundire (2022, p. 1) reflected on the factors affecting employee retention in Zimbabwean companies.

The purpose of the study by Musundire (2021a, p. 97) in an *international journal* article on *teacher education and professional development* was to investigate the "perceptions of school-based managers and" classroom teachers in South Africa regarding the 'missing' link between the peer supervision model of "teacher development and quality of teaching through teamwork."

Another *international* article *journal* on *teacher education and professional development* (Musundire, 2022, p. 1) examined the "effectiveness of the self-directed supervision strategy as a tool for improving teaching quality. Special reference was made to the implementation of the" perceptions of South African school-based managers and educators.

Digital Transformation in Educational Institutions Across All Levels

Against a background similar to that of the study, which is the topic of this chapter, Ansu-Kyeremeh and Goosen (2022) were exploring the socio-economic facets of online inclusive education in Ghana regarding the effects of technological advancements in academia.

Extending Digital Volunteerism Practices to Colleges, Technical, and Higher Education Institutions

The study by Musundire (2021b, p. 33) in an *international journal* article on *digital literacy and digital competence* "was aimed at investigating the impact of lecturers' level of" instructional "knowledge and skills of e-learning, pedagogical attitude, and learners' performance in" the context of "South African private institutions of higher learning".

School Improvement Conditions

The foundational level of the e-capacity model entails variables suggested as conducive to the successful improvement of innovative reforms in school improvement conditions, providing a structured framework for enhancing educational outcomes through technological implementation.

Leadership

Leadership is defined as the development and effective management of these aspects within the limitations and restrictions of the establishment, with the purpose of establishing and delivering the intended outcomes (Lawrence & Tar, 2018). It has been demonstrated through empirical study that *leadership* support has an enormous effect on "teachers' integration of ICT into their" teaching and instructions (Vo, 2019, p. 65). Uluyol and Şahin (2014) also emphasized that despite significant technological developments in schools, *leadership* support is often neglected. The latter authors advocated for school administrators to be fully committed to facilitating teachers' integration of ICTs to realize the full potential value of technological integration fully.

Presenting a realist approach, the *school leadership* and *management* journal article by Carrington, Spina, Kimber, Spooner-Lane and Williams (2021) indicated that *leadership* attributes that promote teamwork, value diversity, support staff and school improvement, as well as place a high importance on the ongoing professional growth of teachers have a favorable effect on morale and decision-making, which in turn leads to improved results for educational institutions. These characteristics promote a climate in which teachers are valued and motivated, which in turn promotes the effectiveness of their education.

In a study conducted by Wyttenbach and Ospino (2022), it was discovered that administrators within Catholic schools are promoting the adoption of technology. Furthermore, when school leaders actively endorse and aid instructors in integrating technology into their professional tasks as well as teaching methodologies, it increases the feasibility of teachers Infusing technology into their pedagogical strategies.

When there is strong *leadership* backing, an educational institution's efforts to integrate ICTs into the teaching environment will be assured. Against the background of the impact of *leadership* on the growth of ICT companies, a *journal* article on *sustainable business and economics* by Madanchian and Taherdoost (2023) asserted that a deficiency in strong *leadership* abilities frequently acts as a major roadblock, preventing planned advancement and hampering the successful achievement of organizational goals. These show that school administrators and teammates must actively participate in providing ICT support; it is not just the ICT coordinator's job. Schools may guarantee that technology integration is thorough and successful by offering assistance for ICTs. This will help to create a cohesive effort to use ICT to improve educational results (Huber, Lupschina, Schwarz, & Krey, 2021).

Similarly, the integration of ICT into educational institutions is a complex and multifaceted process, necessitating a comprehensive approach that involves legislative and organizational frameworks, strategic planning, and collaborative efforts among professionals. Sosa-Díaz, Sierra-Daza, Arriazu-Muñoz, Llamas-Salguero, and Durán-Rodríguez (2022) highlight the critical role of effective *leadership* in coordinating these diverse elements, ensuring successful integration and long-term sustainability. Without strong *leadership* support, these initiatives risk fragmentation and failure to achieve the desired impact. Increasing the involvement of teachers in goal-setting and decision-making processes through *leadership* had been seen as a good way to encourage inclusion and active engagement in the field of education.

Leaders of educational establishments have a vital role to play as far as the effect of government ICT policy and technology *leadership* on teachers' technology integration in their educational institutions is concerned (Rojas Briñez, Duart, & Galvis Panqueva, 2023). That is, it is their responsibility to ensure the training of teachers on how to use ICTs in their daily classroom instruction. They are also responsible for motivating teachers and promoting a spirit of collaboration in their institutions. These measures ensure that teachers are ready and motivated to implement technologies in their classrooms. Besides the support functions for teachers, such comprehensive support is also helpful in ensuring meaningful long-term progress related to ICTs in classrooms.

Similarly, research conducted by Setia and Aufar (2023) asserts the positive effects it has on teachers' ability to include technology in their classroom. National technological regulations that are supportive and offer a strong framework for leaders to effectively push the use of ICTs in education further promotes this positive influence. This in turn provides teachers with the direction and tools they need to successfully use technology to improve learners' outcomes.

According to a *journal* article on *research on technology in education* by Dexter and Richardson (2020), effective technology integration research tell us that the latter is guaranteed by *leadership* of technology strategies that build a community of professional practice, improve professional competence, and grant teachers with the variable and continuous access to continuing education opportunities. These techniques not only increase the skill and knowledge of teachers. Still, they also create an all-involving atmosphere that promotes creativity and the utilization of technology in pedagogy. A *British journal* article on *education* by Amos, Ogoti, and Siamoo (2022) also found in their study that a spirit of shared strategic vision in a participative *leadership* style helps to promote quality education provision among public secondary schools in the Arusha region of Tanzania.

An ICT coordinator can effectively lead the implementation of technology in schools if they are appointed to a formal position, work in a team of coordinators, and directed with their teaching load, assignments and interaction. In an *educational management administration* and *leadership* journal article, Woo (2023) provided a distributed perspective on the *leadership* of ICT coordinators, arguing that such support allows the coordinators to lead the integration of ICTs most effectively.

MAIN FOCUS OF THE CHAPTER

Issues, Problems

This section will present the authors' perspectives on the issues, problems, etc., as these relate to theme of the book on Strengthening Community Engagement and School Leadership Through Digital Volunteerism and arguments supporting the authors' position on Strengthening Teachers and School Leadership Through Digital Transformation. It will also compare and contrast with what had been, or is currently being, done as it relates to the specific topic of the chapter and the main theme of the book.

Challenges Related to Equity, Access, and Digital Inclusion in Volunteerism

The systematic literature review in the chapter by Musundire (2025a, p. 77) as part of a book on *educational philosophy and sociological* foundations *of education* analyzed "peer-reviewed articles that explored challenges and opportunities of differentiated instruction, social justice, and linguistic diversity in South African private schools."

The study reported on by Musundire (2025h, p. 129) examined "the integration of educational robotics and artificial intelligence" in African Science, Technology, Engineering, and Mathematics (STEM) "education, investigating the challenges and opportunities associated with" such incorporation in a book on *Innovations in Educational Robotics* towards *Advancing AI for Sustainable Development*.

The literature-based study in the chapter by Musundire (2025l, p. 355) as part of a book presenting *research methods for educational leadership and management* "aimed to improve educational leadership and management" by understanding and making use of the so-called 'Research Onion' model framework (Saunders, Lewis, & Thornhill, 2019) and its application. "It addressed challenges such as fragmented methodologies, lack of contextual analysis, and limited inclusivity in leadership practices."

An *international journal* article on *applied management theory and research* by Magaisa and Musundire (2021, p. 24) was focused on "addressing lack of commitment challenges by … consultants as a result of" the relationship between and/or"ineffectiveness of transformational leadership and other motivation factors at" South African management consulting firms.

In a book on *AI strategies for social entrepreneurship and sustainable economic development*, the chapter by Musundire (2025d, p. 307) was using "73 articles related to educational barriers, opportunities, and prospects in science, technology, and innovation (STI) for potential female entrepreneurs in South Africa".

Participation in Decision Making

This can be achieved by seamlessly integrating ICTs into the curriculum. Through this approach, students can enhance their critical thinking, problem-solving, and communication proficiencies, simultaneously accessing and adeptly utilizing information from digital resources. It develops interesting and dynamic learning environments that encourage innovation, teamwork, and creativity (Vanderlinde & Van Braak, 2010).

In reputable Irish schools, teachers tended to avoid utilizing ICT when they lacked the required level of confidence. Based on their degrees of confidence, past experiences, or ideas about the function of technology within the educational environment, teachers' perceptions of the positive aspects as well as difficulties connected with using technology can vary (Anderson & Putman, 2020).

Moreover, as seen in the dynamics of technological advancement and the consequent incessant changes, there is a consequently rapid shift in the educational system's methodologies. Teachers are well-positioned to incorporate the new developments and continually adjust the training and learning methodologies. On the flip side, teachers are better custodians of the set policies and regulations, and their involvement ensures an appreciation and understanding of the rules pertaining to content and delivery. Take for example active teacher participation in school governance of the school, this not only ensures decisions are made with learners and the institution's interest in mind, but it also engenders a mindset of accountability and control calling for their commitment and accountability (Kiprop-Marakis, 2021).

According to Top, Baser, Akkus, Akayoglu, and Gurer (2021), teacher involvement in decision making concerning ICT training is essential in ensuring the training matches educators' desires and goals by improving the smooth incorporation of technology into teaching methodologies and, in turn, enriching students' learning journeys.

For teachers and parents, being involved in academic processes leads to their perception of a higher level of involvement and preparation in terms of both technology and pedagogy, as well as to the notion that they can handle responses more efficiently to any unexpected changes. The hands-on engagement of educators in the implementation of ICT integration into school education is the key to effective implementation and maintaining this process (Rickert & Skinner, 2022).

Kali, McKenney, and Sagy (2015) stated that the choice of approaches to the implementation of technology-enhanced learning depends on the level of instructor's participation and engagement. Therefore, an enhanced knowledge of how teachers can be involved in this process and creating ways to provide and support this involvement causes the emergence of approaches that increase the importance and value of ICT deployment. However, in its turn, it is necessary to conduct more research to identify the best ways to do this.

Professional Collegiality

There are two popular meanings of *collegiality* in the workplace. The first is the faculty members' active participation in their institution's administration. It is widely acknowledged in academia that a cooperative sector relies heavily on collaborative and constructive interactions among its members (Hammer, et al., 2019). Collegial behaviors, such as support, respect, and willingness to contribute, are crucial for maintaining high morale and effectiveness within academic departments. Research has shown that such behaviors significantly contribute to institutional effectiveness. In a survey of faculty satisfaction or dissatisfaction in the workplace, collegiality within the department or school was reported as the most common issue (Ambrose, Huston, & Norman, 2005).

The collegiality and collaborative endeavors among educators have significant importance in driving innovations and advancements in the education system, including ICT integration. In actual practice, recent studies have highlighted the significance of informal learning networks rooted in practical experiences for the continual professional growth of instructors (Ball & Forzani, 2011). To create efficient methods of instruction that prioritize collaborative expertise and group learning, professional collegiality is crucial.

Doorgakant and Baichoo (2021) also believe that professional collegiality at educational settings can improve performance and personal well-being, as academics embrace the notion to foster emotional as well as social intelligence. Furthermore, the development of professional peer relationships in academia can help researchers to be professionally satisfied and to thrive through both personal and professional change (Garbett & Thomas, 2020).

While it is rarely fully assessed and frequently mentioned, professional collegiality is important in the academic review procedures. Depending on the discipline and kind of academic institution, collegiality can have different meanings. A more cooperative and encouraging learning environment can be created by promoting professional collegiality, which will benefit the entire educational institution (Dawson, et al., 2022).

Teachers' Information and Communication Technology Competence

The ability to use a range of ICT applications efficiently for various reasons is referred to as ICT competency. Various researchers had demonstrated that teachers' attitudes and ICT proficiency affect their later encounters with technology as well as their initial usage of it (Lund, Furberg, Bakken, & Engelien, 2014). According to Korukluoğlu, Alci, and Rubach (2023), teachers' basic ICT skills encompass a variety of professional abilities, including thinking critically, and general competencies, ICTs are utilized for educational progress, decision-making, managing change, collaborative efforts, and efficient communication.

ICT literacy, according to Hew and Brush (2007), is required for instructors to be able to use ICTs effectively. Allowing educators to easily infuse technology into their teaching strategies enhances the learning and participation of students results. Further, ICT literacy empowers educators to use cutting-edge teaching techniques in the contemporary classroom and adjust to changing emerging digital trends. Three categories were used to separate ICT literacy:

1. Fundamental ICT knowledge and abilities, such as operating computers and spreadsheets;
2. Pedagogical ICT skills, such as knowing how ICT affects teachers' roles, learners' motivation, and learning outcomes; and
3. Classroom abilities to manage the classroom, which are essential for a smooth ICT integration process and include setting up the classroom to ensure equal access to ICT for every learner and efficiently resolving their technical issues.

The absence of teaching proficiency in ICT is a major obstacle that hinders educators from embedding ICT within their pedagogy. This shortfall frequently leads to teachers feeling less assured about using digital tools proficiently in the classroom. Consequently, investing in ICT-focused training and initiatives for professional development for teachers can cater for this challenge as well as enable teachers to make use of ICTs to enhance the educational process (Mumtaz, 2000).

Instructors are often preoccupied with technological tasks, from launching applications, adjusting electronic interactive boards to ensuring tablet access and administering tech-integrated classrooms (Lachand-Pascal, Michel, Serna, & Tabard, 2022). ICT competency requires continual professional development to stay abreast and updated with the rapidly evolving technology environment because which remains dynamic rather than fixed. To stay current in their industry, educators must routinely update their knowledge of cutting-edge resources and effective teaching techniques (Sadik & Ottenbreit-Leftwich, 2023).

In today's educational environment, information literacy is a crucial ability. It helps students to organize, process, and use information in an efficient manner. Information literacy is essential for assisting pupils in navigating the wide variety of knowledge that is accessible throughout today's digital environment, claimed Aghauche, Nkamnebe, and Nkamnebe (2019). Aničić and Bušelić (2021) had underlined the importance of ICT skills learnt in school as playing a crucial role in defining instructors' preparedness to use ICT in their instruction. On the other hand, studies highlight that more youthful and less experienced instructors express an intention to use ICT, but a proportion of educators lack a fundamental understanding of its justification and how it could benefit their instruction. Additionally, time constraints, heavy instructional loads, and equipment restrictions emerge as significant impediments to the effective integration of technologies in teaching and beyond (Ngao, Sang, & Kihwele, 2022).

Also, Henderson and Milman (2020) noted that teachers employ a diverse range of digital tools, including student management systems, video conferencing platforms, and educational apps, within their educational settings. This integration has led to increased efficiency in tasks like assigning homework, assessing the performance of learners, and giving feedback to learners and stakeholders. Teaching staff are committed to integrating ICT into teaching practice, though they are often cautious due to external constraints, which leads them to evolve pedagogy incrementally (Lavrenova, Lalak, & Molnar, 2020).

Moreover, instructors need ample time to familiarize themselves with as well as explore ICT tools, including the process of trial and error, to become fully competent in utilizing these for the goal of instructing and learning. This is crucial because teachers are responsible for their pupils. They therefore need to continuously improve their teaching methods through ICT integration to ensure an effective and technologically advanced learning culture (Tayaban, 2022). Teachers have limited digital literacy skills in content creation, information literacy, and problem-solving but satisfactory skills in communicating and collaborating using digital content. Although some teachers may encounter difficulties with certain aspects of digital literacy, such as content creation and problem-solving, they generally excel in utilizing digital platforms to communicate and collaborate with digital resources (Garzón-Artacho, Sola-Martínez, Romero-Rodríguez, & Gómez-García, 2021).

Teachers' Actual Use of Information and Communication Technologies

The e-capacity model considers "teachers' actual use of ICTs", in connection with teachers' ICT adoption as, an extra intermediary phase or a steady factor (Vanderlinde & Van Braak, 2010, p. 546). Also, instructors' hands-on engagement with

ICT is viewed as a forecaster. Several research studies indicate that the willingness of teachers to employ ICT is greatly impacted by the nature and proficiency level of ICT skills they acquire during their academic courses (Agyei & Voogt, 2011). However, studies highlight that while more youthful and less experienced instructors showed an intent to use ICT, a certain number of instructors did not understand the fundamental justification for technology use and thus cast doubt on how it could be useful to their instruction. Along with these challenges, time restraints, hefty instructional loads, and equipment restrictions were apparent as major roadblocks to incorporating technology (Ngao, et al., 2022). Studies show that recently appointed teachers lack sufficient readiness to effectively integrate technology into instructional methods in their classrooms (Tondeur, et al., 2012).

Both the e-capacity model and the framework suggested by Kozma (2003) take into account how teachers utilize ICTs. Facilitators' and instructors' utilization of ICTs is seen as an additional intermediate layer or factor in the process, rather than being central to our model. Stated differently, the real-world ICT use by instructors is regarded as an independent variable as opposed to a dependent one. ICT use has been reported and conceptualized in a variety of ways in earlier research. Certain academics concentrate on "the amount of time students spend using ICT, the amount of time" it is used in classrooms, or the number of specific computer apps that are used (Bourgonjon, 2015, p. 4).

Niederhauser and Stoddart (2001) concentrated on educational applications usage, making a distinction between a flexible constructivist program and a skills-based transmission program. Many scholars view ICT usage as a multifaceted process, emphasizing that ICT can be incorporated in various ways within classroom settings. In this particular situation, the study of ICT usage is concerned with a more intricate phenomenon that relates to different categories of usage.

According to a study by Rajput, et al. (2020), about 2 per cent of secondary school teachers used ICT to teach specific subjects, and only 0.5 per cent of teachers integrated ICT as a fundamental part of their daily teaching practice. The majority of teachers use technologies for purposes such as creating lesson plans, calculating learners' scores and delivering instruction using interactive PowerPoint presentations. Yet, they rarely use telecommunications devices to communicate with their learners directly (Niem, Veriñ, & Alcantara, 2020).

Teachers use ICTs to collaborate and interact with each other, and such use are often made without adequate know-how among many teachers; this gives evidence that professional development programs for teachers should boost efforts in ICTs related knowledge and experience. Possibly, these programs can make sure that through more comprehensive training, when teachers are adequately prepared on how to use the technologies in an efficient manner (García-Valcárcel & Mena, 2021).

Akram, Abdelrady, Al-Adwan, and Ramzan (2022) noted that teachers positively perceived ICT integration, especially as a game-changer, in the educational field. Some think that it not only enhances the ability of the teachers to deliver their instructions but also adds fun and interactions to the lesson, which in turn engages students and increases their interest. An analysis administered by Giovannella (2022) brought to light that 36% of instructors have the perception of adopting ICT into their pedagogical practice and it was possible because of collaboration among the teachers and learners.

Finally, using the survey method, Pinto and Leite (2020) also found that teachers are now incorporating more ICTs in the teaching space to complement the conventional teaching and instructional methods with the online teaching-learning process. The prime advantage of doing so is to foster the corresponding activities as well as increase the level of activity and variability of the learning processes taking place.

SOLUTIONS AND RECOMMENDATIONS

This section will discuss solutions and recommendations in dealing with the issues or problems presented in the preceding section.

Solutions Related to Equity, Access, and Digital Inclusion in Volunteerism

Beyond volunteerism, the chapter by Stolz, Fürst and Mundle (2012) discussed real world learning to foster responsible leadership, serve patients and develop innovative solutions to healthcare challenges in a book on *Corporate Volunteering*.

Finally, a document on locally-owned solutions delivering impact in the context of volunteerism and community resilience by Chadwick and Fadel (2020, p. 3) concluded "that resilience is not an end state but an on-going process of change and transformation, and that volunteers are constantly shaping their communities".

Recommendations

The chapter on barriers, opportunities, and prospects regarding social justice realities for women leaders in South African schools by Musundire (2025e, p. 93) as part of a book on *new horizons in leadership: inclusive explorations in health, technology, and education* presented findings of a "systematic literature review making use of findings, conclusions and recommendations from 32 articles related to female school principals".

Information and Communication Technologies Policy Planning

Findings and derived challenges concerning how school leaders should support ICT integration at schools as described in the *school leadership* and *management* journal article by Rojas Briñez, et al. (2023) indicated that the ICT vision and strategy for the inclusion and adoption of ICTs in education, teachers' pedagogical training and enhancement, curriculum and school computerization, as well as all infrastructure, hardware, software, and financial resources for integration to be used in high-quality education, are all related to *information and communication technologies policy planning*.

The study reported on by Kilag, et al. (2022) stated that to be able to carry out ICT so that the material is transferred into learning activities to adhere to education. Generally, a plan of some kind is needed. This strategy describes the anticipated workflow that the university seeks to realize. The report explores the impact of ICT on learning, making a series of general recommendations on ICT usage. Consequently, educators in educational settings that have an ICT strategy centered around shared goals are more prone to regularly incorporate ICT into their lesson plans.

Kundu (2021) highlighted that an ICT policy plan entails more than just hardware and internet access; it also involves the inclusion and adoption of ICT into the educational curriculum. He underscores the significance of regularly evaluating the ICT policy plan, stating that ongoing assessment is as crucial as its initial creation. Essentially, ICT policy planning is a continual and progressive procedure.

ICT in education is impacted by several factors, including infrastructure, education for teachers, policy and legislation, educational programs, instructional resources, as well as assessment (Tay, Lim, & Lim, 2015). Likewise, Tairab and Ronghuai (2017) illustrated that ICT policy plays a pivotal role in driving educational progress within the K–12 system of Sudan.

A *technology, knowledge and learning* journal article on creating a future ready information technology policy for national education systems by Zagami, et al. (2018) argued that national policies regarding ICT integration in education are vital in the effort of preparing students with the competencies and understanding needed to excel in a knowledge-based society. These policies have a dramatic effect on education as they provide well-stated best practices, resources, and models for how to integrate technology into the curricula and instruction. The effective national ICT policy for educational institutions reflects updating their curricula, lesson plans, and practices to deliver high-quality teaching that would increase student success and employability (Sar & Misra, 2020).

ICTs can be the game changer in those parts of the developing world with an opportunity to create fabulous educational institutions. Development preparation and work will need to persist (Cette, Clerc, & Bresson, 2015). Nevertheless, there are notable disparities in how educational infrastructure, syllabus development, and training initiatives are implemented, and the inclusion of ICTs into the educational setting are approached in economically disadvantaged nations, particularly in sub-Saharan countries (Mominó & Carrere, 2016).

Implementing government policies to integrate ICT into pedagogical training and advancement is a multifaceted venture that depends on a deep understanding of its various dimensions. It requires addressing five critical areas for improvement: effective management strategies, adequate financial resources, streamlined technology procurement procedures, comprehensive ICT training programs, and assessment of the impact of ICT on pedagogy (Younie, 2006).

An *educational technology research and development* journal article by Hew and Brush (2007) discussed current (at the time) knowledge gaps and recommendations for future research directions with regard to integrating technologies into K-12 teaching and learning.

FUTURE RESEARCH DIRECTIONS

This section will discuss future and emerging trends, as well as provide insight about the future of the theme of the book on Strengthening Community Engagement and School Leadership Through Digital Volunteerism from the perspective of the chapter focus on Strengthening Teachers and School Leadership Through Digital Transformation. The viability of a paradigm, model, implementation issues of proposed programs, etc., may be included in this section. If appropriate, the section will suggest future research opportunities within the domain of the topic.

Future Research Directions: Innovation, Emerging Trends, and the Evolving Role of Digital Volunteerism in Education

Drawing on extant literature, the methodological study by Ngulube (2015, p. 125) in an *African journal* article on *library, archives and information science* provided emerging trends (at the time) based on "a content analysis of research procedures employed in knowledge management (KM) research".

Schools' Vision of Information and Communication Technologies Integration

Case Studies and Empirical Research on Digital Volunteerism Impact

The Ghanian government is actively encouraging the assimilation of ICTs within scholarly domains through the provision of essential resources and policies. Nonetheless, it is the responsibility of individual schools to create a holistic vision for ICT integration that suits their specific requirements, goals, and future ambitions. This entails aligning ICT strategies that supports the institution's comprehensive academic goals strategically to ensure that technologies act as valuable tools in improving teaching and learning experiences (Ghavifekr & Rosdy, 2015).

The *vision* and objectives of schools significantly impact the degree and method of ICT integration in educational activities. Additionally, a *journal* article on *educational administration* by Yuen, Law and Wong (2003) presenting *case studies* of ICT integration in teaching and learning, ICT implementation and school *leadership* indicated that the historical background of a school affects the adoption and utilization of ICTs within its pedagogical structure.

As stated by Goh and Sigala (2020), resistance to change among administrators and educators can hinder how ICTs are assimilated into the educational system and training. This blockage is perhaps due to the reverence of the orthodox teaching techniques or the fear of technological repercussions on the educational outputs. In the absence of a comprehensive digital strategy, or a systems-wide view of how to best integrate ICTs, they might overlook key opportunities to improve student outcomes in the classroom. ICT resources can be used ineffectively and have limited educational effects if strategic planning and mutual comprehension are lacking (Costa, Castaño-Muñoz, & Kampylis, 2021).

Similarly, within their scholarly work about the effective use of ICTs in schools, Kalita and Kumar (2020) implied that for optimal efficiency integrating technology, schools should have a clear vision. Besides, together with considerable benefits, the integration of technological tools can be connected with some challenges. To implement this may pose tough challenges for instructors implementing a number of ICTs, and students can resist this integration if schools have no vision for ICT integration.

Sancho-Gil, Rivera-Vargas, and Miño-Puigcercós (2020) highlighted that having a narrow vision of the adoption of ICTs in education can turn into the main barrier, which does not enable to achieve significant improvements and transformations. Such an approach makes it possible to dismiss the complex nature of education. Overlooking the complexity of academic work in this way leads to the inefficient allocation of valuable public resources, which could otherwise be utilized more effectively for educational advancements.

Utilizing contemporary ICTs simplifies access to the worldwide information market and facilitates the adoption of emerging global educational trends. Computer technology integration stimulates student desire for learning and scientific inquiry, opens new channels for creativity, and provides opportunities for the development of a variety of professional abilities (Lomos, Luyten, & Tieck, 2023). Moreover, ICT-infused education encourages increased learner engagement. The constructivist approach to learning, which emphasizes realistic and learner-centered experiences, is improved through the utilization of ICTs.

Application of Digital Volunteerism in Early Childhood Development Centers

Digital Volunteerism in Primary and Secondary Schools

An *international journal* article on *emerging* trends related to, and *issues in, early childhood education* by Kilag, et al. (2022) considered ICT integration in *primary* school classrooms in the time of the pandemic in the light of the cognitive development theory of Piaget (1964).

CONCLUSION

This last section will provide discussion of the overall coverage of the chapter and concluding remarks.

The chapter provided a detailed examination of the e-capacity model (Vanderlinde & Van Braak, 2010), highlighting its relevance in appreciating the complexity of ICT integration in educational contexts. It emphasized the call for a well-rounded approach that evaluates the interconnected aspects of an educational institution's structure, technical infrastructure, and human resources. It delved into the various challenges these institutions face, like insufficient technological infrastructure, inadequate capacity-building initiatives, and teachers' resistance to change.

The literature review identified challenges teachers and school leadership face during ICT integration. It also suggested a framework designed to manage and overcome the identified challenges in other to promote effective and thorough integration of ICTs in education. The review of literature also brings to light the main importance of ICT integration in education which includes high academic performance of students, individualized learning experience for students and also increasing collaboration and maximal engagements among teachers and learners. It was also realized that the integration of ICTs in education makes learners boost their computer literacy as well as promote critical thinking skills among learners in diverse educational settings.

The chapter probed several strategies that can be adopted to integrate ICTs into education. Factors like geographical settings of learners, the formation and implementation of educational policies and the availability of the needed technological infrastructure in schools. After considering this factors, valuable insight was gained on how these factors foster the effective use of ICTs in instructional practices showing best practices and areas that need improvement.

Lastly, it was stressed that teachers collaborate among each other in other to overcome challenges in ICT integration and ensure the equal utilization of technological enhanced teaching as well as learning. The importance of a comprehensive approach that is made up of organizational, pedagogical, and technological considerations was emphasized. This framework provides the foundation for evaluating the preparedness of teachers and educational institutions to apply the e-capacity model to adapt the new curriculum to include ICTs. The subsequent section of this thesis will present the research plan and methodology employed.

REFERENCES

Adade, R., & Goosen, L. (2024). Teachers and Schools Navigating Virtual Worlds and the Metaverse for Enhanced E-Learning: Evaluating an E-Capacity Model Approach. In Chafiq, N., Cummins, P., Al-Qatawneh, K., & El Imadi, I. (Eds.), *Navigating Virtual Worlds and the Metaverse for Enhanced E-Learning* (pp. 134–152). IGI Global., DOI: 10.4018/979-8-3693-1034-2.ch006

Aghauche, E. E., Nkamnebe, C. B., & Nkamnebe, E. C. (2019). Information literacy skills of undergraduates in Paul University Awka, Anambra state. *UNIZIK Journal of Research in Library and Information Science*, 4(1/2), 94–109.

Agyei, D. D., & Voogt, J. M. (2011). Exploring the potential of the will, skill, tool model in Ghana: Predicting prospective and practising teachers' use of technology. *Computers & Education*, 56(1), 91–100. DOI: 10.1016/j.compedu.2010.08.017

Akram, H., Abdelrady, A. H., Al-Adwan, A. S., & Ramzan, M. (2022). Teachers' perceptions of technology integration in Teaching-Learning Practices: A Systematic Review. *Frontiers in Psychology*, 13, 920317. Advance online publication. DOI: 10.3389/fpsyg.2022.920317 PMID: 35734463

Ambrose, S., Huston, T., & Norman, M. (2005). A qualitative method for assessing faculty satisfaction. *Research in Higher Education*, 46(7), 803–830. DOI: 10.1007/s11162-004-6226-6

Amos, O., Ogoti, E., & Siamoo, P. (2022). Shared Strategic Vision in Participative Leadership Style and Quality Education Provision in Public Secondary Schools in Arusha Region, Tanzania. *Brock Journal of Education*, 10(7), 51–74. DOI: 10.37745/bje.2013/vol10n7pp5174

Anderson, S. E., & Putman, R. S. (2020). Special education teachers' experience, confidence, beliefs, and knowledge about integrating technology. *Journal of Special Education Technology*, 35(1), 37–50. DOI: 10.1177/0162643419836409

Aničić, K., & Bušelić, V. (2021). Importance of Generic Skills of ICT Graduates-Employers, Teaching Staff, and Students Perspective. *IEEE Transactions on Education*, 64(3), 245–252. DOI: 10.1109/TE.2020.3034958

Ansu-Kyeremeh, E. K., & Goosen, L. (2022). Exploring the Socioeconomic Facet of Online Inclusive Education in Ghana: The Effects of Technological Advancement in Academia. In Garcia, M. (Ed.), *Socioeconomic Inclusion During an Era of Online Education* (pp. 47–66). IGI Global., DOI: 10.4018/978-1-6684-4364-4.ch003

Ball, D., & Forzani, F. (2011). Teaching skillful teaching. *Educational Leadership*, *68*(4), 40–45.

Bourgonjon, J. (2015). *Video game literacy: Social, cultural and educational perspectives.* (Doctoral dissertation). Ghent University.

Carrington, S., Spina, N., Kimber, M., Spooner-Lane, R., & Williams, K. (2021). Leadership attributes that support school improvement: A realist approach. *School Leadership & Management*, *42*(2), 151–169. DOI: 10.1080/13632434.2021.2016686

Cette, G., Clerc, C., & Bresson, L. (2015). Contribution of ICT Diffusion to Labour Productivity Growth: The United States, Canada, the Eurozone, and the United Kingdom, 1970-2013. *International Productivity Monitor*, *28*, 81–88.

Chadwick, A., & Fadel, B. (2020). *Volunteerism and Community Resilience: Locally Owned Solutions Delivering Impact.* Emirates Foundation. Retrieved from https://www.iave.org/iavewp/wp-content/uploads/2020/07/Volunteerism-and-Community-Resilience-Locally-Owned-Solutions-Delivering-Impact.pdf

Costa, P., Castaño-Muñoz, J., & Kampylis, P. (2021). Capturing schools' digital capacity: Psychometric analyses of the Selfie self-reflection tool. *Computers & Education*, *162*, 104080. Advance online publication. DOI: 10.1016/j.compedu.2020.104080

Dawson, D., Morales, E., McKiernan, E. C., Schimanski, L. A., Niles, M. T., & Alperin, J. P. (2022). The role of collegiality in academic review, promotion, and tenure. *PLoS One*, *17*(4), e0265506. Advance online publication. DOI: 10.1371/journal.pone.0265506 PMID: 35385489

Dexter, S., & Richardson, J. W. (2020). What does technology integration research tell us about the leadership of technology? *Journal of Research on Technology in Education*, *52*(1), 17–36. DOI: 10.1080/15391523.2019.1668316

Doorgakant, Y. M., & Baichoo, R. R. (2021). Collegiality as a Fundamental Professional Value in an Academic Setting: A Case Study in a Teacher Education Institution in a Small Island Developing State. *Pedagogical Quarterly/Kwartalnik Pedagogiczny, 66*(4), 52-70.

Garbett, D., & Thomas, L. (2020). Developing inter-collegial friendships to sustain professional wellbeing in the academy. *Teachers and Teaching*, *26*(3-4), 295–306. DOI: 10.1080/13540602.2020.1832062

García-Valcárcel, A., & Mena, J. (2021). In-service teachers' use of ICT for the Promotion of Collaborative Professional Learning. In *Research Anthology on Facilitating New Educational Practices Through Communities of Learning* (pp. 287–301). IGI Global. DOI: 10.4018/978-1-7998-7294-8.ch015

Garzón-Artacho, E., Sola-Martínez, T., Romero-Rodríguez, J. M., & Gómez-García, G. (2021). Teachers' perceptions of digital competence at the lifelong learning stage. *Heliyon*, *7*(7), e07513. Advance online publication. DOI: 10.1016/j.heliyon.2021.e07513 PMID: 34401558

Ghavifekr, S., & Rosdy, W. A. (2015). Teaching and learning with technology: Effectiveness of ICT integration in schools. *International Journal of Research in Education and Science*, *1*(2), 175–191. DOI: 10.21890/ijres.23596

Giovannella, C. (2022). Between awareness and acceptance: A more mature school teachers' perspective on integrated learning one year after the pandemic outbreak. [s]. *Interaction Design and Architecture*, (52), 23–43. DOI: 10.55612/s-5002-052-002

Goh, E., & Sigala, M. (2020). Integrating Information & Communication Technologies (ICT) into classroom instruction: Teaching tips for hospitality educators from a diffusion of innovation approach. *Journal of Teaching in Travel & Tourism*, *20*(2), 156–165. DOI: 10.1080/15313220.2020.1740636

Hammer, D. P., Bynum, L. A., Carter, J., Hagemeier, N. E., Kennedy, D. R., Khansari, P., Stamm, P., & Crabtree, B. (2019). Revisiting faculty citizenship. *American Journal of Pharmaceutical Education*, *83*(4), 7378. Advance online publication. DOI: 10.5688/ajpe7378 PMID: 31223170

Henderson, J., & Milman, N. B. (2020). The technology acceptance model: Considerations for online educators. *Distance Learning : for Educators, Trainers, and Leaders*, *17*(3), 104–107. DOI: 10.1108/DL-02-2021-0014

Hew, K. F., & Brush, T. (2007). Integrating technology into K-12 teaching and learning: Current knowledge gaps and recommendations for future research. *Educational Technology Research and Development*, *55*(3), 223–252. DOI: 10.1007/s11423-006-9022-5

Huber, S., Lupschina, R., Schwarz, M., & Krey, K. (2021). Peer-coaching and Inclusive Collaborative Learning using ICT. *Pedagógusképzés*, *20*(1), 99–109. DOI: 10.37205/TEL-hun.2021.1.05

Kali, Y., McKenney, S., & Sagy, O. (2015). Teachers as designers of technology enhanced learning. *Instructional Science*, *43*(2), 173–179. DOI: 10.1007/s11251-014-9343-4

Kalita, H., & Kumar, K. (2020). Digital Technology Integration in Different Educational Fields: Design, Architecture, Tourism, and Business Engineering. In *Methodologies and Outcomes of Engineering and Technological Pedagogy* (pp. 112–131). IGI Global. DOI: 10.4018/978-1-7998-2245-5.ch008

Kilag, O. K., Ignacio, R., Lumando, E. B., Alvez, G. U., Abendan, C. F., Quiñanola, N. M. P., & Sasan, J. M. (2022). ICT Integration in Primary School Classrooms in the time of Pandemic in the Light of Jean Piaget's Cognitive Development Theory. *International Journal of Emerging Issues in Early Childhood Education, 4*(2), 42–54. DOI: 10.31098/ijeiece.v4i2.1170

Kiprop-Marakis, J. (2021). Effect of Teacher Participation on Decision-making Processes on Performance in Secondary Schools in Mombasa County, Kenya. *East African Journal of Education Studies, 4*(1), 29–36. DOI: 10.37284/eajes.4.1.437

Korukluoğlu, P., Alcı, B., & Rubach, C. (2023). Reliability and validity of the Turkish version of the teachers' basic ICT competence beliefs scale. *International Journal of Assessment Tools in Education, 10*(1), 29–55. DOI: 10.21449/ijate.995005

Kozma, R. B. (2003). Technology and classroom practices: An international study. *Journal of Research on Technology in Education, 36*(1), 1–14. DOI: 10.1080/15391523.2003.10782399

Kundu, A. (2021). A sound framework for ICT integration in Indian teacher education. *International Journal of Teacher Education and Professional Development, 4*(1), 49–67. DOI: 10.4018/IJTEPD.2021010104

Lachand-Pascal, V., Michel, C., Serna, A., & Tabard, A. (2022). Challenges and Opportunities for Multi-Device Management in Classrooms. *ACM Transactions on Computer-Human Interaction, 29*(6), 1–27. DOI: 10.1145/3519025

Lavrenova, M., Lalak, N., & Molnar, T. (2020). Preparation of Future Teachers for Use of ICT in Primary School. *Revista Romaneasca pentru Educatie Multidimensionala, 12*, 185-195. DOI: 10.18662/rrem/12.1sup1/230

Lawrence, J. E., & Tar, U. A. (2018). Factors that influence teachers' adoption and integration of ICT in teaching/learning process. *Educational Media International, 55*(1), 79–105. DOI: 10.1080/09523987.2018.1439712

Lomos, C., Luyten, J. W., & Tieck, S. (2023). Implementing ICT in classroom practice: What else matters besides the ICT infrastructure? *Large-Scale Assessments in Education, 11*(1), 1–28. DOI: 10.1186/s40536-022-00144-6 PMID: 36686619

Lund, A., Furberg, A., Bakken, J., & Engelien, K. L. (2014). What does professional digital competence mean in teacher education? *Nordic journal of digital literacy, 9*(4), 280-298.

Madanchian, M., & Taherdoost, H. (2023). The impact of leadership on the growth of ICT companies. *Journal of Sustainable Business and Economics, 6*(4), 20–27. DOI: 10.30564/jsbe.v6i4.5874

Magaisa, G. M., & Musundire, A. (2021). Relationship Between Transformational Leadership and Commitment of Consultants in South African Management Consulting Firms. [IJAMTR]. *International Journal of Applied Management Theory and Research, 3*(2), 24–37. DOI: 10.4018/IJAMTR.2021070103

Magaisa, G. M., & Musundire, A. (2022). Factors affecting employee retention in Zimbabwean companies. *International Journal of Applied Management Theory and Research, 4*(1), 1–20. Advance online publication. DOI: 10.4018/IJAMTR.288507

Mominó, J. M., & Carrere, J. (2016). A model for obtaining ICT indicators in education. *Working papers on education policy, 3*. Retrieved from https://unesdoc.unesco.org/ark:/48223/pf0000244268

Mumtaz, S. (2000). Factors affecting teachers' use of information and communications technology: A review of the literature. *Journal of Information Technology for Teacher Education, 9*(3), 319–342. DOI: 10.1080/14759390000200096

Musundire, A. (2021a, July). Peer supervision: A missing link between teacher development and quality of teaching–perceptions of school managers and classroom teachers in South Africa. [IJTEPD]. *International Journal of Teacher Education and Professional Development, 4*(2), 97–115. DOI: 10.4018/IJTEPD.2021070107

Musundire, A. (2021b, October). The Impact of E-Learning Instructional Knowledge on Pedagogical Attitude and Learner Performance: The Context of South African Private Institutions of Higher Learning. [IJDLDC]. *International Journal of Digital Literacy and Digital Competence, 12*(4), 33–53. DOI: 10.4018/IJDLDC.2021100103

Musundire, A. (2022). The Effectiveness of Self-Directed Supervision on Improving Quality of Teaching: Perceptions of South African School-Based Managers and Educators. [IJTEPD]. *International Journal of Teacher Education and Professional Development, 5*(1), 1–17. Advance online publication. DOI: 10.4018/IJTEPD.304873

Musundire, A. (2025a). Exploring Challenges and Opportunities of the Social Justice Philosophy in Education in South African Private Schools: Differentiated Instruction, Linguistic Diversity, Equity, and Inclusion. In *Educational Philosophy and Sociological Foundation of Education* (pp. 77-102). IGI Global.

Musundire, A. (2025b). Indiscipline and crime in South African secondary schools: The place of the African Ubuntu philosophy. In *Educational Philosophy and Sociological Foundation of Education* (pp. 103–132). IGI Global.

Musundire, A. (2025c). Effectiveness of the Connoisseurship Supervision Model on Quality of Teaching in the Context of Developmental Supervision: The Case of South African P-12 Education System. In *Reimagining the P-20 Landscape for School Leadership Learning* (pp. 457–482). IGI Global Scientific Publishing.

Musundire, A. (2025d). Systemstic Literature Analysis of Educational Barriers, Opportunities, and Innovation in Science, Technology, and Innovation: The Case of Potential Female Entrepreneurs in South Africa. In *AI Strategies for Social Entrepreneurship and Sustainable Economic Development* (pp. 307-334). IGI Global.

Musundire, A. (2025e). Social Justice Realities for Women Leaders in South African Schools: Barriers, Opportunities, and Prospects. In *New Horizons in Leadership: Inclusive Explorations in Health, Technology, and Education* (pp. 93-120). IGI Global Scientific Publishing.

Musundire, A. (2025f). Chatbots as virtual leaders: Supporting decision-making and strategic planning in Australian secondary schools. In *Chatbots in educational leadership and management* (pp. 1–28). IGI Global Scientific Publishing. DOI: 10.4018/979-8-3693-8734-4.ch001

Musundire, A. (2025g). Integrating Chatbots Into Educational Management Systems in the Global Intuitions of Higher Learning: Streamlining Administrative Tasks. In *Chatbots in educational leadership and management* (pp. 53-72). IGI Global Scientific Publishing.

Musundire, A. (2025h). Integrating Educational Robotics and Artificial Intelligence With African Educational Perspectives in Science, Technology, Engineering, and Mathematics: Challenges and Opportunities. In *Innovations in Educational Robotics: Advancing AI for Sustainable Development* (pp. 129-156). IGI Global Scientific Publishing.

Musundire, A. (2025i). The Relationship Between Knowledge Management Systems, Transformational Leadership, and Organizational Adaptability: The Case of South African Private Institutions of Higher Learning. In *Leveraging Technology for Organizational Adaptability* (pp. 197-222). IGI Global Scientific Publishing.

Musundire, A. (2025j). Indigenous vs. Eurocentric Teaching Methods: The Place of Afro-Centric Games in South African Primary School Mathematics Curriculum. In *Enabling Indigenous Knowledge Systems in Action Research and Action Learning* (pp. 357-378). IGI Global Scientific Publishing.

Musundire, A. (Ed.). (2025k). *Research Methods for Educational Leadership and Management*. IGI Global., Retrieved from https://www.igi-global.com/book/research-methods-educational-leadership-management/356342 DOI: 10.4018/979-8-3693-9425-0

Musundire, A. (2025l). Understanding the Research Onion and Its Application in Educational Leadership and Management Research: Making Use of Saunders' Research Model. In *Research Methods for Educational Leadership and Management* (pp. 355-384). IGI Global Scientific Publishing.

Musundire, A. (2025m). Understanding the Research Process and Its Application in Educational Leadership and Management: Making Use of Ngulube's Research Model. In *Research Methods for Educational Leadership and Management* (pp. 385-414). IGI Global Scientific Publishing.

Ngao, A. I., Sang, G., & Kihwele, J. E. (2022). Understanding teacher educators' perceptions and practices about ICT integration in teacher education program. *Education Sciences*, *12*(8), 549. Advance online publication. DOI: 10.3390/educsci12080549

Ngulube, P. (2015). Trends in research methodological procedures used in knowledge management studies. *African Journal of Library Archives and Information Science*, *25*(2), 125–143.

Niederhauser, D. S., & Stoddart, T. (2001). Teachers' instructional perspectives and use of educational software. *Teaching and Teacher Education*, *17*(1), 15–31. DOI: 10.1016/S0742-051X(00)00036-6

Niem, M. M., Veriñ, R. U., & Alcantara, E. C. (2020). Teaching and learning with technology: Ramification of ICT integration in Mathematics Education. *Southeast Asian Mathematics Education Journal*, *10*(1), 27–40. DOI: 10.46517/seamej.v10i1.83

Piaget, J. (1964). Part I: Cognitive development in children: Piaget development and learning. *Journal of Research in Science Teaching*, *2*(3), 176–186. DOI: 10.1002/tea.3660020306

Pinto, M., & Leite, C. (2020). Digital Technologies in support of students learning in Higher Education: Literature review. *Digital Education Review*, (37), 343–360. DOI: 10.1344/der.2020.37.343-360

Rajput, N., Bukhari, S., Noonari, N., Solangi, G., Soomro, M., & Dahri, A. (2020). From Perspective to Practice: Gauging the Awareness and Integration Level of ICT in Teaching Process at Secondary Level in District Shaheed Benazirabad, Pakistan. *Modern Applied Science*, *14*(8), 23. Advance online publication. DOI: 10.5539/mas.v14n8p23

Rickert, N. P., & Skinner, E. A. (2022). Parent and teacher warm involvement and student's academic engagement: The mediating role of self-system processes. *The British Journal of Educational Psychology, 92*(2), 667–687. DOI: 10.1111/bjep.12470 PMID: 34697805

Rojas Briñez, D. K., Duart, J. M., & Galvis Panqueva, Á. H. (2023). Findings and derived challenges concerning how school leaders should support ICT integration at schools. *School Leadership & Management, 43*(5), 497–524. DOI: 10.1080/13632434.2023.2237514

Sadik, O., & Ottenbreit-Leftwich, A. T. (2023). Understanding U.S. secondary computer science teachers' challenges and needs. *Computer Science Education, 34*(2), 252–284. DOI: 10.1080/08993408.2023.2209474

Sancho-Gil, J., Rivera-Vargas, P., & Miño-Puigcercós, R. (2020). Moving beyond the predictable failure of Ed-Tech initiatives. *Learning, Media and Technology, 45*(1), 61–75. DOI: 10.1080/17439884.2019.1666873

Sar, A., & Misra, S. N. (2020, December). A study on policies and implementation of information and communication technology (ICT) in Educational Systems. *Materials Today: Proceedings.* Advance online publication. DOI: 10.1016/j.matpr.2020.10.507

Saunders, M. N., Lewis, P., & Thornhill, A. (2019). Research methods for business students (Eighth ed.). Harlow: Pearson education limited.

Setia, S., & Aufar, S. M. (2023). The effect of government ICT policy and Technology leadership on Teacher's Technology Integration. *QALAMUNA: Jurnal Pendidikan, Sosial. Dan Agama, 15*(1), 341–352. DOI: 10.37680/qalamuna.v15i1.2332

Sosa-Díaz, M. J., Sierra-Daza, M. C., Arriazu-Muñoz, R., Llamas-Salguero, F., & Durán-Rodríguez, N. (2022). "Edtech Integration Framework in schools": Systematic review of the literature. *Frontiers in Education, 7*, 895042. Advance online publication. DOI: 10.3389/feduc.2022.895042

Stolz, I., Fürst, M., & Mundle, D. (2012). Beyond volunteerism! Real world learning to foster responsible leadership, serve patients and develop innovative solutions to healthcare challenges. In Wehner, T., & Gentile, C. (Eds.), *Corporate Volunteering: Unternehmen im Spannungsfeld von Gemeinschaft und Gesellschaft (AT)*. Springer Gabler.

Tairab, A., & Ronghuai, H. (2017). Analyzing ICT Policy in K-12 Education in Sudan (1990-2016). *World Journal of Education, 7*(1), 71–82. DOI: 10.5430/wje.v7n1p71

Tay, L. Y., Lim, C. P., & Lim, S. K. (2015). Differences in ICT usage across subject areas: A case of an elementary school in Singapore. *Journal of Educational Computing Research*, *53*(1), 75–94. DOI: 10.1177/0735633115585930

Tayaban, A. D. (2022). Students' and Teachers' Perspectives on ICT Integration in Learning Process During Pandemic. *International Journal of Multidisciplinary: Applied Business and Education Research*, *3*(12), 2622–2630. DOI: 10.11594/ijmaber.03.12.15

Tondeur, J., Van Braak, J., Sang, G., Voogt, J., Fisser, P., & Ottenbreit-Leftwich, A. (2012). Preparing pre-service teachers to integrate technology in education: A synthesis of qualitative evidence. *Computers & Education*, *59*(1), 134–144. DOI: 10.1016/j.compedu.2011.10.009

Top, E., Baser, D., Akkus, R., Akayoglu, S., & Gurer, M. D. (2021). Secondary School Teachers' preferences in the process of individual technology mentoring. *Computers & Education*, *160*, 104030. Advance online publication. DOI: 10.1016/j.compedu.2020.104030

Uluyol, Ç., & Şahin, S. (2014). Elementary School Teachers' ICT use in the classroom and their motivators for using ICT. *British Journal of Educational Technology*, *47*(1), 65–75. DOI: 10.1111/bjet.12220

Vanderlinde, R. (2011). *School-based ICT policy planning in a context of curriculum reform*. (Proefschrift: Doctor in de Pedagogische Wetenschappen). Universiteit Gent.

Vanderlinde, R., & Van Braak, J. (2010). The e-capacity of primary schools: Development of a conceptual model and scale construction from a school improvement perspective. *Computers & Education*, *55*(2), 541–553. DOI: 10.1016/j.compedu.2010.02.016

Vo, P. T. (2019). *An investigation of ICT policy implementation in an EFL teacher education program in Vietnam*. Edith Cowan University.

Woo, D. (2023). The leadership of ICT coordinators: A distributed perspective. *Educational Management Administration & Leadership*, *51*(2), 308–323. DOI: 10.1177/1741143220979714

Wyttenbach, M., & Ospino, H. (2022). Hispanic teachers and leaders in Catholic schools: Special issue introduction. *Journal of Catholic Education*, *25*(2). Advance online publication. DOI: 10.15365/joce.2502002022

Younie, S. (2006). Implementing government policy on ICT in education: Lessons learnt. *Education and Information Technologies*, *11*(3-4), 385–400. DOI: 10.1007/s10639-006-9017-1

Yuen, A., Law, N., & Wong, K. (2003). ICT implementation and school leadership: Case studies of ICT integration in teaching and learning. *Journal of Educational Administration*, *41*(2), 158–170. DOI: 10.1108/09578230310464666

Zagami, J., Bocconi, S., Starkey, L., Wilson, J., Gibson, D., Downie, J., Malyn-Smith, J., & Elliott, S. (2018). Creating Future Ready Information Technology Policy for National Education Systems. *Technology. Knowledge and Learning*, *23*(3), 495–506. DOI: 10.1007/s10758-018-9387-7

Zenda, E. T., Musundire, A., & Mumanyi, O. (2020). The Impact of Organisational Change Management Theoretical Perspective in the Context of Zimbabwe's Cash Crisis on Small to Medium Enterprises and their Consequent Adaptation Strategies. [IJSR]. *International Journal of Scientific Research*, *9*(8), 1256–1265.

Chapter 8
The Digital Pulse of Volunteerism:
Tools That Drive Engagement and Impact

Ananya Pandey
http://orcid.org/0000-0002-2419-6314
Christ University, Bangalore, India

ABSTRACT

Volunteering has changed as a result of the digital age, which has increased chances for involvement beyond time and location restrictions. In addition to assessing and enhancing social effect, this chapter examines the technological tools and platforms that help organizations recruit, engage, and retain volunteers. Using case studies and real-world examples, it looks at data-driven monitoring frameworks, gamification strategies, recruitment tools, and collaboration platforms. Issues like data privacy, the digital divide, and the dangers of relying too much on technology at the detriment of interpersonal relationships are also covered in the conversation. The chapter emphasizes how digital innovation can improve community participation and support long-lasting social change by fusing theoretical models with practical applications. Future trends and policy issues are discussed to help businesses create digital volunteer ecosystems that are ethical, inclusive, and productive.

DOI: 10.4018/979-8-3373-5722-5.ch008

INTRODUCTION

Social change has always been centered on volunteerism. People have donated their time and talents to causes bigger than themselves for ages, whether it is supporting community projects, aiding neighbors in need, or contributing knowledge to projects that enhance the well-being of all. This culture of service has historically flourished in in-person settings, such as a community clean-up at the park, a reading circle for disadvantaged kids at the town library, or a grassroots initiative launched from a small community hall. The strength of these interactions, which were frequently small in scope, came from the immediate personal connection, the common goal, and the observable consequences. However, the definition of volunteerism has changed significantly during the past 20 years. With the advent of social media, cellphones, and high-speed internet, practically every type of civic engagement now includes a digital component. By tutoring a student via video conference, interpreting paperwork for an international aid organization, or writing code for a nonprofit's software project, a volunteer can now support a cause without ever having the opportunity to see the beneficiaries in person. By removing regional restrictions and facilitating worldwide cooperation, the digital realm has broadened the scope of volunteer programs. This change has brought with it demands and complications of its own, but it has also created opportunities that were almost unthinkable for earlier generations. Volunteering's "digital pulse" is becoming just as important as its human heartbeat. In addition to making volunteer recruiting easier, digital platforms also foster communities of practice, enable real-time contact across continents, and offer data-driven insights into the results of projects. Organizations of various sizes, from local grassroots NGOs to large international humanitarian agencies, are using digital tools to engage volunteers, maintain their involvement, and increase the effectiveness of their work. This change is becoming a fundamental component of contemporary public engagement, not just a convenience.

However, there is a paradox in this digital progress. Reaching possible volunteers has never been simpler, but maintaining their commitment over time continues to be a constant struggle. People may sign up for several causes but find it difficult to remain actively involved in any one of them due to the "scatter effect" caused by the multitude of internet opportunities. Furthermore, it might be challenging to promote a true sense of belonging and mutual accountability when there is no in-person interaction. Engagement runs the risk of turning transactional rather than transformative in the absence of the unofficial ties and customs of face-to-face involvement (Pandey, 2025). The problem of determining the actual impact of volunteer programs in this digital environment is equally urgent. Although the abundance of metrics—such as hours worked, activities finished, and digital badges obtained—offers quantitative insights, they could not adequately represent the more profound, qualitative results that characterize effective volunteer involvement. For example, how can the long-term empowerment of a rural community be measured? How can analytics and dashboards represent the intangible advantages of interpersonal relationships or cultural exchange? The conflict between the effectiveness of digital technology and the fundamentally human aspect of volunteer labor is brought to light by these queries. These problems are made worse by worries about access and equity. Digital platforms can bring people together from different continents, but they can also keep out folks who don't have dependable internet access, digital literacy, or the newest gadgets. The potential for perpetuating current disparities is significant, and if digital volunteerism is not well planned, it may inadvertently favor some groups over others. This quickly developing subject is further complicated by issues with algorithmic bias, cybersecurity, and data privacy.

In light of this, this chapter aims to thoroughly examine the relationship between digital technologies and volunteer involvement. The goal is to comprehend how these tools are changing the volunteer experience from recruiting to retention, from task execution to quantifiable impact, rather than just listing prominent platforms or technology. The chapter will give a comprehensive picture of what it means to "volunteer" in the digital era by looking at both the benefits and drawbacks of digitization. This chapter's ultimate goal is to shed light on a fundamental reality: technology can increase the scope and influence of volunteers when used carefully, but it must be used with caution, compassion, and a steadfast dedication to inclusivity. In the ensuing decades, the digital tools we select and how we use them will influence not only the future of volunteerism but also the fundamental structure of civic life.

THEORETICAL AND CONCEPTUAL FOUNDATIONS

Human solidarity has long been reflected in volunteering, which is the act of providing time, abilities, or resources to others without anticipating financial gain. However, the term's meaning and complexity have grown in modern discourse. The various types of volunteerism that exist today are influenced by technology, global interconnectedness, and the evolving character of society. Usually, academics make a distinction between various forms of volunteer work. Formal volunteerism takes place in formal organizations with defined roles and reporting lines, including government programs, nonprofits, or charities (Musick & Wilson, 2008). On the other hand, without an official structure, informal volunteerism develops naturally throughout communities through local problem-solving initiatives, mutual aid organizations, or neighbors assisting neighbors (United Nations Volunteers, 2018). These categories can be further refined to include skill-based volunteering, where participants draw on professional knowledge in fields like law, IT, or education; episodic volunteerism, where people contribute in short-term, project-based settings; and virtual volunteering, where the entire process—including recruitment, training, collaboration, and service delivery—occurs online (Bussell & Forbes, 2002; Cravens & Ellis, 2014).

One of the most notable developments over the last three decades is the shift in volunteerism from a largely community-based practice to a worldwide networked phenomena. In the past, volunteerism was confined to certain geographic areas and was coordinated by civic associations, religious institutions, and neighborhood associations. Many of these barriers have been broken down by globalization and the expansion of the internet. Today, a student in Mumbai may use video conferencing to teach English to rural students in Southeast Asia, while someone in Nairobi can create communication materials for an NGO in Vancouver. The trend toward transnational volunteer networks has been further accelerated by the advent of global issues including pandemics, refugee crises, and climate change (Hustinx et al., 2010). Not only has digital technology sped up this trend, but it has also completely changed the parameters of who, where, and how volunteers can participate.

Frameworks for Digital Transformation

It is impossible to comprehend the rapid rise of digital adoption in volunteer management without examining well-established theories of social interaction and technology acceptance.

Model of Technology Acceptance (TAM)

Davis (1989) created the Technology Acceptance Model, which is still a commonly used framework for comprehending how users interact with new technology. It suggests that people's willingness to embrace a certain instrument is influenced by two main factors: perceived utility and perceived ease of use. Perceived utility in the context of volunteering may have to do with how well a platform matches volunteers with worthwhile opportunities, whereas perceived ease of use refers to how easy it is for users with different levels of digital literacy to utilize. Adoption rates among potential volunteers may rise if a mobile volunteer coordination software, for instance, has an easy-to-use interface and a transparent impact-tracking dashboard.

Unified Theory of Acceptance and Use of Technology (UTAUT)

The Unified Theory of Acceptance and Use of Technology (Venkatesh et al., 2003) expands upon TAM by combining several theories to offer a more thorough perspective. According to UTAUT, the main factors influencing the adoption of technology are social influence, performance expectancy, effort expectancy, and facilitating conditions. When it comes to volunteering, this implies that in addition to convenience and personal utility, volunteers are impacted by a platform's social endorsement (e.g., peer recommendations) and the availability of supporting infrastructure (e.g., accessible customer support, available training).

Social Capital and Network Theory

Network theory and the idea of social capital provide a deeper understanding of the relationship dynamics of volunteer communities, whereas TAM and UTAUT concentrate on individual decision-making. Densely connected communities can more efficiently share resources, information, and support, according to network theory, which highlights the composition and strength of links among social groupings (Borgatti et al., 2009). According to Putnam (2000), social capital is the networks, norms, and trust that support group action. These types of capital are developed in online volunteer communities via frequent engagement, open communication, and shared impact stories. Volunteer commitment tends to increase when digital platforms effectively foster a sense of belonging through discussion boards, recognition programs, and real-time collaboration.

Conceptual Framework

A conceptual model that places digital technologies at the center of contemporary volunteer participation and provides a clear route to quantifiable social impact is the result of combining these theoretical insights. The concept starts with digital tools, which include anything from project management systems and impact analytics dashboards to communication applications and recruitment platforms. Based on TAM and UTAUT, these tools need to be accessible and helpful, with infrastructure that promotes long-term use. According to the network theory viewpoint, these platforms need to facilitate the development of relationships, which would promote volunteers' shared identity and sense of trust. Volunteer engagement is the model's next step. In this case, digital technologies affect both long-term retention and initial participation. Gamification, chances for skill development, and open impact reporting are a few examples of engagement strategies. Strongly engaged volunteer communities frequently exhibit high social capital, with members more eager to assist one another, coordinate duties, and exchange expertise. Ultimately, the model produces quantifiable societal benefit. Monitoring and evaluation technologies that record both qualitative results (better well-being, more community skills) and quantitative data (hours volunteered, beneficiaries served) are integrated into effective digital volunteer systems. Organizations can enhance their strategy and make sure that volunteer efforts result in noticeable gains in the well-being of society by integrating real-time analytics with feedback loops.

Network connections and social capital serve as reinforcing feedback loops that keep the cycle going over time. The suggested structure can be seen as a linear yet dynamic flow: Digital Tools → Volunteer Engagement → Social Impact.

MAPPING THE DIGITAL TOOL ECOSYSTEM

Volunteer organizations are no longer restricted to using conventional outreach techniques in the digitally linked world of today. Rather, they function within an extensive ecosystem of resources that not only facilitate every phase of the volunteer journey, but also work together to provide smooth experiences. It helps to think of this ecosystem as consisting of several important tool categories, each addressing specific needs: recruiting, cooperation and communication, task management, gamification, and impact measurement. These tools become much more than individual utilities when they are carefully combined to create a synergistic infrastructure that drives engagement and significant effect.

Platforms for Hiring

Digital recruiting platforms act as the first point of contact between organizations in need of volunteers and prospective volunteers. These websites, which include Idealist, VolunteerMatch, and the United Nations' Online Volunteering service, offer searchable databases with possibilities classified by geographic region, time commitment, and area of interest. In order to suggest possibilities that fit a volunteer's interests and skill set, they frequently incorporate machine learning algorithms (Hustinx et al., 2020). Hiring has become more focused as a result of the transition from passive listing boards to interactive, data-driven matchmaking, which shortens the time between an individual expressing interest and their active engagement. Furthermore, a lot of these platforms include social media, allowing volunteers to share opportunities with their peers and using network effects to increase reach.

Tools for Cooperation and Communication

It becomes crucial to keep up good communication after volunteers are onboarded. Distributed teams can collaborate, share updates, and solve problems in real time with the help of platforms like Zoom, Microsoft Teams, and Slack. These platforms provide avenues for information dissemination, virtual orientations, and feedback loop facilitation for volunteer coordinators. Volunteers in various time zones can stay involved without being constrained by synchronous meetings thanks to asynchronous communication tools like message boards and threaded discussions (Bennett & Segerberg, 2013). Additionally, combining task tracking, file sharing, and instant messaging into a single interface lowers friction and facilitates more seamless coordination.

Tools for Project and Task Management

In addition to communication, organized workflows are necessary for successful volunteer programs. Coordinators can assign tasks, establish deadlines, and track progress using Kanban boards, Gantt charts, and other project management views on platforms like Trello, Asana, and Monday.com. By enabling all participants to see how their duties contribute to the larger project goals, these tools improve transparency (Kapoor et al., 2018). Even complicated volunteer projects, like disaster relief or extensive fundraising, can move forward in an orderly and timely manner because of the features that allow attachment of documents, tracking of dependencies, and automated reminders.

Tools for Gamification and Engagement

Maintaining long-term involvement in volunteer work is one of the ongoing challenges. This difficulty is addressed by gamification tactics that use digital resources to boost human motivation for achievement, acknowledgment, and community status. Volunteers are rewarded with features like leaderboards, point systems, and digital badges for reaching milestones like completed tasks or hours of service (Hamari et al., 2014). Bounty-style challenges are used by some groups, in which volunteers do predetermined tasks in exchange for prizes or public recognition. In addition to offering a feeling of achievement, these instruments encourage healthy competition, which can strengthen dedication. Crucially, when done well, gamification preserves intrinsic motivation by tying rewards to organizational and personal values instead of just extrinsic ones.

Platforms for Impact Measurement

It's crucial for organizations and volunteers to comprehend the observable results of voluntary effort. Dashboards offered by impact measurement platforms monitor contributions to corporate objectives, which are frequently linked to more general frameworks such as the Sustainable Development Goals (SDGs) of the UN. To ensure transparency and credibility, advanced systems use blockchain technology to produce tamper-proof records of volunteer hours and deliverables (Tapia & Maldonado, 2022). These platforms may create reports for stakeholders, visualize beneficiary reach, and compile data from many programs. These methods help volunteers understand the importance of their contributions and promote continued involvement by giving them transparent feedback on their influence.

Interoperability and Integration

Although each type of tool has a specific function, the greatest advantages arise when they work together as a cohesive ecosystem. Discovery on a recruitment platform, onboarding via a communication tool, task distribution via a project management platform, engagement maintained through gamification elements, and effect documented in a measurement dashboard could all be the first steps in a digital volunteer journey. Data can move across various systems with ease because of interoperability, which is made possible by cross-platform connections and application programming interfaces (APIs). A personal profile on a gamification platform, for example, can be automatically updated by volunteer hours recorded in a project management application. This update then appears on the impact dashboard of the company.

By reducing the need for redundant data entry or switching between unrelated systems, this integration improves the volunteer experience and lessens administrative load. Because organizations can monitor the entire volunteer lifespan, from first contact to long-term impact, it also makes richer analytics possible. However, to handle concerns like user consent, data privacy, and interoperability between proprietary systems, integration necessitates meticulous preparation (Smith & Cordery, 2021). The digital tool ecosystem for volunteering is essentially a network of interconnected applications that are intended to draw in, empower, and keep volunteers while making sure that their efforts are accurately tracked and shared. The complexity of this ecosystem will increase along with technology, opening up new possibilities for efficiency, inclusivity, and global reach.

DRIVING VOLUNTEER ENGAGEMENT THROUGH DIGITAL TOOLS

Digital tools are more than just convenient in today's volunteer environment; they are powerful motivators that profoundly influence how individuals commit, maintain motivation, acquire new skills, and experience a sense of belonging to causes.

Strategies for Hiring with AI-Powered Matching

In order to match people with the causes that most appeal to them, contemporary volunteer platforms are depending more and more on AI-driven matching. Volunteers are directed toward positions that match their abilities, interests, availability, and location rather than having to manually search through openings, making the experience far more engaging and effective for everyone involved (Ordonez, n.d.; NGOs.ai, n.d.). Algorithms that consider variables such as organizational requirements and volunteer preferences, for instance, might produce extremely compatible matches, increasing volunteer satisfaction right away (Ordonez, n.d.; NGOs.ai, n.d.). Furthermore, technologies like chatbots and virtual assistants now manage first-time questions, expedite onboarding, and provide customized advice—reducing administrative burden while enhancing the sense of personalization (NGOs.ai, n.d.).

Gamification and Recognition for Retention and Motivation

Long-term volunteer engagement frequently depends on internal incentive and acknowledgment, which is where gamification excels. Points, badges, leaderboards, challenges, and other game-like elements are included into volunteer platforms to turn repetitive activities into engaging, fulfilling experiences (Wikipedia, 2025; Galaxy Digital, 2024). Once volunteers accomplish goals, programs can give them digital badges, publicly recognize their accomplishments, or use leaderboards to promote healthy competition (Galaxy Digital, 2024). In order to generate both personal fulfillment and natural advocacy, some nonprofits trade accrued points for branded merchandise, such as volunteer T-shirts or comparable tokens (VolunteerHub blog, n.d.). According to studies, companies that use gamified systems frequently witness a 30–70% increase in volunteer participation because volunteers feel appreciated, inspired, and have a sense of fun achievement (MoldStud; VolunteerHub blog, n.d.). Additionally, retention increases when volunteers receive points for going "above and beyond," particularly when acknowledgment is conveyed in a clear and consistent manner (VolunteerHub blog, n.d.).

Developing Capabilities with Micro-Credentials and E-Learning

Serving others can be just as much a part of volunteering as personal development. Micro-credentialing platforms and e-learning modules are excellent for fulfilling that dual function. These systems enable volunteers to study at their own pace, get feedback, and obtain certifications that verify their contributions, whether through organized online modules or bite-sized digital instruction. A program where corporate volunteers tutor youngsters through structured, virtual reading sessions is one example, albeit it is not precisely a micro-credential program. Through remote e-training and supported engagement, volunteers acquired both teaching and digital facilitation abilities, as seen by the significant improvement in students' reading levels, which averaged about three reading levels (Innovations for Learning, n.d.).

Case Study: An NGO Uses Digital Tools to Increase Volunteer Retention

Take the example of "Open Hand Atlanta," a legitimate nonprofit that has effectively integrated gamification into its volunteer program. Volunteers contributed hours or finished tasks using a program called LeaderTree, earning points for their work that could be redeemed for material goods like branded clothing. In addition to acknowledging individual efforts, this gamified framework promoted healthy competition and increased corporate awareness. Consequently, Open Hand Atlanta saw major improvements in volunteer retention and cost savings of hundreds of thousands of dollars (VolunteerHub blog, n.d.). Real-time recognition encouraged volunteers to become more involved since they felt appreciated. Essentially, the straightforward process of allocating point values and openly sharing advancement strengthened dedication and gave volunteering a sense of purpose and fulfillment.

MEASURING AND ENHANCING AI IMPACT

In the context of social action today, the idea of effect has developed into a more organized and fact-based understanding that goes beyond anecdotal reports of kindness. Impact in volunteerism refers to the material and immaterial changes that volunteers make to their communities and to the lives of those they serve (Rochester et al., 2010). Because of its dual character, effect cannot be quantified solely by output, such as the quantity of events hosted, but also by more profound results, such as improved skills, altered behavior over time, or heightened community resilience. From a quantitative standpoint, some variables offer a distinct starting point for comprehending the scope of volunteerism. The overall number of volunteer hours, the number of beneficiaries directly served, and the number of projects successfully finished are examples of common metrics (Salamon et al., 2017). To donors, legislators, and the general public, these metrics assist organizations in proving their effectiveness and accountability. An NGO focused on health, for example, would state that in a given year, its volunteers conducted 10,000 hours of community health checks, reaching 25,000 people in underprivileged areas. Qualitative measurements, on the other hand, are just as important as they capture aspects that cannot be quantified. Volunteering frequently improves participants' personal development, creates cultural bridges, and cultivates social trust (Wilson, 2012). By allowing beneficiaries and volunteers to share their lived experiences, focus groups, interviews, and storytelling provide the best understanding of these characteristics. For instance, a youth mentorship program might be able to show that mentees have not only done better academically but have also grown more confident and had better interpersonal skills—outcomes that are important but might not be seen in statistical reports. Importantly, a well-rounded approach that incorporates both quantitative and qualitative viewpoints offers a more thorough and reliable picture of the worth of volunteering to society.

Tools for Measuring Digital Impact

The quick development of digital technologies has changed how nonprofits monitor and assess their work. While some situations still employ traditional pen-and-paper reporting techniques, real-time digital dashboards that compile project data and provide decision-makers with rapid access to it are gradually replacing them (Deane, 2020). Metrics like volunteer hours, regional coverage, beneficiary demographics, and activity completion rates are frequently incorporated into these dashboards.

Reporting using mobile devices has proved especially useful in situations when volunteers work in remote or resource-constrained environments. Volunteers can geotag their service areas, upload photos, and register activities using mobile applications, which guarantees that data is recorded reliably and on time (Berkman & Glass, 2020). Because of this immediacy, data loss is minimized and gaps or problems can be found while projects are still in progress. The emergence of participatory monitoring tools, which include community members and volunteers in the impact assessment process, is another noteworthy development (Estrella & Gaventa, 2022). Organizations can obtain insights rooted in local viewpoints by letting beneficiaries provide feedback directly through community forums, voice notes, or smartphone surveys. In addition to improving the caliber of data gathered, this participatory strategy builds community trust in organizations. There are factors to take into account when using these digital technologies. They improve speed and accuracy, but they also raise concerns about data privacy, digital literacy, and fair access to technology. Hybrid strategies that combine offline data gathering with subsequent digital integration can still be required in areas with poor internet availability.

Data-Driven Decision Making

The ultimate goal of impact measurement is to help make better decisions, not just to generate reports. Organizations can better allocate resources, create programs that address real needs, and pinpoint areas for development by using data-driven decision making (Bryson et al., 2021). For instance, an analytics-based environmental volunteer network finds that poor post-planting maintenance lowers the survival rates of tree-planting initiatives in some areas. They improve the program's long-term ecological benefit by modifying tactics—possibly by training local caregivers or setting up follow-up visits—after detecting this tendency through data. Patterns in volunteer participation itself can also be found through data analysis. Organizations can look at the root issues, such as workload, recognition, or expectations alignment, and modify their engagement tactics if analytics show that retention rates decline beyond the first three months of volunteering. Additionally, businesses can convey their impact in ways that are widely accepted by aligning measurement with global frameworks like the Sustainable Development Goals (SDGs) of the United Nations (United Nations, 2015). Volunteer projects can make a stronger case for support and cultivate cross-sector relationships by connecting their activities and results to particular SDG targets. However, the ethics and caliber of the data gathered determine how valuable data-driven approaches are. Conclusions can be misled by poorly constructed surveys, biased sampling, or a lack of contextual knowledge. Therefore, it is still crucial to combine statistical analysis with human judgment to make sure that data interpretation accurately captures the nuanced reality of social change activity (Mertens, 2015).

CHALLENGES, LIMITATIONS AND ETHICAL CONCERNS

Without a question, the quick adoption of digital tools in volunteer work has increased participation, efficiency, and worldwide reach. But these developments come with difficult problems that need careful consideration. Large-scale coordination is made possible by digital platforms, but they can also unintentionally prejudice, alienate, or exclude particular people and communities. Accessibility, privacy, technological dependence, and inclusivity raise ethical and practical concerns. To guarantee that technology facilitates human connection rather than replaces it, these issues must be addressed.

Accessibility and the Digital Divide

Access to digital volunteerism is still unequal across many socioeconomic and geographic situations, despite its potential. The difference between people and communities who have easy access to digital technologies and those who do not is known as the "digital divide" (Van Dijk, 2020). A lack of digital knowledge, poor gear, expensive data plans, and restricted internet availability can all be obstacles for volunteers working in low-resource environments. For example, whereas their urban counterparts may have no trouble accessing the same resources, a rural community health volunteer in a remote area of sub-Saharan Africa would find it difficult to engage in online training modules that demand high-speed internet.

A type of "digital exclusion" may result from these differences, thereby marginalizing those who might otherwise be able and willing to contribute. The problem is not just one of infrastructure; it is also one of inclusivity in terms of language and culture. Platforms created largely for Western audiences or in English may inadvertently put those from various cultural backgrounds or speakers of other languages at a disadvantage. According to academics, digital inclusion necessitates both having access to technology and having the ability to utilize it effectively (Helsper, 2021). Volunteer programs have the potential of escalating rather than reducing social inequality if intentional design decisions are not made that take into consideration the varied requirements of users.

Security and Privacy of Data

The handling of personal information is another urgent issue. Sensitive information such as location, expertise, contact information, and even identification documents are frequently gathered via volunteer platforms. Platforms occasionally collect performance indicators as well, such feedback scores or volunteer hours logged. Such data presents serious privacy and security hazards even while it can enhance program coordination and impact measurement. In addition to harming individuals, unauthorized access, data breaches, and information misuse can also undermine trust in the organizations concerned (Zwitter & Boisse-Despiaux, 2018). For instance, if a volunteer's involvement information is unintentionally revealed when they are working in a politically delicate setting, they could be in grave risk. High privacy requirements are mandated by data protection laws, such as the General Data Protection Regulation (GDPR) of the EU, however compliance varies among international volunteer programs. Therefore, ethical responsibility requires that organizations use safe storage methods, gather only the information that is necessary, and keep volunteers informed about the use of their data.

An Excessive Dependence on technology

Even though digital technologies provide previously unheard-of efficiency, there is growing fear that an excessive dependence on technology could compromise the human component at the core of volunteerism. When interactions are conducted solely through screens, the relational component—the empathy, trust, and camaraderie developed through in-person interaction—may be compromised. Virtual mentoring programs, for example, might make it possible for volunteers to connect with mentees who live far away, but they might also find it difficult to match the emotional impact of face-to-face interactions. Furthermore, volunteer programs that rely too much on technology may be susceptible to interruptions. Activities may be abruptly stopped by program discontinuance, cyberattacks, or system outages, leaving volunteers unable to carry on with their job. Resilience in digital systems necessitates redundancy, backup plans, and an awareness that technology is a tool to support human connections and decision-making, not to replace them, as noted by West and Allen (2020).

Inclusivity and Algorithmic Bias

New ethical issues arise as volunteer platforms use increasingly complex tools, like AI-driven matching systems. Algorithmic bias happens when automated systems replicate and reflect current social injustices, frequently as a result of skewed or inadequate training data (Noble, 2018). This could mean that, even if they have the requisite skills and enthusiasm, members of particular groups—like older adults, individuals with disabilities, or members of underrepresented ethnic backgrounds—are less likely to be matched with opportunities when it comes to volunteer recruiting. These biases can be subtle and challenging to identify, particularly in cases where algorithms are opaque and private. For instance, a platform that gives preference to candidates who have past experience volunteering online may unintentionally leave out those from rural areas who are just as talented but haven't had the opportunity to do so. Thus, to stop the quiet exclusion of underrepresented groups, inclusive design and frequent algorithmic audits are crucial.

FUTURE DIRECTIONS AND POLICY IMPLICATIONS

With the increasing integration of cutting-edge technologies like blockchain, augmented and virtual reality (AR/VR), artificial intelligence (AI), and the Internet of Things (IoT), the digital landscape influencing volunteers is far from static. For example, AI is being used more and more to match volunteers with opportunities that fit their availability, motivations, and skill set, which makes recruitment more individualized and efficient (Mora et al., 2021). These solutions enable organizations to proactively manage retention issues by analyzing volunteer history, evaluating engagement levels, and even forecasting attrition threats. Contrarily, blockchain provides an unchangeable, transparent way to document volunteer contributions, whether they take the shape of hours worked, knowledge shared, or results attained, increasing credibility and confidence among stakeholders (Tapscott & Tapscott, 2018). Before beginning on-the-ground work, volunteers can experience virtual surroundings thanks to AR and VR, which offer intriguing opportunities for immersive training and orientation (Yoon et al., 2020). Such tools can be especially helpful in humanitarian relief, health outreach, and disaster response, when being familiar with the operational context beforehand can greatly increase readiness. From environmental cleanup operations that record the amount of rubbish collected to medical volunteer missions that use sensor networks to track essential supplies, IoT devices are enabling real-time monitoring of activities. Despite their potential, these inventions need to be carefully evaluated for accessibility, ethical consequences, and scalability.

Long-Term Digital Volunteering

Digitalization is incredibly efficient, but it's important to think about how these solutions will affect the environment. Energy-efficient platforms and green technologies must be thoughtfully incorporated into digital volunteerism to be sustainable. The carbon footprint of digital activities can be decreased by using cloud computing that is fueled by renewable energy sources, low-bandwidth communication technologies, and reusing outdated technology (Hilty & Aebischer, 2015). Another aspect that organizations cannot ignore is the ethical sourcing of software and hardware. Device procurement frequently depends on supply chains linked to labor conditions and resource extraction, which may be at odds with the very humanitarian ideals that volunteerism aims to preserve (Bocken et al., 2016). By including supplier transparency and sustainability audits into procurement procedures, it is ensured that the infrastructure supporting volunteerism does not sustain social injustices or environmental damage.

Suggestions for Policy

Frameworks that place a strong focus on inclusivity, openness, and ethical responsibility ought to direct the governance of digital volunteering. Fundamentally, explicit data protection regulations are required, particularly when sensitive personal data is collected by AI and IoT systems (Floridi et al., 2018). By revealing the standards used to match volunteers to positions, for example, transparency in algorithmic decision-making can help reduce mistrust and remove biases. Making thoughtful design decisions is necessary for inclusivity. Although effective, automated systems run the danger of leaving out people who are not digitally literate, reside in places with poor connectivity, or are members of underrepresented communities in training datasets (Noble, 2018). Investments in multilingual platform interfaces, capacity building, and hybrid models that blend online and offline engagement are necessary to address this. National governments and international organizations could work together to create certification requirements for digital volunteer platforms that satisfy sustainability, accessibility, and ethical standards. Volunteering's future depends on balancing technology advancement with the human element of service. Ensuring that volunteers in the digital age continue to be impactful, equitable, and sustainable will require policies that recognize the dual nature of digital tools—their ability to empower and exclude.

CONCLUSION

This chapter traces the evolving pulse of volunteerism in the digital age, demonstrating how technology has evolved from a mere tool to an essential collaborator in organizing, maintaining, and mobilizing volunteer activity. The conversation outlined the wide range of platforms and apps that facilitate hiring, improve teamwork, encourage drive, and track results. We observed how advancements like real-time analytics, gamification features, and AI-driven matching may greatly increase participation rates and enhance the caliber of engagement. The case studies also showed that, when used carefully, digital technologies can increase the scope and results of volunteer programs in addition to streamlining procedures. However, the timeless reality that volunteering is ultimately a human endeavor hides beneath the data dashboards and computational efficiencies. The empathy, dedication, and sense of purpose that motivate people to freely donate their time cannot be replaced by technology, even though it may bring strangers together across countries and precisely organize work. Therefore, the efforts that combine the ease of digital technologies with the warmth of meaningful relationship-building and human acknowledgment are the most successful. Not only is it excellent practice to balance these aspects, but it also protects against the possibility that volunteering will become a transactional endeavor. In the future, it will be crucial to investigate how digital volunteerism develops in various industries, resource situations, and cultural contexts. Tools that work well in one nation or cause might not work well in another. The nuanced ways that institutional support, digital literacy, and local values influence the uptake and effects of technology in volunteer programs should be the subject of future studies. We can only guarantee that the digital pulse of voluntarism stays inclusive, robust, and fundamentally human by gaining such cross-cultural and cross-sector insights.

REFERENCES

Bennett, W. L., & Segerberg, A. (2013). *The logic of connective action: Digital media and the personalization of contentious politics.* Cambridge University Press. DOI: 10.1017/CBO9781139198752

Berkman, L. F., & Glass, T. (2020). *Social integration, social networks, social support, and health.* Social Epidemiology. Oxford University Press.

Bocken, N. M. P., Short, S. W., Rana, P., & Evans, S. (2016). A literature and practice review to develop sustainable business model archetypes. *Journal of Cleaner Production, 65*, 42–56. DOI: 10.1016/j.jclepro.2013.11.039

Borgatti, S. P., Mehra, A., Brass, D. J., & Labianca, G. (2009). Network analysis in the social sciences. *Science, 323*(5916), 892–895. DOI: 10.1126/science.1165821 PMID: 19213908

Bryson, J. M., Crosby, B. C., & Bloomberg, L. (2021). Public value governance: Moving beyond traditional public administration and the New Public Management. *Public Administration Review, 81*(1), 3–19. DOI: 10.1111/puar.13271

Bussell, H., & Forbes, D. (2002). Understanding the volunteer market: The what, where, who and why of volunteering. *International Journal of Nonprofit and Voluntary Sector Marketing, 7*(3), 244–257. DOI: 10.1002/nvsm.183

Cravens, J., & Ellis, S. J. (2014). *The last virtual volunteering guidebook: Fully integrating online service into volunteer involvement.* Energize, Inc.

Davis, F. D. (1989). Perceived usefulness, perceived ease of use, and user acceptance of information technology. *Management Information Systems Quarterly, 13*(3), 319–340. DOI: 10.2307/249008

Deane, S. (2020). Digital transformation in the nonprofit sector: Case studies and best practices. *The Nonprofit Quarterly, 27*(3), 45–53.

Estrella, M., & Gaventa, J. (2022). *Who counts reality? Participatory monitoring and evaluation: A literature review.* IDS Working Paper 70, Institute of Development Studies.

Floridi, L., Cowls, J., Beltrametti, M., Chatila, R., Chazerand, P., Dignum, V., Luetge, C., Madelin, R., Pagallo, U., Rossi, F., Schafer, B., Valcke, P., & Vayena, E. (2018). AI4People—An ethical framework for a good AI society: Opportunities, risks, principles, and recommendations. *Minds and Machines, 28*(4), 689–707. DOI: 10.1007/s11023-018-9482-5 PMID: 30930541

Galaxy Digital. (2024, April 23). *Gamifying volunteerism for enhanced engagement.* https://www.galaxydigital.com/blog/how-to-gamify-volunteerism-and-increase-engagement

Hamari, J., Koivisto, J., & Sarsa, H. (2014). Does gamification work? — A literature review of empirical studies on gamification. *Proceedings of the 47th Hawaii International Conference on System Sciences*, 3025–3034. DOI: 10.1109/HICSS.2014.377

Helsper, E. J. (2021). *The digital disconnect: The social causes and consequences of digital inequalities.* SAGE Publications. DOI: 10.4135/9781526492982

Hilty, L. M., & Aebischer, B. (2015). ICT for sustainability: An emerging research field. In Hilty, L. M., & Aebischer, B. (Eds.), *ICT Innovations for Sustainability* (pp. 3–36). Springer., DOI: 10.1007/978-3-319-09228-7_1

Hustinx, L., Handy, F., & Cnaan, R. A. (2010). Volunteering. In Taylor, R. (Ed.), *Third sector research* (pp. 549–572). Springer., DOI: 10.1007/978-1-4419-5707-8_7

Hustinx, L., Handy, F., Cnaan, R. A., & Kang, C. (2020). The changing landscape of volunteering: A review of recent literature. *Voluntas, 31*(5), 1016–1036. DOI: 10.1007/s11266-020-00241-4

Innovations for Learning. (n.d.). *Innovations for learning.* In *Wikipedia*. Retrieved August 14, 2025, from https://en.wikipedia.org/wiki/Innovations_for_Learning

Kapoor, K., Dwivedi, Y. K., Piercy, N. F., & Williams, M. D. (2018). Examining the role of project management in improving organizational performance. *International Journal of Project Management, 36*(3), 384–397. DOI: 10.1016/j.ijproman.2017.10.002

Mertens, D. M. (2015). *Research and evaluation in education and psychology: Integrating diversity with quantitative, qualitative, and mixed methods*. Sage Publications.

MoldStud. (n.d.). *Custom software for volunteer recruitment in non-profits*. https://moldstud.com/articles/p-custom-software-for-non-profit-virtual-volunteer-recruitment

Mora, H., Gilart-Iglesias, V., Pérez-del Hoyo, R., & Andújar-Montoya, M. D. (2021). Volunteerism and technology: A review of platforms and digital practices. *Voluntas, 32*(2), 245–260. DOI: 10.1007/s11266-020-00271-9

Musick, M. A., & Wilson, J. (2008). *Volunteers: A social profile*. Indiana University Press.

NGOs.ai. (n.d.). *AI for volunteer management and recruitment*. https://ngos.ai/wes/ai-for-volunteer-management-and-recruitment

Noble, S. U. (2018). *Algorithms of oppression: How search engines reinforce racism*. NYU Press. DOI: 10.18574/nyu/9781479833641.001.0001

Ordonez, K. (n.d.). *AI in volunteer management: Identifying and retaining volunteers with AI*. LinkedIn. https://www.linkedin.com/pulse/ai-volunteer-management-identifying-retaining-kevin-ordonez-aaip-c7ekc

Pandey, A. (2025). The Transformative Potential of Artificial Intelligence in Building Sustainable Agricultural Systems: Innovations, Challenges, and Future Directions. In *AI and Ecological Change for Sustainable Development* (pp. 161-182). IGI Global Scientific Publishing.

Putnam, R. D. (2000). *Bowling alone: The collapse and revival of the American community*. Simon & Schuster.

Rochester, C., Paine, A. E., & Howlett, S. (2010). *Volunteering and society in the 21st century*. Palgrave Macmillan. DOI: 10.1057/9780230279438

Salamon, L. M., Sokolowski, S. W., & Haddock, M. A. (2017). Measuring the economic value of volunteer work globally: Concepts, estimates, and a roadmap to the future. *Nonprofit and Voluntary Sector Quarterly, 46*(5), 893–911. DOI: 10.1177/0899764017721770

Smith, K., & Cordery, C. (2021). Digital governance in nonprofit organizations: Challenges and opportunities. *Nonprofit Management & Leadership*, *31*(4), 593–611. DOI: 10.1002/nml.21453

Tapia, A., & Maldonado, E. (2022). Blockchain for social impact: Transparency in humanitarian aid and volunteerism. *Journal of Humanitarian Innovation and Technology*, *4*(2), 45–62. DOI: 10.1080/26753814.2022.2028724

Tapscott, D., & Tapscott, A. (2018). *Blockchain revolution: How the technology behind bitcoin and other cryptocurrencies is changing the world*. Penguin.

United Nations. (2015). *Transforming our world: The 2030 Agenda for Sustainable Development*. United Nations. https://sdgs.un.org/2030agenda

United Nations Volunteers. (2018). *State of the world's volunteerism report: The thread that binds*. United Nations Volunteers Programme.

Van Dijk, J. (2020). *The digital divide*. Polity Press.

Venkatesh, V., Morris, M. G., Davis, G. B., & Davis, F. D. (2003). User acceptance of information technology: Toward a unified view. *Management Information Systems Quarterly*, *27*(3), 425–478. DOI: 10.2307/30036540

VolunteerHub. (n.d.). *3 ways to increase engagement with gamification*. https://volunteerhub.com/blog/3-ways-to-increase-engagement-with-gamification

West, D. M., & Allen, J. R. (2020). *Turning point: Policymaking in the era of artificial intelligence*. Brookings Institution Press. DOI: 10.5040/9780815751113

Wikipedia. (2025). *Gamification*. In *Wikipedia*. Retrieved August 14, 2025, from https://en.wikipedia.org/wiki/Gamification

Wilson, J. (2012). Volunteerism research: A review essay. *Nonprofit and Voluntary Sector Quarterly*, *41*(2), 176–212. DOI: 10.1177/0899764011434558

Yoon, S., Oh, J., & Choi, H. (2020). Immersive learning using virtual reality: A systematic review. *Educational Technology Research and Development*, *68*(6), 3221–3242. DOI: 10.1007/s11423-020-09882-2

Zwitter, A., & Boisse-Despiaux, M. (2018). Big data ethics: Risks and opportunities. *Big Data & Society, 5*(2), 1–6.

KEY TERMS AND DEFINITIONS

Volunteering Online: The act of using digital tools or online platforms to donate time, abilities, or knowledge to a cause. By removing time and location constraints, this type of involvement enables people to support groups or communities without having to be physically present.

Tools for Engagement: Software features, platforms, or applications created to draw in, engage, and inspire volunteers to continue working on a project. These might be anything from gamified challenges and interactive dashboards to straightforward lines of communication that motivate and connect people.

Evaluation of Impact: Collecting and evaluating data in order to comprehend the concrete and intangible outcomes of volunteer projects. It aims to evaluate how volunteer labor has enhanced lives, bolstered communities, or aided certain development objectives, going beyond simply tallying hours spent.

Gamification: Gamification refers to the strategic use of elements traditionally found in games—such as leaderboards, achievement levels, badges, and point systems—within settings that are not inherently game-based. In the context of volunteerism, these components are incorporated into programs or platforms to boost motivation, sustain participation, and create a sense of progress. By framing tasks and milestones in a playful, rewarding way, gamification can transform routine activities into engaging experiences. This approach not only fosters a spirit of friendly competition but also strengthens personal commitment, making volunteers feel recognized, valued, and accomplished in their contributions toward a shared goal.

Retention of Volunteers: The capacity of an organization or program to sustain the engagement of its volunteers over time. Volunteer retention is frequently correlated with their sense of support and value as well as the significance of their work.

Volunteering Based on Skills: A type of volunteer work where people donate their professional skills—like marketing, IT, design, or legal counsel—to support a cause. This method frequently produces results with a significant impact since it directly draws on specialist knowledge.

The Digital Divide: The digital divide refers to the gap separating individuals, communities, or regions that enjoy regular, reliable access to modern information and communication technologies (ICTs) from those who lack such access. This disparity may stem from differences in infrastructure, affordability, digital literacy, or social and economic conditions. In the context of volunteerism, it can limit participation in online initiatives, leaving certain groups excluded from opportunities to contribute or benefit. Bridging this divide is essential to ensure that digital volunteer platforms are inclusive, equitable, and reflective of diverse voices, skills, and experiences across different societal and geographic boundaries.

Platforms for Online Hiring: Online resources that connect volunteers with charitable organizations. They frequently connect people to opportunities that fit their availability, interests, and skill set by using recommendation algorithms or search criteria.

Making Decisions Based on Data: A method of managing programs that is based on data rather than conjecture, such as analytics, surveys, or performance indicators. It assists organizations in improving their volunteerism strategy for increased impact and involvement.

Tools for Virtual Collaboration: Tools for virtual collaboration are digital platforms and applications designed to enable individuals or teams to work together effectively without being physically present in the same location. These tools provide shared online spaces for communication, document management, and project coordination. Examples include cloud-based file storage systems, collaborative work environments, and video conferencing software. They allow real-time information sharing, collective problem-solving, and synchronized workflow management, bridging geographical distances and time zones. By integrating features such as instant messaging, task tracking, and shared editing, virtual collaboration tools enhance productivity, maintain team cohesion, and support flexible, remote, or hybrid work arrangements across diverse sectors.

Compilation of References

Acs, Z. J., Song, A. K., Szerb, L., Audretsch, D. B., & Komlósi, É. (2021). The evolution of the global digital platform economy: 1971–2021. *Small Business Economics*, *57*(4), 1629–1659. DOI: 10.1007/s11187-021-00561-x

Adade, R., & Goosen, L. (2024). Teachers and Schools Navigating Virtual Worlds and the Metaverse for Enhanced E-Learning: Evaluating an E-Capacity Model Approach. In Chafiq, N., Cummins, P., Al-Qatawneh, K., & El Imadi, I. (Eds.), *Navigating Virtual Worlds and the Metaverse for Enhanced E-Learning* (pp. 134–152). IGI Global., DOI: 10.4018/979-8-3693-1034-2.ch006

Adjekum, A., Blasimme, A., & Vayena, E. (2018). Elements of trust in digital health systems: Scoping review. *Journal of Medical Internet Research*, *20*(12), e11254. DOI: 10.2196/11254 PMID: 30545807

Aftab, W., Siddiqui, F., Tasic, H., Perveen, S., Siddiqi, S., & Bhutta, Z. (2020). Implementation of health and health-related sustainable development goals: Progress, challenges and opportunities – a systematic literature review. *BMJ Global Health*, *5*(8), e002273. DOI: 10.1136/bmjgh-2019-002273 PMID: 32847825

Aghauche, E. E., Nkamnebe, C. B., & Nkamnebe, E. C. (2019). Information literacy skills of undergraduates in Paul University Awka, Anambra state. *UNIZIK Journal of Research in Library and Information Science*, *4*(1/2), 94–109.

Agyei, D. D., & Voogt, J. M. (2011). Exploring the potential of the will, skill, tool model in Ghana: Predicting prospective and practising teachers' use of technology. *Computers & Education, 56*(1), 91–100. DOI: 10.1016/j.compedu.2010.08.017

Akhtar-Schuster, M., Stringer, L., & Barger, N. (2024). Fast-tracking action on the sustainable development goals by enhancing national institutional arrangements. *PLoS One, 19*(3), e0298855. DOI: 10.1371/journal.pone.0298855 PMID: 38507393

Akram, H., Abdelrady, A. H., Al-Adwan, A. S., & Ramzan, M. (2022). Teachers' perceptions of technology integration in Teaching-Learning Practices: A Systematic Review. *Frontiers in Psychology, 13*, 920317. Advance online publication. DOI: 10.3389/fpsyg.2022.920317 PMID: 35734463

Alan, Ş., Baysan, C., Gümren, M., & Kubilay, E. (2021). Building Social Cohesion in Ethnically Mixed Schools: An Intervention on Perspective Taking. *The Quarterly Journal of Economics, 136*(4), 2147–2194. DOI: 10.1093/qje/qjab009

Alfes, K., Shantz, A., & Bailey, C. (2015). Enhancing volunteer engagement to achieve desirable outcomes: What can non-profit employers do? *Voluntas, 27*(2), 595–617. DOI: 10.1007/s11266-015-9601-3

Ali, F., Paswan, S., Bennett, G., Pradhan, R., Nadagouda, S., & Choudhury, S. (2021). Leveraging digital platforms for disseminating health and nutrition information during COVID-19: Reflections from project samvad in india. *Journal of Global Health Reports, 5*. Advance online publication. DOI: 10.29392/001c.22121

Alkusaibati, W. (2024). Digitalized co-production of emergency response: using volunteers as first responders.. https://doi.org/DOI: 10.3384/9789180756488

Allmann, K., & Blank, G. (2021). Rethinking digital skills in the era of compulsory computing: Methods, measurement, policy and theory. *Information Communication and Society, 24*(6), 837–855. DOI: 10.1080/1369118X.2021.1874475

Almudhaybri, T. (2025). The role of faculty members at Qassim University in digital volunteering in light of Saudi Arabia's vision 2030. *IJESA*, *4*(4), 337–372. DOI: 10.59992/IJESA.2025.v4n4p14

Alnofeli, K. K., Akter, S., & Yanamandram, V. (2025). Unlocking the power of AI in CRM: A comprehensive multidimensional exploration. *Journal of Innovation & Knowledge*, *10*(3), 100731. DOI: 10.1016/j.jik.2025.100731

Alonso, R., Thoene, U., & Benavides, D. (2020). Social computing applications as a resource for newly arrived refugees in Kronoberg, Sweden. *Digital Policy Regulation and Governance*, *23*(1), 21–44. DOI: 10.1108/DPRG-05-2020-0063

Ambrose, S., Huston, T., & Norman, M. (2005). A qualitative method for assessing faculty satisfaction. *Research in Higher Education*, *46*(7), 803–830. DOI: 10.1007/s11162-004-6226-6

Amos, O., Ogoti, E., & Siamoo, P. (2022). Shared Strategic Vision in Participative Leadership Style and Quality Education Provision in Public Secondary Schools in Arusha Region, Tanzania. *Brock Journal of Education*, *10*(7), 51–74. DOI: 10.37745/bje.2013/vol10n7pp5174

Anderson, S. E., & Putman, R. S. (2020). Special education teachers' experience, confidence, beliefs, and knowledge about integrating technology. *Journal of Special Education Technology*, *35*(1), 37–50. DOI: 10.1177/0162643419836409

Aničić, K., & Bušelić, V. (2021). Importance of Generic Skills of ICT Graduates-Employers, Teaching Staff, and Students Perspective. *IEEE Transactions on Education*, *64*(3), 245–252. DOI: 10.1109/TE.2020.3034958

Ansu-Kyeremeh, E. K., & Goosen, L. (2022). Exploring the Socioeconomic Facet of Online Inclusive Education in Ghana: The Effects of Technological Advancement in Academia. In Garcia, M. (Ed.), *Socioeconomic Inclusion During an Era of Online Education* (pp. 47–66). IGI Global., DOI: 10.4018/978-1-6684-4364-4.ch003

Anthony, B.Jr. (2024). The role of community engagement in urban innovation towards the co-creation of smart sustainable cities. *Journal of the Knowledge Economy, 15*(2), 567–589. DOI: 10.1007/s13132-023-01176-1

Asteria, D., Surpi, N., Brotosusilo, A., & Suja'i, I. (2023). Integration of local capacity building in countering false information about disaster into community-based disaster risk management. *IOP Conference Series. Earth and Environmental Science, 1275*(1), 012028. DOI: 10.1088/1755-1315/1275/1/012028

Ayamga, M., Lawani, A., Akaba, S., & Birindwa, A. (2023). Developing institutions and inter-organizational synergies through digitalization and youth engagement in African agriculture: The case of "africa goes digital". *Land (Basel), 12*(1), 199. DOI: 10.3390/land12010199

Baalharith, I., & Aboshaiqah, A. (2024). Virtual healthcare revolution: Understanding nurse competencies and roles. *SAGE Open Nursing, 10*, 23779608241271703. Advance online publication. DOI: 10.1177/23779608241271703 PMID: 39161935

Ball, D., & Forzani, F. (2011). Teaching skillful teaching. *Educational Leadership, 68*(4), 40–45.

Barkay, T. (2012). Employee volunteering: Soul, body and CSR. *Social Responsibility Journal, 8*(1), 48–62. DOI: 10.1108/17471111211196566

Basheva, O. A., & Ermolaeva, P. O. (2024). "Digital volunteering concept: Definition and models for analysis." *Handbook of Environmental Policy and Law*. https://doi.org/DOI: 10.1007/978-3-031-30231-2_26-1

Basheva, D., & Ermolaeva, P. (2025). Digital competence and volunteer engagement in online environments. *Voluntas, 36*(1), 45–59.

Basheva, О., & Ермолаева, П. (2020). The phenomenon of digital volunteerism in emergency situations: Its essence, types and theoretical framework. *Vestnik Instituta Sotziologii, 11*(1), 49–71. DOI: 10.19181/vis.2020.11.1.625

Belina, A. (2023). Digital volunteering through a volunteering crowdsourcing platform: lessons from tudu.org.pl. Voluntary Sector Review, 14(3), 557-566. https://doi.org/DOI: 10.1332/204080522X16546738241352

Bennett, W. L., & Segerberg, A. (2013). *The logic of connective action: Digital media and the personalization of contentious politics*. Cambridge University Press. DOI: 10.1017/CBO9781139198752

Berkman, L. F., & Glass, T. (2020). *Social integration, social networks, social support, and health*. Social Epidemiology. Oxford University Press.

Blyznyuk, T., & Sobakar, M. (2024). Risks in volunteer activities during the war in Ukraine. *Ukrainian Journal of Applied Economics*, 9(2), 39–43. DOI: 10.36887/2415-8453-2024-2-6

Bocken, N. M. P., Short, S. W., Rana, P., & Evans, S. (2016). A literature and practice review to develop sustainable business model archetypes. *Journal of Cleaner Production*, 65, 42–56. DOI: 10.1016/j.jclepro.2013.11.039

Bonina, C., Koskinen, K., Eaton, B., & Gawer, A. (2021). Digital platforms for development: Foundations and research agenda. *Information Systems Journal*, 31(6), 869–902. DOI: 10.1111/isj.12326

Boppre, B., Reed, S., & Belisle, L. (2022). "real students helping others": Student reflections on a research-based service-learning project in a gender and victimization course. *Journal of Experiential Education*, 46(3), 281–303. DOI: 10.1177/10538259221134873

Borgatti, S. P., Mehra, A., Brass, D. J., & Labianca, G. (2009). Network analysis in the social sciences. *Science*, 323(5916), 892–895. DOI: 10.1126/science.1165821 PMID: 19213908

Bouarar, A., Mouloudj, S., Umar, T., & Mouloudj, K. (2023). Antecedents of physicians' intentions to engage in digital volunteering work: An extended technology acceptance model (TAM) approach. *Journal of Integrated Care*, 31(4), 285–299. DOI: 10.1108/JICA-03-2023-0017

Bourgonjon, J. (2015). *Video game literacy: Social, cultural and educational perspectives*. (Doctoral dissertation). Ghent University.

Bowser, A., Shilton, K., Preece, J., & Warrick, E. (2017). Accounting for privacy in citizen science., 2124-2136. https://doi.org/DOI: 10.1145/2998181.2998305

Briones, R., & Janoski, T. (2021). Digital volunteering and civic engagement in education. *Nonprofit and Voluntary Sector Quarterly*, *50*(3), 560–580. DOI: 10.1177/08997640211999142

Briones, R., & Janoski, T. (2021). Volunteer engagement and organizational impact in educational settings: Evidence from digital platforms. *Nonprofit and Voluntary Sector Quarterly*, *50*(2), 345–365. DOI: 10.1177/0899764020965152

Brix, J. (2019). Innovation capacity building. *The Learning Organization*, *26*(1), 12–26. DOI: 10.1108/TLO-08-2018-0143

Bryson, J. M., Crosby, B. C., & Bloomberg, L. (2021). Public value governance: Moving beyond traditional public administration and the New Public Management. *Public Administration Review*, *81*(1), 3–19. DOI: 10.1111/puar.13271

Buckler, A., Twiner, A., & Power, T. (2025). "I had to adjust my character so I was able to help": How community volunteers in rural Zimbabwe developed as educators in a context of crisis and school closures. *Journal of Educational Change*, *26*(4), 631–655. DOI: 10.1007/s10833-025-09535-2

Bussell, H., & Forbes, D. (2002). Understanding the volunteer market: The what, where, who and why of volunteering. *International Journal of Nonprofit and Voluntary Sector Marketing*, *7*(3), 244–257. DOI: 10.1002/nvsm.183

Buyakova, C. & Malkova, I. (2021). Volunteering as a form of students' educational activities in the context of the university's third mission. Vysshee Obrazovanie v Rossii = Higher Education in Russia, 30(8-9), 69-79. DOI: 10.31992/0869-3617-2021-30-8-9-69-79

Caldron, P., Impens, A., Pavlova, M., & Groot, W. (2015). A systematic review of social, economic and diplomatic aspects of short-term medical missions. *BMC Health Services Research*, *15*(1), 380. Advance online publication. DOI: 10.1186/s12913-015-0980-3 PMID: 26373298

Caligiuri, P., Mencin, A., & Jiang, K. (2013). Win–win–win: The influence of company-sponsored volunteerism programs on employees, NGOs, and business units. *Personnel Psychology*, *66*(4), 825–860. DOI: 10.1111/peps.12019

Caridà, A., Colurcio, M., & Melia, M. (2022). Digital platform for social innovation: Insights from volunteering. *Creativity and Innovation Management*, *31*(4), 678–690. DOI: 10.1111/caim.12499

Carrington, S., Spina, N., Kimber, M., Spooner-Lane, R., & Williams, K. (2021). Leadership attributes that support school improvement: A realist approach. *School Leadership & Management*, *42*(2), 151–169. DOI: 10.1080/13632434.2021.2016686

Cette, G., Clerc, C., & Bresson, L. (2015). Contribution of ICT Diffusion to Labour Productivity Growth: The United States, Canada, the Eurozone, and the United Kingdom, 1970-2013. *International Productivity Monitor*, *28*, 81–88.

Chadwick, A., & Fadel, B. (2020). *Volunteerism and Community Resilience: Locally Owned Solutions Delivering Impact*. Emirates Foundation. Retrieved from https://www.iave.org/iavewp/wp-content/uploads/2020/07/Volunteerism-and-Community-Resilience-Locally-Owned-Solutions-Delivering-Impact.pdf

Chow, C., Goh, S., Tan, C., Wu, H., & Shahdadpuri, R. (2021). Enhancing frontline workforce volunteerism through exploration of motivations and impact during the COVID-19 pandemic. *International Journal of Disaster Risk Reduction*, *66*, 102605. DOI: 10.1016/j.ijdrr.2021.102605 PMID: 34603950

Christensen, C., Ehrenberg, N., & Christiansson, J. (2022). "Volunteer-based IT helpdesks as ambiguous quasi-public services—A case study from two Nordic countries." *Nordic Human-Computer Interaction*, 6(CSCW). Article, *45*, 1–20. DOI: 10.1145/3534567

Chui, C., & Chan, C. (2019). The role of technology in reconfiguring volunteer management in nonprofits in Hong Kong: Benefits and discontents. *Nonprofit Management & Leadership*, *30*(1), 89–111. DOI: 10.1002/nml.21369

Clandinin, D. J., & Connelly, F. M. (2000). *Narrative inquiry: Experience and story in qualitative research*. Jossey-Bass.

Cnaan, R. A., Handy, F., & Wadsworth, M. (1996). Defining who is a volunteer: Conceptual and empirical considerations. *Nonprofit and Voluntary Sector Quarterly*, *25*(3), 364–383. DOI: 10.1177/0899764096253006

Costa, P., Castaño-Muñoz, J., & Kampylis, P. (2021). Capturing schools' digital capacity: Psychometric analyses of the Selfie self-reflection tool. *Computers & Education*, *162*, 104080. Advance online publication. DOI: 10.1016/j.compedu.2020.104080

Cravens, J., & Ellis, S. J. (2014). *The last virtual volunteering guidebook: Fully integrating online service into volunteer involvement*. Energize, Inc.

Crittenden, V. L., & Hager, M. A. (2025). Digital volunteerism and civic engagement in the digital age. *Journal of Nonprofit & Public Sector Marketing*, *37*(1), 1–15.

Cuadra, J., & Cotoron, V. (2025). Addressing false information through local capacity building in community-based disaster risk management. *Jàambá*, *17*(1), a1836. Advance online publication. DOI: 10.4102/jamba.v17i1.1836 PMID: 40357013

Danganan, C. G., & Gamboa, A. G. (2025). Unveiling the Dynamic Landscape: Exploring Practices, Challenges, and Resilience Strategies of Digital Leaders in Secondary Education. *Journal of Cultural Analysis and Social Change*, *587*, 587–598. Advance online publication. DOI: 10.64753/jcasc.v10i3.2457

Davis, F. D. (1989). Perceived usefulness, perceived ease of use, and user acceptance of information technology. *Management Information Systems Quarterly*, *13*(3), 319–340. DOI: 10.2307/249008

Dawson, D., Morales, E., McKiernan, E. C., Schimanski, L. A., Niles, M. T., & Alperin, J. P. (2022). The role of collegiality in academic review, promotion, and tenure. *PLoS One*, *17*(4), e0265506. Advance online publication. DOI: 10.1371/journal.pone.0265506 PMID: 35385489

De Filippi, F., Coscia, C., Cocina, G. G., Lazzari, G., & Manzo, S. (2022). Digital participatory platforms for civic engagement: A new way of participating in society? Analysis of case studies in four EU countries. *International Journal of Urban Planning and Smart Cities*, *1*(1), 1–21. DOI: 10.4018/IJUPSC.2020010101

Deane, S. (2020). Digital transformation in the nonprofit sector: Case studies and best practices. *The Nonprofit Quarterly*, *27*(3), 45–53.

Dekel, G., Geldenhuys, M., & Harris, J. (2022). Exploring the value of organizational support, engagement, and psychological wellbeing in the volunteer context. *Frontiers in Psychology*, *13*, 915572. Advance online publication. DOI: 10.3389/fpsyg.2022.915572 PMID: 36160559

Den Broeder, L., South, J., Rothoff, A., Bagnall, A.-M., Azarhoosh, F., van der Linden, G., Bharadwa, M., & Wagemakers, A. (2022). Community engagement in deprived neighbourhoods during the COVID-19 crisis: Perspectives for more resilient and healthier communities. *Health Promotion International*, *37*(6), daac123. Advance online publication. DOI: 10.1093/heapro/daab098 PMID: 34297841

Denzin, N. K., & Lincoln, Y. S. (2018). *The SAGE handbook of qualitative research* (5th ed.). SAGE Publications.

Denzin, N. K., & Lincoln, Y. S. (2018). *The Sage handbook of qualitative research* (5th ed.). Sage.

Dexter, S., & Richardson, J. W. (2020). What does technology integration research tell us about the leadership of technology? *Journal of Research on Technology in Education, 52*(1), 17–36. DOI: 10.1080/15391523.2019.1668316

Digitalized Co-production and Volunteerism in Emergency Response. A literature review. (2023). *Proceedings of the . . . International ISCRAM Conference.* https://doi.org/DOI: 10.59297/ARQO2281

Dinca, L. G., & Diaconita, V. (2024). "Enhancing the involvement level of volunteer students in the academic community: Efficient usage of digital resources." *Proceedings of the 23rd International Conference on Informatics in Economy*, 49–58. https://doi.org/DOI: 10.1007/978-981-96-0161-5_5

Doorgakant, Y. M., & Baichoo, R. R. (2021). Collegiality as a Fundamental Professional Value in an Academic Setting: A Case Study in a Teacher Education Institution in a Small Island Developing State. *Pedagogical Quarterly/Kwartalnik Pedagogiczny, 66*(4), 52-70.

Dube, B. (2025). Digital literacy initiatives and community participation in Zimbabwean schools. *African Educational Research Journal, 13*(1), 45–56.

Dubé, M. (2025). Youth activism and the power of social media to drive social change. *International Journal for Multidisciplinary Research, 7*(2), 42967. Advance online publication. DOI: 10.36948/ijfmr.2025.v07i02.42967

Education Coalition of Zimbabwe. (2017, October 12). Inclusive Education Indaba 2017. https://ecozi.co.zw/the-inclusive-education-indaba-2017/

Ehsan, M. M., & Zaidan, E. (2024). Exploring internet inclusivity and effectiveness of e-learning initiatives during the pandemic – a comparative analysis. *Frontiers in Education, 8*, 1301135. Advance online publication. DOI: 10.3389/feduc.2023.1301135

Eickelmann, B., & Gerick, J. (2017). Learning with digital media: A cross-national analysis of ICT use in schools. *Computers & Education, 111*, 1–12. https://doi.org/10.1016/j.compedu.2017.04.001

Elboj-Saso, C., Cortés-Pascual, A., Íñiguez-Berrozpe, T., Lozano-Blasco, R., & Quílez-Robres, A. (2021). Emotional and educational accompaniment through dialogic literary gatherings: A volunteer project for families who suffer digital exclusion in the context of COVID-19. *Sustainability (Basel), 13*(4), 1890. DOI: 10.3390/su13031206

Epstein, J. L. (2018). *School, family, and community partnerships: Preparing educators and improving schools* (2nd ed.). Westview Press.

Erdreich, L. (2025). Digital Well-Being and Superdigital Citizenship: A Class Comparison of Parenting Practices for Remote Learning. *Social Justice Research, 38*(3), 332–351. DOI: 10.1007/s11211-025-00454-4

Estévez, M., Ballestar, M. T., & Sáinz, J. (2025). Market research and knowledge using Generative AI: The power of Large Language Models. *Journal of Innovation & Knowledge, 10*(5), 100796. DOI: 10.1016/j.jik.2025.100796

Estrella, M., & Gaventa, J. (2022). *Who counts reality? Participatory monitoring and evaluation: A literature review.* IDS Working Paper 70, Institute of Development Studies.

Eveleigh, A., Jennett, C., Blandford, A., Brohan, P., & Cox, A. (2014). Designing for dabblers and deterring drop-outs in citizen science., 2985-2994. https://doi.org/DOI: 10.1145/2556288.2557262

Fasanmi, O. O., Olusanya, B. B., & Oyenuga, M. O. (2024).. . *Entrepreneurial Training as a Retirement Succorance for Nigerian Retirees Twist, 19*(4), 137–147. DOI: 10.5281/zenodo.10049652#321

Flick, U. (2019). *An introduction to qualitative research* (6th ed.). Sage.

Floridi, L., Cowls, J., Beltrametti, M., Chatila, R., Chazerand, P., Dignum, V., Luetge, C., Madelin, R., Pagallo, U., Rossi, F., Schafer, B., Valcke, P., & Vayena, E. (2018). AI4People—An ethical framework for a good AI society: Opportunities, risks, principles, and recommendations. *Minds and Machines*, *28*(4), 689–707. DOI: 10.1007/s11023-018-9482-5 PMID: 30930541

Forteh, E., Ngemenya, M., Kwalar, G., Alembong, E., Tanue, E., Kibu, O., & Nsagha, D. (2025). Determinants of the use of digital one health amongst medical and veterinary students at the University of Buea, Cameroon. https://doi.org/DOI: 10.1101/2025.04.16.25325946

Galaxy Digital. (2024, April 23). *Gamifying volunteerism for enhanced engagement*. https://www.galaxydigital.com/blog/how-to-gamify-volunteerism-and-increase-engagement

Garbett, D., & Thomas, L. (2020). Developing inter-collegial friendships to sustain professional wellbeing in the academy. *Teachers and Teaching*, *26*(3-4), 295–306. DOI: 10.1080/13540602.2020.1832062

García-Valcárcel, A., & Mena, J. (2021). In-service teachers' use of ICT for the Promotion of Collaborative Professional Learning. In *Research Anthology on Facilitating New Educational Practices Through Communities of Learning* (pp. 287–301). IGI Global. DOI: 10.4018/978-1-7998-7294-8.ch015

Garzón-Artacho, E., Sola-Martínez, T., Romero-Rodríguez, J. M., & Gómez-García, G. (2021). Teachers' perceptions of digital competence at the lifelong learning stage. *Heliyon*, *7*(7), e07513. Advance online publication. DOI: 10.1016/j.heliyon.2021.e07513 PMID: 34401558

Ghamrawi, N., Shal, T., & Ghamrawi, N. A. R. (2024). Leadership development in virtual communities of practice: The case of school principals from the GCC Region. *Education and Information Technologies*, *29*(17), 23897–23916. Advance online publication. DOI: 10.1007/s10639-024-12784-y

Ghavifekr, S., & Rosdy, W. A. (2015). Teaching and learning with technology: Effectiveness of ICT integration in schools. *International Journal of Research in Education and Science*, *1*(2), 175–191. DOI: 10.21890/ijres.23596

Giovannella, C. (2022). Between awareness and acceptance: A more mature school teachers' perspective on integrated learning one year after the pandemic outbreak. [s]. *Interaction Design and Architecture*, (52), 23–43. DOI: 10.55612/s-5002-052-002

Giraudet, L.-G., Apouey, B., Arab, H., Baeckelandt, S., Bégout, P., Berghmans, N., Blanc, N., Boulin, J.-Y., Buge, É., Courant, D., Dahan, A., Fabre, A., Fourniau, J.-M., Gaborit, M., Granchamp, L., Guillemot, H., Jeanpierre, L., Landemore, H., Laslier, J., & Tournus, S. (2022). "Co-construction" in deliberative democracy: Lessons from the French Citizens' Convention for Climate. *Humanities & Social Sciences Communications*, *9*(1), 207. DOI: 10.1057/s41599-022-01212-6 PMID: 35757681

Goh, E., & Sigala, M. (2020). Integrating Information & Communication Technologies (ICT) into classroom instruction: Teaching tips for hospitality educators from a diffusion of innovation approach. *Journal of Teaching in Travel & Tourism*, *20*(2), 156–165. DOI: 10.1080/15313220.2020.1740636

Goodall, J. (2021). Digital volunteering and leadership capacity in schools: Global lessons. *Journal of Educational Leadership*, *15*(1), 45–62.

Goodall, J. (2021). *Supporting parent engagement in schools: Insights from research and practice*. Routledge.

Grosman-Rimon, L., & Wegier, P. (2024). With advancement in health technology comes great responsibility – ethical and safety considerations for using digital health technology: A narrative review. *Medicine*, *103*(33), e39136. DOI: 10.1097/MD.0000000000039136 PMID: 39151529

Gurstein, M. (2007, December 19). What is community informatics (and why does it matter)? arXiv. https://doi.org//arXiv.0712.3220DOI: 10.48550

Hamari, J., Koivisto, J., & Sarsa, H. (2014). Does gamification work? — A literature review of empirical studies on gamification. *Proceedings of the 47th Hawaii International Conference on System Sciences*, 3025–3034. DOI: 10.1109/HICSS.2014.377

Hamerman, E., & Schneider, A. (2017). The role of disgust sensitivity in volunteer recruitment and retention. *International Journal of Nonprofit and Voluntary Sector Marketing*, *23*(2), e1597. Advance online publication. DOI: 10.1002/nvsm.1597

Hammer, D. P., Bynum, L. A., Carter, J., Hagemeier, N. E., Kennedy, D. R., Khansari, P., Stamm, P., & Crabtree, B. (2019). Revisiting faculty citizenship. *American Journal of Pharmaceutical Education*, *83*(4), 7378. Advance online publication. DOI: 10.5688/ajpe7378 PMID: 31223170

Helsper, E. J. (2021). *The digital disconnect: The social causes and consequences of digital inequalities*. SAGE Publications. DOI: 10.4135/9781526492982

Henderson, A. T., Mapp, K. L., Johnson, V. R., & Davies, D. (2019). *Beyond the bake sale: The essential guide to family-school partnerships*. The New Press.

Henderson, J., & Milman, N. B. (2020). The technology acceptance model: Considerations for online educators. *Distance Learning : for Educators, Trainers, and Leaders*, *17*(3), 104–107. DOI: 10.1108/DL-02-2021-0014

Herodotou, C., Aristeidou, M., Miller, G., Ballard, H., & Robinson, L. (2020). What do we know about young volunteers? an exploratory study of participation in zooniverse. *Citizen Science: Theory and Practice*, *5*(1), 2. Advance online publication. DOI: 10.5334/cstp.248 PMID: 35795590

Hew, K. F., & Brush, T. (2007). Integrating technology into K-12 teaching and learning: Current knowledge gaps and recommendations for future research. *Educational Technology Research and Development*, *55*(3), 223–252. DOI: 10.1007/s11423-006-9022-5

Hilty, L. M., & Aebischer, B. (2015). ICT for sustainability: An emerging research field. In Hilty, L. M., & Aebischer, B. (Eds.), *ICT Innovations for Sustainability* (pp. 3–36). Springer., DOI: 10.1007/978-3-319-09228-7_1

Hine, C. (2024). Making sense of digital volunteering: relational and temporal aspects of the digital volunteer experience. Voluntary Sector Review, 1-19. DOI: 10.1332/20408056Y2024D000000032

Hine, C. (2015). *Ethnography for the internet: Embedded, embodied and everyday.* Bloomsbury Academic.

Hine, C. (2024). Digital participation and volunteering in networked communities. *New Media & Society*, 26(2), 1021–1038.

Hlungwani, P. M. (2025). Bridging the digital divide to promote inclusive education in Zimbabwean rural secondary schools: A case of Mwenezi District. *International Journal of Development and Sustainability*, 14(4), 344–359. DOI: 10.63212/IJDS24120201

Hubballi, R. B., Selvakumar, P., Seenivasan, R., Basava Aradhya, S. G., Dinesh, N., & Seelam, P. K. (2025). Overview of Current AI Technologies in Education. In Kyei-Blankson, L., & Ntuli, E. (Eds.), *Transformative AI Practices for Personalized Learning Strategies* (pp. 1–26). IGI Global Scientific Publishing., DOI: 10.4018/979-8-3693-8744-3.ch001

Huber, S., Lupschina, R., Schwarz, M., & Krey, K. (2021). Peer-coaching and Inclusive Collaborative Learning using ICT. *Pedagógusképzés*, 20(1), 99–109. DOI: 10.37205/TEL-hun.2021.1.05

Hustinx, L., Cnaan, R. A., & Handy, F. (2019). *Navigating theories of volunteering: A life-course and cross-cultural perspective.* Springer.

Hustinx, L., Cnaan, R., & Handy, F. (2019). Navigating theories of volunteering: A mixed-methods approach. *Voluntas*, 30(3), 431–450. DOI: 10.1007/s11266-019-00148-7

Hustinx, L., Handy, F., & Cnaan, R. A. (2010). Volunteering. In Taylor, R. (Ed.), *Third sector research* (pp. 549–572). Springer., DOI: 10.1007/978-1-4419-5707-8_7

Hustinx, L., Handy, F., Cnaan, R. A., & Kang, C. (2020). The changing landscape of volunteering: A review of recent literature. *Voluntas*, *31*(5), 1016–1036. DOI: 10.1007/s11266-020-00241-4

Iefimova, G. V., & Pashchenko, K. O. (2025). "The role of social media in promoting volunteer initiatives and shaping communities." *Problemy Ekonomiky*, 1(1), 112–125. https://problecon.com/article/view/2025-volunteer-socialmedia

Iglesias, R. S., Carrolaggi, P., & Randaccio, S. (2023). "Learning helping: Inclusive education of adults through virtual volunteering." *EDULEARN23 Proceedings*, 15(1), 1123–1132. https://library.iated.org/view/IGLESIAS2023LEA

Indama, V. (2022). Digital governance: Citizen perceptions and expectations of online public services. *ISSLP*, *1*(2), 12–18. DOI: 10.61838/kman.isslp.1.2.3

Indra, R., Ritonga, M., & Kustati, M. (2022). E-leadership of the school principals in implementing online learning during COVID-19 pandemic at public senior high schools. *Frontiers in Education*, *7*, 973274. Advance online publication. DOI: 10.3389/feduc.2022.973274

Innovations for Learning. (n.d.). *Innovations for learning*. In *Wikipedia*. Retrieved August 14, 2025, from https://en.wikipedia.org/wiki/Innovations_for_Learning

International Institute for Capacity Building in Africa. (2024, January). Zimbabwe: Education Country Brief. UNESCO.

Iraqi, A. (2025). Towards a new form of volunteering 2.0: a survey at apsopad international. jlsdgr, 5(1), e02548. https://doi.org/DOI: 10.47172/2965-730X.SDGsReview.v5.n01.pe02548

Jabbar, A., Astuti, Y., Ahmad, J., Adnan, A. A., & Putra, A. (2026). Bridging digital transformation and local wisdom: Towards inclusive and sustainable public service delivery in indigenous communities. *Frontiers in Sustainability*, *6*, 1715580. Advance online publication. DOI: 10.3389/frsus.2025.1715580

Jete, R., & Farah, R. (2024). "Empowering communities through digital skills training in Simeulue Village." *Pengabdian: Jurnal Abdimas*, 4(1), 45–52. https://journal.ypidathu.or.id/index.php/pengabdian/article/view/123

Jiang, L., & Gu, M. M. (2022). Understanding youths' civic participation online: A digital multimodal composing perspective. *Learning, Media and Technology*, 47(2), 149–162. DOI: 10.1080/17439884.2022.2044849

Jiwei, R. (2023). Research on digital empowerment to facilitate quality development of volunteerism in new era. *International Journal of Frontiers in Sociology*, 5(2), 88–97. https://www.francis-press.com/papers/12345

Joshi, D. R., Adhikari, K. P., Chapai, K. P. S., & Bhattarai, A. R. (2023). Effectiveness of online training on digital pedagogical skills of remote area teachers in Nepal. *International Journal of Professional Development Learners and Learning*, 5(2), ep2311. Advance online publication. DOI: 10.30935/ijpdll/13666

Kalita, H., & Kumar, K. (2020). Digital Technology Integration in Different Educational Fields: Design, Architecture, Tourism, and Business Engineering. In *Methodologies and Outcomes of Engineering and Technological Pedagogy* (pp. 112–131). IGI Global. DOI: 10.4018/978-1-7998-2245-5.ch008

Kali, Y., McKenney, S., & Sagy, O. (2015). Teachers as designers of technology enhanced learning. *Instructional Science*, 43(2), 173–179. DOI: 10.1007/s11251-014-9343-4

Kamerāde, D., Clark, A., Goodall, C., Parker, C., & Vasilica, C. (2024). "Bridging the digital divide: Challenges and opportunities for disabled adults in volunteering." *University of Greenwich Repository*. https://gala.gre.ac.uk/id/eprint/42356

Kangana, N., Kankanamge, N., De Silva, C., Goonetilleke, A., Mahamood, R., & Ranasinghe, D. (2024). Bridging community engagement and technological innovation for creating smart and resilient cities: A systematic literature review. *Smart Cities*, 7(1), 45–62. DOI: 10.3390/smartcities7060147

Kapoor, K., Dwivedi, Y. K., Piercy, N. F., & Williams, M. D. (2018). Examining the role of project management in improving organizational performance. *International Journal of Project Management*, *36*(3), 384–397. DOI: 10.1016/j.ijproman.2017.10.002

Kappelides, P., Cuskelly, G., & Hoye, R. (2018). The influence of volunteer recruitment practices and expectations on the development of volunteers' psychological contracts. *Voluntas*, *30*(1), 259–271. DOI: 10.1007/s11266-018-9986-x

Kelder, J., Crawford, J., Al-Naabi, I., & To, L. (2025). Enhancing digital productivity and capability in higher education through authentic leader behaviors: A cross-cultural structural equation model. *Education and Information Technologies*, *30*(12), 17751–17767. DOI: 10.1007/s10639-025-13422-x

Kilag, O. K., Ignacio, R., Lumando, E. B., Alvez, G. U., Abendan, C. F., Quiñanola, N. M. P., & Sasan, J. M. (2022). ICT Integration in Primary School Classrooms in the time of Pandemic in the Light of Jean Piaget's Cognitive Development Theory. *International Journal of Emerging Issues in Early Childhood Education*, *4*(2), 42–54. DOI: 10.31098/ijeiece.v4i2.1170

Kiprop-Marakis, J. (2021). Effect of Teacher Participation on Decision-making Processes on Performance in Secondary Schools in Mombasa County, Kenya. *East African Journal of Education Studies*, *4*(1), 29–36. DOI: 10.37284/eajes.4.1.437

Korukluoğlu, P., Alcı, B., & Rubach, C. (2023). Reliability and validity of the Turkish version of the teachers' basic ICT competence beliefs scale. *International Journal of Assessment Tools in Education*, *10*(1), 29–55. DOI: 10.21449/ijate.995005

Kotte, K. R., Attaluri, V., & Selvakumar, P. (2025). Revolutionising Retail Banking with AI and Virtual Technologies AI-Driven Financial Training. In Nair, A. J., Manohar, S., Limbu, Y. B., & Huhmann, B. A. (Eds.), *Intersecting Natural Language Processing and FinTech Innovations in Service Marketing* (pp. 421–440). IGI Global Scientific Publishing., DOI: 10.4018/979-8-3693-9944-6.ch020

Kozma, R. B. (2003). Technology and classroom practices: An international study. *Journal of Research on Technology in Education, 36*(1), 1–14. DOI: 10.1080/15391523.2003.10782399

Kumar, D., Sunder, N., Sabatés, R., & Wadhwa, W. (2024). Improving children's foundational learning through community-school participation: Experimental evidence from rural India. *Labour Economics, 91*, 102615. DOI: 10.1016/j.labeco.2024.102615

Kundu, A. (2021). A sound framework for ICT integration in Indian teacher education. *International Journal of Teacher Education and Professional Development, 4*(1), 49–67. DOI: 10.4018/IJTEPD.2021010104

Kunnathully, K., Satyanarayana, P., Anute, N., Sharma, M., Sureshkrishna, G., & Manjunath, T. C. (2025). Propaganda, Social Media and AI. In Vieira, A., Joaquim, A., & Duarte, A. (Eds.), *Digital Populism and the Use of Neo-Propaganda and Fake News* (pp. 19–38). IGI Global Scientific Publishing., DOI: 10.4018/979-8-3693-9999-6.ch002

Lachand-Pascal, V., Michel, C., Serna, A., & Tabard, A. (2022). Challenges and Opportunities for Multi-Device Management in Classrooms. *ACM Transactions on Computer-Human Interaction, 29*(6), 1–27. DOI: 10.1145/3519025

Laurean Sanchez, S. D. (2024). "Expanding market reach: A comprehensive strategy for scaling Dashboa's services to global eCommerce markets." *Theseus.fi*. https://www.theseus.fi/bitstream/handle/10024/874290/Laurean_Sanchez_Sergio_Daniel.pdf

Lavrenova, M., Lalak, N., & Molnar, T. (2020). Preparation of Future Teachers for Use of ICT in Primary School. *Revista Romaneasca pentru Educatie Multidimensionala, 12*, 185-195. DOI: 10.18662/rrem/12.1sup1/230

Lawrence, J. E., & Tar, U. A. (2018). Factors that influence teachers' adoption and integration of ICT in teaching/learning process. *Educational Media International*, *55*(1), 79–105. DOI: 10.1080/09523987.2018.1439712

Lawrence, K. C., & Fakuade, O. V. (2021). Parental involvement, learning participation and online learning commitment of adolescent learners during the COVID-19 lockdown. *Research in Learning Technology*, *29*, 2544. DOI: 10.25304/rlt.v29.2544

Lee, S., Hui, J., & Dillahunt, T. R. (2025). "Sociocultural factors in digital skills learning: A community-based intervention among US public housing adults." *Proceedings of the ACM on Human-Computer Interaction*, 9(CSCW1), Article 123, 1–26. https://doi.org/DOI: 10.1145/3711070

Lee, C., Goh, D., Sin, S., Osop, H., & Theng, Y. (2019). A crowdsourcing approach to explore helping motives in a smart city: A preliminary analysis. *Proceedings of the Association for Information Science and Technology*, *56*(1), 701–702. DOI: 10.1002/pra2.142

Li-li, P., & Jialin, N. (2023). Practices and reflections on volunteer service in higher education institutions: A case study of a certain university in Shenzhen, China. *Frontiers in Educational Research*, *6*(19). Advance online publication. DOI: 10.25236/FER.2023.061921

Li, T. (2024). Analysis of personal privacy risks and protection countermeasures under the privacy paradox dimension. *TSSEHR*, *11*, 509–515. DOI: 10.62051/tsnrh462

Liu, T., Li, S., Yang, R., Liu, S., & Chen, G. (2019). Job preferences of undergraduate nursing students in eastern China: A discrete choice experiment. *Human Resources for Health*, *17*(1), 1. Advance online publication. DOI: 10.1186/s12960-018-0335-3 PMID: 30606232

Lomos, C., Luyten, J. W., & Tieck, S. (2023). Implementing ICT in classroom practice: What else matters besides the ICT infrastructure? *Large-Scale Assessments in Education*, *11*(1), 1–28. DOI: 10.1186/s40536-022-00144-6 PMID: 36686619

López, M., Rijpma, A., Moor, T., & Reijerink, J. (2023). Behind the crowdsourcing platform: Assessing volunteer recruitment and engagement instruments. *Nonprofit and Voluntary Sector Quarterly*, *53*(6), 1381–1409. DOI: 10.1177/08997640231212839

Lough, B. (2019). The state of volunteering infrastructure globally. *Voluntaris Zeitschrift Für Freiwilligendienste*, *7*(1), 22–43. DOI: 10.5771/2196-3886-2019-1-22

Lund, A., Furberg, A., Bakken, J., & Engelien, K. L. (2014). What does professional digital competence mean in teacher education? *Nordic journal of digital literacy, 9*(4), 280-298.

Lunga, P. (2024). Community participation and school governance in Zimbabwean education. *Journal of Educational Development in Africa*, *9*(2), 102–118.

Luz, A. (2025). "The role of digital platforms in enhancing the market reach of small businesses in rural America." *Preprints.org*. https://www.theseus.fi/bitstream/handle/10024/874290/Laurean_Sanchez_Sergio_Daniel.pdf

Madanchian, M., & Taherdoost, H. (2023). The impact of leadership on the growth of ICT companies. *Journal of Sustainable Business and Economics*, *6*(4), 20–27. DOI: 10.30564/jsbe.v6i4.5874

Madjid, H., & Safriani, A. (2023). Asset-based approach community service for developing digital textbook in secondary language (l2) teacher education. [Indonesian Journal of English Teaching]. *Ijet*, *12*(1), 104–117. DOI: 10.15642/ijet2.2023.12.1.104-117

Madsen, K., & Brix, J. (2024). Building capacity for digital innovation—A game-study. *Creativity and Innovation Management*, *34*(2), 486–499. DOI: 10.1111/caim.12650

Magaisa, G. M., & Musundire, A. (2021). Relationship Between Transformational Leadership and Commitment of Consultants in South African Management Consulting Firms. [IJAMTR]. *International Journal of Applied Management Theory and Research*, *3*(2), 24–37. DOI: 10.4018/IJAMTR.2021070103

Magaisa, G. M., & Musundire, A. (2022). Factors affecting employee retention in Zimbabwean companies. *International Journal of Applied Management Theory and Research*, 4(1), 1–20. Advance online publication. DOI: 10.4018/IJAMTR.288507

Ma, J., Cui, J., & Zhang, Q. (2023). A "Motivation" model of couple support for digital technology use among rural older adults. *Frontiers in Psychology*, 14, 1095386. Advance online publication. DOI: 10.3389/fpsyg.2023.1095386 PMID: 36818095

Mangena, O., & Chidakwa, N. (2024). The efficacy of inclusive education practices in Zimbabwean rural schools: Challenges and opportunities. *Educational Challenges*, 29(2), 225–246. DOI: 10.34142/2709-7986.2024.29.2.15

Manshadi, V., & Rodilitz, S. (2022). Online policies for efficient volunteer crowdsourcing. *Management Science*, 68(9), 6572–6590. DOI: 10.1287/mnsc.2021.4220

Mao, G., Fernandes-Jesus, M., Ntontis, E., & Drury, J. (2021). What have we learned about COVID-19 volunteering in the UK? A rapid review of the literature. *BMC Public Health*, 21(1), 1470. DOI: 10.1186/s12889-021-11390-8 PMID: 34320922

Marah, T., Pradhan, H., & SHUHOOD, F. (2024). Youth participation in global governance: opportunities and challenges. JoGaPA, 2(1), 238-249. https://doi.org/DOI: 10.70248/jogapa.v2i1.1718

Martono, M., Dewantara, J., Efriani, E., & Prasetiyo, W. (2021). The national identity on the border: Indonesian language awareness and attitudes through multi-ethnic community involvement. *Journal of Community Psychology*, 50(1), 111–125. DOI: 10.1002/jcop.22505 PMID: 33465246

Mason, D., Chen, L., & Lall, S. (2021). Can institutional support improve volunteer quality? An analysis of online volunteer mentors. *Voluntas*, 33(3), 641–655. DOI: 10.1007/s11266-021-00351-9

Mertens, D. M. (2015). *Research and evaluation in education and psychology: Integrating diversity with quantitative, qualitative, and mixed methods.* Sage Publications.

Miao, Q., Schwarz, S., & Schwarz, G. (2021). Responding to COVID-19: Community volunteerism and coproduction in China. *World Development, 137*, 105128. DOI: 10.1016/j.worlddev.2020.105128 PMID: 32834397

Mittos, A., Malin, B., & Cristofaro, E. (2018). Systematizing genome privacy research: A privacy-enhancing technologies perspective. *Proceedings on Privacy Enhancing Technologies. Privacy Enhancing Technologies Symposium, 2019*(1), 87–107. DOI: 10.2478/popets-2019-0006

MoldStud. (n.d.). *Custom software for volunteer recruitment in non-profits.* https://moldstud.com/articles/p-custom-software-for-non-profit-virtual-volunteer-recruitment

Momdjian, L., Manegre, M., & Gutiérrez-Colón, M. (2024). Assessing and bridging the digital competence gap: a comparative study of Lebanese student teachers and in-service teachers using the digcompedu framework. https://doi.org/DOI: 10.21203/rs.3.rs-4711655/v1

Mominó, J. M., & Carrere, J. (2016). A model for obtaining ICT indicators in education. *Working papers on education policy, 3.* Retrieved from https://unesdoc.unesco.org/ark:/48223/pf0000244268

Mora, H., Gilart-Iglesias, V., Pérez-del Hoyo, R., & Andújar-Montoya, M. D. (2021). Volunteerism and technology: A review of platforms and digital practices. *Voluntas, 32*(2), 245–260. DOI: 10.1007/s11266-020-00271-9

Mudzengerere, P. (2017). [Title of work on framework for digital community volunteering in Zimbabwe]. [Publisher or institution].

Mulder, M., Rapp, J., Hamby, A., & Weaver, T. (2015). Consumer transformation through volunteer service experiences. *Service Industries Journal, 35*(15-16), 865–882. DOI: 10.1080/02642069.2015.1090981

Mumtaz, S. (2000). Factors affecting teachers' use of information and communications technology: A review of the literature. *Journal of Information Technology for Teacher Education*, 9(3), 319–342. DOI: 10.1080/14759390000200096

Munemo, R. (2018). Differently abled learners' experiences of inclusive education systems in Zimbabwe: Case studies of three selected high schools in Chitungwiza (Unpublished MEd thesis). University of Zimbabwe.

Muresherwa, P. (2020). [Title of empirical study on infrastructure/leadership practice in Zimbabwe]. [Publisher or institution].

Musick, M. A., & Wilson, J. (2018). *Volunteers: A social profile*. Indiana University Press.

Musundire, A. (2025a). Exploring Challenges and Opportunities of the Social Justice Philosophy in Education in South African Private Schools: Differentiated Instruction, Linguistic Diversity, Equity, and Inclusion. In *Educational Philosophy and Sociological Foundation of Education* (pp. 77-102). IGI Global.

Musundire, A. (2025d). Systemstic Literature Analysis of Educational Barriers, Opportunities, and Innovation in Science, Technology, and Innovation: The Case of Potential Female Entrepreneurs in South Africa. In *AI Strategies for Social Entrepreneurship and Sustainable Economic Development* (pp. 307-334). IGI Global.

Musundire, A. (2025e). Social Justice Realities for Women Leaders in South African Schools: Barriers, Opportunities, and Prospects. In *New Horizons in Leadership: Inclusive Explorations in Health, Technology, and Education* (pp. 93-120). IGI Global Scientific Publishing.

Musundire, A. (2025g). Integrating Chatbots Into Educational Management Systems in the Global Intuitions of Higher Learning: Streamlining Administrative Tasks. In *Chatbots in educational leadership and management* (pp. 53-72). IGI Global Scientific Publishing.

Musundire, A. (2025h). Integrating Educational Robotics and Artificial Intelligence With African Educational Perspectives in Science, Technology, Engineering, and Mathematics: Challenges and Opportunities. In *Innovations in Educational Robotics: Advancing AI for Sustainable Development* (pp. 129-156). IGI Global Scientific Publishing.

Musundire, A. (2025i). The Relationship Between Knowledge Management Systems, Transformational Leadership, and Organizational Adaptability: The Case of South African Private Institutions of Higher Learning. In *Leveraging Technology for Organizational Adaptability* (pp. 197-222). IGI Global Scientific Publishing.

Musundire, A. (2025j). Indigenous vs. Eurocentric Teaching Methods: The Place of Afro-Centric Games in South African Primary School Mathematics Curriculum. In *Enabling Indigenous Knowledge Systems in Action Research and Action Learning* (pp. 357-378). IGI Global Scientific Publishing.

Musundire, A. (2025l). Understanding the Research Onion and Its Application in Educational Leadership and Management Research: Making Use of Saunders' Research Model. In *Research Methods for Educational Leadership and Management* (pp. 355-384). IGI Global Scientific Publishing.

Musundire, A. (2025m). Understanding the Research Process and Its Application in Educational Leadership and Management: Making Use of Ngulube's Research Model. In *Research Methods for Educational Leadership and Management* (pp. 385-414). IGI Global Scientific Publishing.

Musundire, A. (2021a, July). Peer supervision: A missing link between teacher development and quality of teaching–perceptions of school managers and classroom teachers in South Africa. [IJTEPD]. *International Journal of Teacher Education and Professional Development, 4*(2), 97–115. DOI: 10.4018/IJTEPD.2021070107

Musundire, A. (2021b, October). The Impact of E-Learning Instructional Knowledge on Pedagogical Attitude and Learner Performance: The Context of South African Private Institutions of Higher Learning. [IJDLDC]. *International Journal of Digital Literacy and Digital Competence*, *12*(4), 33–53. DOI: 10.4018/IJDLDC.2021100103

Musundire, A. (2022). The Effectiveness of Self-Directed Supervision on Improving Quality of Teaching: Perceptions of South African School-Based Managers and Educators. [IJTEPD]. *International Journal of Teacher Education and Professional Development*, *5*(1), 1–17. Advance online publication. DOI: 10.4018/IJTEPD.304873

Musundire, A. (2025b). Indiscipline and crime in South African secondary schools: The place of the African Ubuntu philosophy. In *Educational Philosophy and Sociological Foundation of Education* (pp. 103–132). IGI Global.

Musundire, A. (2025c). Effectiveness of the Connoisseurship Supervision Model on Quality of Teaching in the Context of Developmental Supervision: The Case of South African P-12 Education System. In *Reimagining the P-20 Landscape for School Leadership Learning* (pp. 457–482). IGI Global Scientific Publishing.

Musundire, A. (2025f). Chatbots as virtual leaders: Supporting decision-making and strategic planning in Australian secondary schools. In *Chatbots in educational leadership and management* (pp. 1–28). IGI Global Scientific Publishing. DOI: 10.4018/979-8-3693-8734-4.ch001

Musundire, A. (Ed.). (2025k). *Research Methods for Educational Leadership and Management*. IGI Global., Retrieved from https://www.igi-global.com/book/research-methods-educational-leadership-management/356342 DOI: 10.4018/979-8-3693-9425-0

Mutyavaviri, P. N. (2016). Educational managers' understanding and experiences of the implementation of inclusive education: Evidence from selected urban primary schools in Zimbabwe (Unpublished MEd thesis). University of KwaZulu-Natal.

Mutyavaviri, C. (2016). Challenges in implementing inclusive education in Zimbabwean schools. *Zimbabwe Journal of Educational Research*, *28*(2), 45–60.

Naicker, S. (2019). Inclusive education in Africa: Policy and practice perspectives. *International Journal of Inclusive Education*, *23*(7–8), 720–735.

Naqshbandi, K. Z., Jeon, Y.-H., & Ahmadpour, N. (2022). Exploring volunteer motivation, identity and meaning-making in digital science-based research volunteering. *International Journal of Human-Computer Interaction*, *39*(20), 4090–4111. DOI: 10.1080/10447318.2022.2109246

Naqshbandi, K., Liu, C., Taylor, S., Lim, R., Ahmadpour, N., & Calvo, R. (2020). "i am most grateful." using gratitude to improve the sense of relatedness and motivation for online volunteerism. *International Journal of Human-Computer Interaction*, *36*(14), 1325–1341. DOI: 10.1080/10447318.2020.1746061

Naqshbandi, M. M., Tabche, I., & Choudhary, N. (2022). Digital volunteering and technology adoption: The role of motivation and self-efficacy. *Information Technology & People*, *35*(6), 1963–1985.

Ncube, A. (2024). Community participation and inclusive schooling in Southern Africa. *Education and Society*, *42*(1), 59–74.

Ngao, A. I., Sang, G., & Kihwele, J. E. (2022). Understanding teacher educators' perceptions and practices about ICT integration in teacher education program. *Education Sciences*, *12*(8), 549. Advance online publication. DOI: 10.3390/educsci12080549

NGOs.ai. (n.d.). *AI for volunteer management and recruitment.* https://ngos.ai/wes/ai-for-volunteer-management-and-recruitment

Ngulube, P. (2015). Trends in research methodological procedures used in knowledge management studies. *African Journal of Library Archives and Information Science*, *25*(2), 125–143.

Ngwarati, C., & Muchemwa, S. (2024). Challenges in implementing inclusive education in Zimbabwean schools. *Journal of Special Education in Africa*, *8*(1), 33–48.

Niederhauser, D. S., & Stoddart, T. (2001). Teachers' instructional perspectives and use of educational software. *Teaching and Teacher Education*, *17*(1), 15–31. DOI: 10.1016/S0742-051X(00)00036-6

Niem, M. M., Veriñ, R. U., & Alcantara, E. C. (2020). Teaching and learning with technology: Ramification of ICT integration in Mathematics Education. *Southeast Asian Mathematics Education Journal*, *10*(1), 27–40. DOI: 10.46517/seamej.v10i1.83

Noble, S. U. (2018). *Algorithms of oppression: How search engines reinforce racism*. NYU Press. DOI: 10.18574/nyu/9781479833641.001.0001

Noor, A. F., Sonedi, S., Azman, M. N. A., Khunaifi, A. R., Dwiningrum, S. I. A., & Haryanto, D. (2021). The Multicultural Education Paradigm Pattern: A Case Study in Muhammadiyah Junior High School in Palangka Raya, Indonesia. *Perspectives of Science and Education*, *52*(4), 297. DOI: 10.32744/pse.2021.4.19

Noronha, M., Lyra, L., Souza, L., Silva, R., & Cahen, F. (2023). International digital competencies maximizing lean internationalization in healthcare startups. *International Journal of Health Management Review*, *9*, e0334. DOI: 10.37497/ijhmreview.v9i00.334

Nowakowska, I. (2021). Age, frequency of volunteering, and present-hedonistic time perspective predict donating items to people in need, but not money to combat COVID-19 during lock-down. *Current Psychology (New Brunswick, N.J.)*, *42*(20), 17329–17339. DOI: 10.1007/s12144-021-01993-0 PMID: 34177212

Nursey-Bray, M., & Masud-All-Kamal, M. (2022). Building community resilience through youth volunteering: Towards a new model. *Regional Studies*, *56*(7), 1123–1135. DOI: 10.1080/00343404.2022.2045070

O'Neil, K., Vettern, R., Maaß, S., Harrington, R., Robideau, K., Mc-Glaughlin, P. C., & Gauley, J. (2023). Equipping Extension Professionals to Lead Volunteer Systems: An Evaluation of an Online Course. *Journal of Human Sciences and Extension*, 12. Advance online publication. DOI: 10.55533/2325-5226.1348

Okunade, B. A., Adewusi, O. E., & Adediran, F. E.Beatrice Adedayo OkunadeOlolade Elizabeth AdewusiFoluke Eyitayo AdediranBukola A, OdulajaRosita Ebere DaraojimbaJustice Chika Igbokwe. (2024). Technology in community development: A comparative review of USA and African Projects. *International Journal of Science and Research Archive*, *11*(1), 1195–1202. DOI: 10.30574/ijsra.2024.11.1.0183

Omale, S. A., Yusuf, S. O., Oyenuga, M. O., Ikemefuna, M., Ojo, S. S., & Momodu, I. D. (2024). Organizational Learning in the Post-COVID-19 Era: A Prerequisite for Stakeholder Satisfaction. Twist 19(3), 265-272 https://twistjournal.net/twist/article/view/339

Omale, S. A., Oyenuga, M. O., Abdullahi, D., & Madu, I. (2024). Moderating Role of Entrepreneurial Education on Innovative Work Behaviour and Resilience of SMEs. *Innovations 77(2)*, 1166-1185https://DOI: 10.13140/RG.2.2.16946.41924

Ordonez, K. (n.d.). *AI in volunteer management: Identifying and retaining volunteers with AI*. LinkedIn. https://www.linkedin.com/pulse/ai-volunteer-management-identifying-retaining-kevin-ordonez-aaip-c7ekc

Oyedele, O. M., & Iember, A. A. (2022). Covid-19 and the Future of Higher Education. *IEEE Technology Policy and Ethics,* 6(4), 1–3. https://doi.org/DOI: 10.1109/NTPE.2021.9778140

Oyedele, M. O., Sunday, A. O., & Abuh, A. I. (2024). Fostering Technological-Enhanced Training and Development for Business Survival and Performance in the New Normal. *Journal of Propulsion Technology*, *45*(3), 1858–1869. https://propulsiontechjournal.com/index.php/journal/article/view/7479

Oyedele, O. M. (2025). Digital Circular Economy: Driving Sustainable Innovation Through Stakeholder Synergy. In Singh, R., & Kumar, V. (Eds.), *Sustainable Innovations and Digital Circular Economy*. Springer., DOI: 10.1007/978-981-96-1064-8_4

Oyenuga, M. O. (2026). Competitive Intelligence in Sustainability and Corporate Social Responsibility (CSR). In R. Marcão & V. Santos (Eds.), *Competitive Intelligence in the Digital Age: Strategies for Business and Technology Leadership* (pp. 65-102). IGI Global Scientific Publishing. https://doi.org/DOI: 10.4018/979-8-3373-2690-0.ch003

Oyenuga, M. O., & Jeresa, S. (2025). Adaptation and Resilience: Private, Public, and Individual Change Makers. In Singh, R., & Filho, W. L. (Eds.), *Climate Neutrality Through Smart Eco-Innovation and Environmental Sustainability. Climate Change Management*. Springer., DOI: 10.1007/978-3-031-83250-5_2

Oyenuga, M. O., Singh, R., Apata, S. B., Khan, S., & Kumar, V. (2025). Digital Technologies and Climate Action. In *Smart Technologies for Climate Change and Net Zero Policies: Practical Approaches Towards Sustainability. Climate Change Management*. Springer., DOI: 10.1007/978-3-031-92221-3_8

Pandey, A. (2025). The Transformative Potential of Artificial Intelligence in Building Sustainable Agricultural Systems: Innovations, Challenges, and Future Directions. In *AI and Ecological Change for Sustainable Development* (pp. 161-182). IGI Global Scientific Publishing.

Pankova, O., & Kasperovych, O. (2022). Ukrainian volunteering under conditions of armed russian aggression: Strengthening capacities through digitalization, platformization and the involvement of ict, network technologies. *Economic Herald of the Donbas*, (2 (68)), 113–123. DOI: 10.12958/1817-3772-2022-2(68)-113-123

Park, C., & Johnston, E. (2017). A framework for analyzing digital volunteer contributions in emergent crisis response efforts. *New Media & Society*, *19*(8), 1308–1327. DOI: 10.1177/1461444817706877

Park, C., & Johnston, E. (2019). Determinants of collaboration between digital volunteer networks and formal response organizations in catastrophic disasters. *International Journal of Organization Theory and Behavior, 22*(2), 155–173. DOI: 10.1108/IJOTB-07-2018-0088

Passey, D., Ntebutse, J. G., Ahmad, M. Y. A., Cochrane, J., Collin, S., Ganayem, A., Langran, E., Mulla, S., Rodrigo, M., Saito, T., Shonfeld, M., & Somasi, S. (2024). M. T., Saito, T., Shonfeld, M., & Somasi, S. (2024). Populations Digitally Excluded from Education: Issues, Factors, Contributions and Actions for Policy, Practice and Research in a Post-Pandemic Era. *Technology Knowledge and Learning, 29*(4), 1733–1750. Advance online publication. DOI: 10.1007/s10758-024-09767-w

Patrício, L., & Ferreira, J. (2023). Strategically redefining university dynamics for the digital age: A qualitative approach. *Strategic Change, 33*(2), 95–106. DOI: 10.1002/jsc.2565

Pattinson, J., Laparidou, D., Akanuwe, J., Scott, A., Sima, C., Lewis, C., & Siriwardena, A. (2023). Volunteering on heritage at risk sites and wellbeing: A qualitative interview study. *Health Expectations, 26*(6), 2485–2499. DOI: 10.1111/hex.13852 PMID: 37589481

Pepper, I., Rogers, C., Turner, J. G., St. Louis, N., & Williams, B. (2024). Enabling student employability through volunteering: Insights from police volunteers studying professional policing degrees in Wales. *Higher Education Skills and Work-Based Learning, 14*(5), 1135–1148. DOI: 10.1108/HESWBL-09-2023-0253

Piaget, J. (1964). Part I: Cognitive development in children: Piaget development and learning. *Journal of Research in Science Teaching, 2*(3), 176–186. DOI: 10.1002/tea.3660020306

Pietilä, I., Meriläinen, N., Varsaluoma, J., & Väänänen, K. (2021). Understanding youths' needs for digital societal participation: Towards an inclusive Virtual Council. *Behaviour & Information Technology, 40*(12), 1275–1290. DOI: 10.1080/0144929X.2021.1912182

Pilemalm, S., Follin, A., & Prytz, E. (2024). Digitalized co-production of emergency response: ICT-enabled dispatch and coordination of volunteers at the emergency site. *Journal of Humanitarian Logistics and Supply Chain Management*, *15*(1), 34–47. DOI: 10.1108/JHLSCM-03-2024-0031

Pilemalm, S., Stenberg, R., & Finnevidsson, E. (2025). *Interdependent digitalized co-production of emergency response: requirements and challenges*. ISCRAM., DOI: 10.59297/9rce7z51

Pilosof, N. P., Welcman, Y., Barrett, M., Oborn, E., & Barrett, S. (2025). Building digital resilience: Leading healthcare transformation through an online community. *Frontiers in Digital Health*, *7*, 1656804. DOI: 10.3389/fdgth.2025.1656804 PMID: 40978698

Pinto, M., & Leite, C. (2020). Digital Technologies in support of students learning in Higher Education: Literature review. *Digital Education Review*, (37), 343–360. DOI: 10.1344/der.2020.37.343-360

Plewa, C., Conduit, J., Quester, P., & Johnson, C. (2014). The impact of corporate volunteering on CSR image: A consumer perspective. *Journal of Business Ethics*, *127*(3), 643–659. DOI: 10.1007/s10551-014-2066-2

Polkinghorne, D. E. (2021). *Narrative research and narrative therapy: Understanding stories in social contexts*. Routledge.

Pukallus, S., & Arthur, C. (2024). Combating hate speech on social media: Applying targeted regulation, developing civil-communicative skills and utilising local evidence-based anti-hate speech interventions. *Journalism and Media*, *5*(2), 467–484. DOI: 10.3390/journalmedia5020031

Putnam, R. D. (2000). *Bowling alone: The collapse and revival of the American community*. Simon & Schuster.

Raïq, H., Rabah, S., Al-Mannai, A. A. M., Malkawi, A. H., Ali, A.-S. M., Tabishat, M., Al-Fahim, F. A. M. S., & Al-Marri, R. H. S. A. (2025). Gender digital divide and political participation in selected Arab countries. *Frontiers in Communication*, *10*, 1703066. Advance online publication. DOI: 10.3389/fcomm.2025.1703066

Rajput, N., Bukhari, S., Noonari, N., Solangi, G., Soomro, M., & Dahri, A. (2020). From Perspective to Practice: Gauging the Awareness and Integration Level of ICT in Teaching Process at Secondary Level in District Shaheed Benazirabad, Pakistan. *Modern Applied Science*, *14*(8), 23. Advance online publication. DOI: 10.5539/mas.v14n8p23

Read, T., Bruce, A., & Olcott, D.Jr. (2024). Development for empowerment: Mobilising online and digital micro-credentials for refugees. *Journal of Learning for Development*, *11*(2), 253–269. DOI: 10.56059/jl4d.v11i2.1357

Redecker, C., & Punie, Y. (2017). *European framework for the digital competence of educators: DigCompEdu*. Publications Office of the European Union.

Ren, J., Guo, J., & Li, H. (2025). Linking digital competence, self-efficacy, and digital stress to perceived interactivity in AI-supported learning contexts. *Scientific Reports*, *15*(1), 33182. DOI: 10.1038/s41598-025-18873-3 PMID: 41006796

Rennó, R., & Novaes, J. (2023). *"Community networks as sustainable infrastructure for digital skills." Digital Literacy and Inclusion: Stories.* Platforms and Practices., DOI: 10.1007/978-3-031-27224-5_5

Rickert, N. P., & Skinner, E. A. (2022). Parent and teacher warm involvement and student's academic engagement: The mediating role of self-system processes. *The British Journal of Educational Psychology*, *92*(2), 667–687. DOI: 10.1111/bjep.12470 PMID: 34697805

Riessman, C. K. (2008). *Narrative methods for the human sciences*. Sage.

Ritchie, B., & Jiang, Y. (2021). Risk, crisis and disaster management in hospitality and tourism: A comparative review. *International Journal of Contemporary Hospitality Management*, *33*(10), 3465–3493. DOI: 10.1108/IJCHM-12-2020-1480

Robinson, J. A., Kocman, D., & Speyer, O. (2021). Meeting volunteer expectations—A review of volunteer motivations in citizen science and best practices for their retention through implementation of functional approaches. *Journal of Science Communication, 20*(2), A03. DOI: 10.22323/2.20020203

Rochester, C., Paine, A. E., & Howlett, S. (2010). *Volunteering and society in the 21st century*. Palgrave Macmillan. DOI: 10.1057/9780230279438

Rojas Briñez, D. K., Duart, J. M., & Galvis Panqueva, Á. H. (2023). Findings and derived challenges concerning how school leaders should support ICT integration at schools. *School Leadership & Management, 43*(5), 497–524. DOI: 10.1080/13632434.2023.2237514

Rotman, D., Hammock, J., Preece, J., Hansen, D., Boston, C., Bowser, A., ... & He, Y. (2014). Motivations affecting initial and long-term participation in citizen science projects in three countries.. https://doi.org/ DOI: 10.9776/14054

Rundel, C., & Salemink, K. (2021). Bridging Digital Inequalities in Rural Schools in Germany: A Geographical Lottery? *Education Sciences, 11*(4), 181. DOI: 10.3390/educsci11040181

Sadik, O., & Ottenbreit-Leftwich, A. T. (2023). Understanding U.S. secondary computer science teachers' challenges and needs. *Computer Science Education, 34*(2), 252–284. DOI: 10.1080/08993408.2023.2209474

Sakthivel, M., Jaganathan, A., & Mohanraj, M. Mohit, Manjunath T, (2025). "Brand Loyalty through AI and Personalisation AI-Generated Content for Financial Marketing". In A J Nair, S Manohar, Y B Limbu & B A Huhmann (Eds.), Intersecting Natural Language Processing and FinTech Innovations in Service Marketing (pp. 77–96). IGI Global Scientific Publishing. https://doi.org/DOI: 10.4018/979-8-3693-9944-6.ch006

Salamon, L. M., Sokolowski, S. W., & Haddock, M. A. (2017). Measuring the economic value of volunteer work globally: Concepts, estimates, and a roadmap to the future. *Nonprofit and Voluntary Sector Quarterly, 46*(5), 893–911. DOI: 10.1177/0899764017721770

Samal, A., & Bhargav, J. S K M, Selvakumar P, Sharma M, T C M, (2025). "Measuring Brand Performance With AI Tools". In Z Hussain, M Sharipudin, A Albattat & A Khan (Eds.), Strategic Brand Management in the Age of AI and Disruption (pp. 279–302). IGI Global Scientific Publishing. https://doi.org/DOI: 10.4018/979-8-3693-9461-8.ch011

Sancho-Gil, J., Rivera-Vargas, P., & Miño-Puigcercós, R. (2020). Moving beyond the predictable failure of Ed-Tech initiatives. *Learning, Media and Technology*, *45*(1), 61–75. DOI: 10.1080/17439884.2019.1666873

Sar, A., & Misra, S. N. (2020, December). A study on policies and implementation of information and communication technology (ICT) in Educational Systems. *Materials Today: Proceedings*. Advance online publication. DOI: 10.1016/j.matpr.2020.10.507

Saunders, M. N., Lewis, P., & Thornhill, A. (2019). Research methods for business students (Eighth ed.). Harlow: Pearson education limited.

Schech, S., Skelton, T., Mundkur, A., & Kothari, U. (2019). International volunteerism and capacity development in nonprofit organizations of the global south. *Nonprofit and Voluntary Sector Quarterly*, *49*(2), 252–271. DOI: 10.1177/0899764019867774

Schneier, B., Shneiderman, B., Wallach, W., Ghazaleh, J., Perakslis, C., Pitt, J., & McDaniel, T. (2020). Istas 2020. *IEEE Technology and Society Magazine*, *39*(3), C2–C2. DOI: 10.1109/MTS.2020.3019850

Sebunya, J., & Gichuki, A. (2024). Digital tools and platforms for enhancing community participation: A review of global practices. *International Journal of Scientific Research*, *12*(2), 77–91. https://edinburgjournals.org/index.php/ijsr/article/view/1123

Selwyn, N. (2020). *Education and technology: Key issues and debates* (2nd ed.). Bloomsbury Academic.

Setia, S., & Aufar, S. M. (2023). The effect of government ICT policy and Technology leadership on Teacher's Technology Integration. *QALAMUNA: Jurnal Pendidikan, Sosial. Dan Agama*, *15*(1), 341–352. DOI: 10.37680/qalamuna.v15i1.2332

Shen, Y., Huang, G., Le, H., Yu, S., Xu, M., Ouyang, J., Fan, Y., & Wang, Q. (2025). 'Cloud for Youth': An implementation research of cloud-based solutions for bridging the digital divide in rural China. *British Journal of Educational Technology*, bjet.70037. Advance online publication. DOI: 10.1111/bjet.70037

Shepherd, C. E., & Bolliger, D. U. (2023). Institutional, program, and professional community: A framework for online higher education. *Educational Technology Research and Development*, *71*(3), 1233–1252. DOI: 10.1007/s11423-023-10214-3 PMID: 37359486

Shoderu, G., Omeleze, S., & Venter, H. (2024). A privacy-compliant process for digital forensics readiness. *International Conference on Cyber Warfare and Security*, 19(1), 337-347. https://doi.org/DOI: 10.34190/iccws.19.1.2055

Simms, J., Trad, A., Richards, K., & Woolf, J. (2024). Examining strategies for undergraduate student volunteer engagement and management in a community-based sport-for-development program. *Recreational Sports Journal*, *48*(1), 75–84. DOI: 10.1177/15588661241236407

Slater, D. J. (2021). Do community citizenship behaviors by leaders enhance team performance? Evidence from the "field.". *The Journal of Values Based Leadership*, *14*(2). Advance online publication. DOI: 10.22543/0733.142.1361

Smith, K., & Cordery, C. (2021). Digital governance in nonprofit organizations: Challenges and opportunities. *Nonprofit Management & Leadership*, *31*(4), 593–611. DOI: 10.1002/nml.21453

Sosa-Díaz, M. J., Sierra-Daza, M. C., Arriazu-Muñoz, R., Llamas-Salguero, F., & Durán-Rodríguez, N. (2022). "Edtech Integration Framework in schools": Systematic review of the literature. *Frontiers in Education*, *7*, 895042. Advance online publication. DOI: 10.3389/feduc.2022.895042

Spillane, J. P., Harris, A., Jones, M., & Mertz, K. (2020). Opportunities and challenges for taking a distributed perspective: Novice school principals' emerging sense of their new position. *British Educational Research Journal*, *46*(1), 97–117. https://doi.org/10.1002/berj.3568

Stathi, A., Withall, J., Agyapong-Badu, S., Barrett, E., Kritz, M., Wills, D., & Fox, K. (2020). Mobilising people as assets for active ageing promotion: a multi-stakeholder perspective on peer volunteering initiatives. https://doi.org/DOI: 10.21203/rs.3.rs-47981/v1

Stein, V., Pentzold, C., Peter, S., & Sterly, S. (2024). Digital political participation for rural development: Necessary conditions and cultures of participation. *The Information Society*, *41*(1), 18–32. DOI: 10.1080/01972243.2024.2407339

Stolz, I., Fürst, M., & Mundle, D. (2012). Beyond volunteerism! Real world learning to foster responsible leadership, serve patients and develop innovative solutions to healthcare challenges. In Wehner, T., & Gentile, C. (Eds.), *Corporate Volunteering: Unternehmen im Spannungsfeld von Gemeinschaft und Gesellschaft (AT)*. Springer Gabler.

Stumbrienė, D., Jevsikova, T., & Kontvainė, V. (2023). Key factors influencing teachers' motivation to transfer technology-enabled educational innovation. *Education and Information Technologies*, *29*(2), 1697–1731. DOI: 10.1007/s10639-023-11891-6 PMID: 37361759

Sui, D., Goodchild, M., & Elwood, S. (2025). Digital divide theory and civic participation in the information age. *Information Communication and Society*, *28*(3), 412–428.

Suklabaidya, S. (2024). "Towards inclusive societies: Leveraging IoT for community development and education." *PhilPapers*. https://philpapers.org/rec/SUKTIS

Sulaimani, A., & Ozuem, W. (2022). Understanding the role of transparency, participation, and collaboration for achieving open digital government goals in oman. *Transforming Government*, *16*(4), 595–612. DOI: 10.1108/TG-04-2022-0044

Sun, P., Morrow-Howell, N., Pawloski, E., & Helbach, A. (2021). Older adults' attitudes toward virtual volunteering during the COVID-19 pandemic. *Journal of Applied Gerontology*, *40*(9), 953–957. DOI: 10.1177/07334648211006978 PMID: 33840232

Susumpow, P., Pansuwan, P., Sajda, N., & Crawley, A. (2014). Participatory disease detection through digital volunteerism., 663-666. https://doi.org/DOI: 10.1145/2567948.2579273

Tairab, A., & Ronghuai, H. (2017). Analyzing ICT Policy in K-12 Education in Sudan (1990-2016). *World Journal of Education*, 7(1), 71–82. DOI: 10.5430/wje.v7n1p71

Tapia, A., & Maldonado, E. (2022). Blockchain for social impact: Transparency in humanitarian aid and volunteerism. *Journal of Humanitarian Innovation and Technology*, 4(2), 45–62. DOI: 10.1080/26753814.2022.2028724

Tapscott, D., & Tapscott, A. (2018). *Blockchain revolution: How the technology behind bitcoin and other cryptocurrencies is changing the world*. Penguin.

Tayaban, A. D. (2022). Students' and Teachers' Perspectives on ICT Integration in Learning Process During Pandemic. *International Journal of Multidisciplinary: Applied Business and Education Research*, 3(12), 2622–2630. DOI: 10.11594/ijmaber.03.12.15

Tay, L. Y., Lim, C. P., & Lim, S. K. (2015). Differences in ICT usage across subject areas: A case of an elementary school in Singapore. *Journal of Educational Computing Research*, 53(1), 75–94. DOI: 10.1177/0735633115585930

Tendeukai, I. C. (2020). School heads' leadership practices in enhancing quality education: Perspectives from six rural day secondary schools of Masvingo District in Zimbabwe (PhD thesis). University of KwaZulu-Natal.

Tendeukai, P. (2020). Community engagement in inclusive education practices in Zimbabwe. *African Educational Research Journal*, 8(3), 521–530.

Theocharis, Y., Boulianne, S., Koc-Michalska, K., & Bimber, B. (2023). Platform affordances and political participation: How social media reshape political engagement. *West European Politics*, 46(4), 788–811. DOI: 10.1080/01402382.2022.2087410

Thewes, C., Sept, A., & Richter, R. (2024). A voluntary divide? Exploring the role of digitalisation in German rural volunteering. *European Countryside, 16*(1), 1–18. DOI: 10.2478/euco-2024-0004

Tijsma, G., Urias, E., & Zweekhorst, M. (2023). Embedding engaged education through community service learning in HEI: A review. *Educational Research, 65*(2), 143–169. DOI: 10.1080/00131881.2023.2181202

Timotheou, S., Miliou, O., Dimitriadis, Y., Villagrá-Sobrino, S., Giannoutsou, N., Cachia, R., Martínez-Monés, A., & Ioannou, A. (2022). Impacts of digital technologies on education and factors influencing schools' digital capacity and transformation: A literature review. *Education and Information Technologies, 28*(6), 6695–6726. DOI: 10.1007/s10639-022-11431-8 PMID: 36465416

Tondeur, J., Van Braak, J., Sang, G., Voogt, J., Fisser, P., & Ottenbreit-Leftwich, A. (2012). Preparing pre-service teachers to integrate technology in education: A synthesis of qualitative evidence. *Computers & Education, 59*(1), 134–144. DOI: 10.1016/j.compedu.2011.10.009

Top, E., Baser, D., Akkus, R., Akayoglu, S., & Gurer, M. D. (2021). Secondary School Teachers' preferences in the process of individual technology mentoring. *Computers & Education, 160*, 104030. Advance online publication. DOI: 10.1016/j.compedu.2020.104030

Tracy, S. J. (2020). *Qualitative research methods: Collecting evidence, crafting analysis, communicating impact* (2nd ed.). Wiley.

Traeger, C., Alfes, K., & Fürstenberg, N. (2022). Perceived organizational support and volunteer outcomes: Evidence from a german environmental nonprofit organization. *Nonprofit and Voluntary Sector Quarterly, 52*(3), 763–786. DOI: 10.1177/08997640221103292

Tripon, C. (2025). Towards Quality Education for All: Integrating EdTech, Mentorship, and Community in Support of SDG 4. *Education Sciences, 15*(9), 1184. DOI: 10.3390/educsci15091184

Uluyol, Ç., & Şahin, S. (2014). Elementary School Teachers' ICT use in the classroom and their motivators for using ICT. *British Journal of Educational Technology, 47*(1), 65–75. DOI: 10.1111/bjet.12220

UNESCO. (2021, April 22). Addressing the needs of learners with disabilities in Zimbabwe. https://www.unesco.org/en/articles/addressing-needs-learners-disabilities-zimbabwe

UNICEF. (2022). *Digital learning and education connectivity in Zimbabwe: Country report*. UNICEF.

UNICEF. (2025). *Digital education and community engagement framework*. UNICEF.

United Nations Volunteers. (2018). *State of the world's volunteerism report: The thread that binds*. United Nations Volunteers Programme.

United Nations. (2015). *Transforming our world: The 2030 Agenda for Sustainable Development*. United Nations. https://sdgs.un.org/2030agenda

Van Dijk, J. (2020). *The digital divide*. Polity Press.

Vanderlinde, R. (2011). *School-based ICT policy planning in a context of curriculum reform*. (Proefschrift: Doctor in de Pedagogische Wetenschappen). Universiteit Gent.

Vanderlinde, R., & Van Braak, J. (2010). The e-capacity of primary schools: Development of a conceptual model and scale construction from a school improvement perspective. *Computers & Education, 55*(2), 541–553. DOI: 10.1016/j.compedu.2010.02.016

Venkatesh, V., Morris, M. G., Davis, G. B., & Davis, F. D. (2003). User acceptance of information technology: Toward a unified view. *Management Information Systems Quarterly, 27*(3), 425–478. DOI: 10.2307/30036540

Villaseñor, R. M. (2024). The Public Service Digitalization in the Philippines towards a national program to capacitate digital frontliners. *Journal of Public Administration and Governance, 14*(2), 164. DOI: 10.5296/jpag.v14i2.22106

VolunteerHub. (n.d.). *3 ways to increase engagement with gamification*. https://volunteerhub.com/blog/3-ways-to-increase-engagement-with-gamification

Vo, P. T. (2019). *An investigation of ICT policy implementation in an EFL teacher education program in Vietnam*. Edith Cowan University.

Warren, M. R., Hong, S., Rubin, C. L., & Uy, P. S. (2009). Beyond the bake sale: A community-based relational approach to parent engagement in schools. *Teachers College Record, 111*(9), 2209–2254. DOI: 10.1177/016146810911100901

Welch, M., & Saltmarsh, J. (2023). "Engaging higher education: Purpose, platforms, and programs for community engagement." *Taylor & Francis*. https://www.taylorfrancis.com/books/edit/10.4324/9781003123456

West, D. M., & Allen, J. R. (2020). *Turning point: Policymaking in the era of artificial intelligence*. Brookings Institution Press. DOI: 10.5040/9780815751113

Whittaker, J., McLennan, B., & Handmer, J. (2015). A review of informal volunteerism in emergencies and disasters: Definition, opportunities and challenges. *International Journal of Disaster Risk Reduction, 13*, 358–368. DOI: 10.1016/j.ijdrr.2015.07.010

Wiggins, A. (2013). Free as in puppies., 1469-1480. https://doi.org/DOI: 10.1145/2441776.2441942

Wikipedia. (2025). *Gamification*. In *Wikipedia*. Retrieved August 14, 2025, from https://en.wikipedia.org/wiki/Gamification

Williamson, B., Eynon, R., & Potter, J. (2020). Pandemic politics, pedagogies and practices: Digital learning in schools. *Learning, Media and Technology, 45*(2), 107–120. DOI: 10.1080/17439884.2020.1761641

Wilson, J. (2012). Volunteerism research: A review essay. *Nonprofit and Voluntary Sector Quarterly, 41*(2), 176–212. DOI: 10.1177/0899764011434558

Woo, D. (2023). The leadership of ICT coordinators: A distributed perspective. *Educational Management Administration & Leadership, 51*(2), 308–323. DOI: 10.1177/1741143220979714

Wu, F., & Nugent, J. B. (2026). Mitigating Life Challenges to Subjective Well-Being Through Civic Engagement: Insights from a Global Perspective. *Social Indicators Research, 181*(2), 52. Advance online publication. DOI: 10.1007/s11205-025-03763-y

Wyttenbach, M., & Ospino, H. (2022). Hispanic teachers and leaders in Catholic schools: Special issue introduction. *Journal of Catholic Education, 25*(2). Advance online publication. DOI: 10.15365/joce.2502002022

Xueying, Y., Arshad, M. A. B., & Lihua, H. (2025). Teacher E-Leadership in the Digital Age: A Systematic Review of Research and Practice [Review of Teacher E-Leadership in the Digital Age: A Systematic Review of Research and Practice]. *International Journal of Academic Research in Business & Social Sciences, 15*(5). Advance online publication. DOI: 10.6007/IJARBSS/v15-i5/25494

Yoon, S., Oh, J., & Choi, H. (2020). Immersive learning using virtual reality: A systematic review. *Educational Technology Research and Development, 68*(6), 3221–3242. DOI: 10.1007/s11423-020-09882-2

Younie, S. (2006). Implementing government policy on ICT in education: Lessons learnt. *Education and Information Technologies, 11*(3-4), 385–400. DOI: 10.1007/s10639-006-9017-1

Yuen, A., Law, N., & Wong, K. (2003). ICT implementation and school leadership: Case studies of ICT integration in teaching and learning. *Journal of Educational Administration, 41*(2), 158–170. DOI: 10.1108/09578230310464666

Zagami, J., Bocconi, S., Starkey, L., Wilson, J., Gibson, D., Downie, J., Malyn-Smith, J., & Elliott, S. (2018). Creating Future Ready Information Technology Policy for National Education Systems. *Technology. Knowledge and Learning, 23*(3), 495–506. DOI: 10.1007/s10758-018-9387-7

Zenda, E. T., Musundire, A., & Mumanyi, O. (2020). The Impact of Organisational Change Management Theoretical Perspective in the Context of Zimbabwe's Cash Crisis on Small to Medium Enterprises and their Consequent Adaptation Strategies. [IJSR]. *International Journal of Scientific Research*, *9*(8), 1256–1265.

Zubeyr, E., Kunasegaran, M., & Kunjiapu, S. (2024). Embracing Youth Volunteerism Through Digital Literacy for a Sustainable Future. *International Journal of Academic Research in Business & Social Sciences*, *14*(4). Advance online publication. DOI: 10.6007/IJARBSS/v14-i4/21420

Zvavahera, P., Garwe, E., Pasipanodya, N., Chigora, P., & Katsande, R. (2024). Digital transformation in Zimbabwean education institutions. *International Journal of Educational Development*, *102*, 102920.

Zwitter, A., & Boisse-Despiaux, M. (2018). Big data ethics: Risks and opportunities. *Big Data & Society*, *5*(2), 1–6.

About the Contributors

Austin Musundire is currently a Research Associate at the University of Limpopo. He obtained his Doctorate of Educational Leadership and Management degree from the University of South Africa and a Master of Education degree in Educational Administration, Planning, and Policy Studies (Educational Leadership and Management) from the Zimbabwe Open University. He also holds a Bachelor of Education degree in Educational Administration, Planning, and Policy Studies from the University of Zimbabwe, along with a Diploma in Education from the same institution. Educational leadership and Management research methods is their main area of academic specialisation

Richard Adade is a doctoral candidate in Educational Research at the University of South Africa. He earned a Bachelor of Education in Information Technology from the University of Cape Coast. His research focuses on technology integration in education, teacher digital capacity, and curriculum implementation. He has teaching experience in Computer Science and ICT and has worked on developing micro eLearning modules using digital tools such as Articulate 360 and Camtasia. His current research examines the capacity of teachers and schools to integrate ICT into Ghana's new curriculum. He is interested in exploring effective pedagogical models that support 21st-century learning and digital inclusion

Kiran C. K is a committed academician and accomplished educator serving as an Assistant Professor in the Department of Computer Application at Dayananda Sagar College of Arts, Science and Commerce,

Bengaluru, Karnataka. With over 12 years of teaching experience in the field of Computer Science and Applications, he has consistently contributed to academic excellence through high-quality instruction, curriculum development, and student-focused mentoring. He holds a Master of Science (MSc) degree in Computer Science and is qualified in the UGC NET, reflecting his strong academic foundation and subject mastery. Over the course of his career, Kiran C. K has developed extensive expertise in teaching undergraduate and postgraduate programs, including BCA, MCA, and MSc courses. His teaching approach blends theoretical clarity with practical exposure, enabling students to build both conceptual understanding and applied technical skills. Known for his structured and outcome-oriented academic methods, he has played an active role in curriculum design and revision, aligning course frameworks with current industry trends and university standards. He has also made significant contributions to institutional quality processes, particularly in NAAC documentation and accreditation-related academic support activities, demonstrating his organizational and compliance capabilities. Beyond classroom teaching, he is deeply involved in student mentoring and academic guidance. He regularly supports learners in project development, career planning, and skill enhancement, fostering a positive and motivating learning environment. His commitment to continuous improvement, collaborative academic culture, and student success makes him a valued member of his institution's academic community.

Hetal Gaglani is an accomplished academician and dedicated educator serving as an Assistant Professor at Ramdeobaba University, Nagpur. Known for her strong academic orientation and student-centered approach, she contributes actively to teaching, research, and institutional development within the higher education ecosystem. With a solid foundation in her discipline, Dr. Gaglani brings clarity, structure, and applied perspective to her teaching methodology. She focuses on building conceptual understanding while connecting theoretical frameworks with practical and industry-relevant applications. Her classroom practices emphasize interactive learning, analytical thinking, and problem-solving, encouraging students to engage deeply with subject matter and develop independent insights. As an Assistant Professor, she plays an important role in curriculum delivery, academic mentoring, and continuous quality improvement initiatives. She supports outcome-based education practices and contributes to curriculum enrichment through updated content, innovative pedagogy, and learner-focused assessment methods. She is also involved in guiding student projects, seminars, and academic activities that enhance research exposure and professional readiness. Dr. Gaglani's academic interests extend to research and scholarly writing. She participates in conferences, workshops, and faculty development programs to stay aligned with emerging trends and advances in her field. Through research engagement and collaboration, she works toward generating meaningful academic and applied contributions. In addition to her teaching and research responsibilities, she contributes to departmental and institutional activities such as organizing academic events, technical sessions, and student development programs. She is valued by colleagues and students alike for her professionalism, supportive mentoring style, and commitment to educational excellence.

Leila Goosen is a full professor in the Department of Science and Technology Education of the University of South Africa. She holds a C2 rating via the South African National Research Foundation. Prof. Goosen was an Associate Professor in the School of Computing, and the module leader and head designer of the fully online signature module for the College for Science, Engineering and Technology, rolled out to over 92,000 registered students since the first semester of 2013. She usually supervises around ten Masters and Doctoral students, and has successfully completed supervision of 43 students at postgraduate level. Previously, she was a Deputy Director at the South African national Department of Education. In this capacity, she was required to develop ICT strategies for implementation. Before that, she had been a lecturer of Information Technology (IT) in the Department for Science, Mathematics and Technology Education in the Faculty of Education of the University of Pretoria. Her research interests have included cooperative work in IT, effective teaching and learning of programming and teacher professional development.

Dhananjay Kulkarni is a Senior Assistant Professor at the Balaji Institute of Management and Human Resource Development (BIMHRD), under Sri Balaji University, Pune. A seasoned academician and management professional, he brings a wealth of experience in teaching, training, and corporate interface. Prof. Kulkarni is known for his dynamic teaching style, practical approach to management education, and dedication to student development. His academic interests lie in the areas of management, leadership, and organizational behavior, where he continually bridges theory with real-world business practices. With a strong commitment to nurturing future leaders, Prof. Kulkarni contributes significantly to the institute's mission of excellence in management education and holistic student growth.

Meenal R. Kale is an accomplished academician and dedicated educator currently serving as an Assistant Professor at Yeshwantrao Chavan College of Engineering, Nagpur. With a strong commitment to teaching, research, and institutional development, she has built a reputation for academic excellence, student mentorship, and professional integrity. Dr. Kale has consistently contributed to higher education through her dynamic teaching approach, blending theoretical foundations with practical applications to enhance student understanding and engagement. Her classroom methodology emphasizes concept clarity, analytical thinking, and problem-solving skills, enabling learners to connect academic knowledge with real-world scenarios. She is known for creating an interactive learning environment that encourages curiosity, participation, and innovation among students. In her role as Assistant Professor, Dr. Kale actively participates in curriculum development, academic planning, and outcome-based education practices. She supports continuous improvement initiatives within her department and contributes to maintaining high academic standards. Her involvement often extends beyond classroom teaching to include mentoring student projects, guiding research activities, and supporting career-oriented skill development. Dr. Kale's research interests include emerging trends and applied areas within her discipline, and she continually works toward expanding her scholarly contributions through publications, conferences, workshops, and collaborative projects. She believes in lifelong learning and regularly updates her knowledge to keep pace with evolving academic and industry developments. She also contributes to institutional responsibilities such as organizing seminars, technical events, faculty development programs, and student enrichment activities. Her collaborative spirit and professional approach make her a valued member of the academic community.

Golden Mabwe, a Bachelor of Laws (Honours) graduate from the University of Zimbabwe and a current Master of Science in Governance and Leadership student with the National University of Science and Technology (NUST), is passionate about governance, leadership ethics, and institutional accountability. With a strong background in legal studies and policy analysis, he seeks to integrate principles of justice, ethical governance, and transformational leadership in public and private institutions. His perspective in governance and leadership is informed by his legal training, which emphasizes fairness, integrity, and the rule of law as essential pillars for sustainable development and societal transformation

Vigilance Matongo, a Bachelor of Arts Honors Degree graduate in Religious Studies from the University of Zimbabwe and a current Master's student in Governance and Leadership, is a dedicated teacher by profession. Passionate about transforming lives and empowering the disadvantaged, Matongo's commitment to service is deeply rooted in personal life experiences and background. With a strong belief in education as a tool for social change, Vigilance strives to influence learners and communities positively through ethical leadership and inclusive educational practices. Her academic and professional journey reflects a drive to integrate governance principles with moral and social responsibility to promote equity and sustainable development

Michael Oyenuga holds a PhD in Marketing and Communication and has over 25 years of experience in scholarly and practitioner roles, spanning education policy, digital transformation, and inclusive learning. His research interests cut across marketing, branding, consumer behaviour, education and sustainability. He is an Associate Professor and the pioneer Assistant Dean at the School of Business, Woxsen University, Hyderabad, India.

P. Selvakumar is currently an Associate Professor in the Department of Science and Humanities at Nehru Institute of Technology, Coimbatore,

Tamil Nadu, India. Prior to joining Nehru Institute of Technology, he held positions as an Assistant Professor in the Department of Science and Humanities various engineering colleges in Coimbatore, Tamil Nadu, India, spanning from 2011 to 2023. Dr.P. Selvakumar's academic and research interests lie primarily in the field of phytochemistry. He has made significant contributions to his field, with an impressive record that includes 30 journal publications, 12 patents, and 20 conference papers. Additionally, he has organized 5 seminars and conferences, further demonstrating his commitment to academic and scientific exchange. Throughout his career, Dr. P.Selvakumar has been recognized for his dedication and excellence in teaching, having been honored with several awards, including the Best Teacher Awards. He holds a prominent position in the academic community, contributing actively to research.

Ananya Pandey is a Research Scholar in School of Law at Christ University, Bangalore. She has her research interests in the field of Constitutional Law, Environment Law, Human Rights, Food Security, Intellectual Property Law and Jurisprudence.

Vijay Uprikar is a passionate Faculty of Marketing Management at Datta Meghe Institute of Management Studies, Nagpur. With over 20 years of blended experience in academics and pharmaceutical industry, he demonstrates a unique blend of corporate insights and academic expertise to the world of marketing education. A firm believer in innovative pedagogy, have developed study materials that hold six copyrights, designed to enhance conceptual clarity in marketing management. His interdisciplinary research explores Mahatma Jotirao Phule's contributions to Entrepreneurial Social Responsibility (ESR), integrating historical and social perspectives into contemporary management frameworks. With a strong foundation in management education, Dr. Uprikar has contributed significantly to the academic and professional development of students through his expertise and dedication. His work focuses on fostering innovation, leadership, and excellence in the field of management. A respected figure in the academic community, Dr. Uprikar continues to play a vital role in shaping future business leaders.

Index

C

Capacity Building 28, 29, 31, 33, 35, 41, 42, 43, 45, 52, 55, 60, 63, 64, 70, 74, 75, 76, 80, 117, 123, 132, 144, 159, 163, 168, 170, 177, 191, 237

Communication 2, 3, 4, 6, 7, 18, 26, 28, 30, 32, 35, 36, 40, 44, 46, 47, 48, 50, 52, 53, 56, 57, 62, 63, 64, 66, 71, 89, 95, 96, 112, 132, 136, 137, 142, 143, 146, 147, 150, 151, 155, 156, 157, 158, 159, 163, 164, 166, 167, 168, 175, 181, 185, 187, 188, 197, 199, 200, 203, 204, 210, 215, 222, 224, 225, 226, 227, 236, 243, 244

Community 1, 2, 3, 4, 5, 6, 7, 8, 9, 10, 11, 12, 13, 14, 15, 16, 17, 18, 19, 22, 23, 24, 25, 26, 27, 28, 30, 31, 32, 33, 34, 35, 38, 39, 40, 41, 42, 43, 44, 46, 50, 52, 57, 63, 64, 65, 66, 67, 72, 74, 76, 78, 82, 85, 86, 87, 88, 89, 90, 91, 92, 93, 94, 95, 96, 97, 98, 100, 101, 102, 103, 104, 105, 106, 107, 108, 109, 111, 112, 113, 115, 116, 117, 118, 119, 120, 121, 122, 123, 124, 125, 126, 127, 128, 129, 130, 131, 132, 133, 134, 135, 136, 137, 138, 139, 140, 141, 142, 143, 144, 145, 146, 147, 149, 150, 152, 153, 154, 155, 156, 157, 158, 159, 160, 161, 162, 163, 164, 165, 166, 168, 169, 170, 171, 172, 173, 174, 175, 176, 177, 178, 179, 180, 181, 182, 183, 184, 185, 186, 187, 188, 189, 190, 191, 195, 196, 202, 204, 209, 219, 220, 221, 222, 224, 226, 230, 231, 232, 233, 241

Community Engagement 1, 2, 3, 4, 5, 6, 8, 9, 11, 12, 13, 14, 15, 16, 18, 19, 22, 31, 33, 41, 57, 65, 72, 85, 88, 103, 105, 115, 116, 117, 118, 119, 120, 121, 122, 123, 124, 125, 126, 127, 128, 130, 131, 132, 133, 134, 135, 138, 139, 140, 141, 142, 143, 146, 147, 149, 152, 153, 154, 157, 158, 159, 160, 163, 172, 174, 175, 176, 178, 181, 182, 183, 186, 187, 188, 189, 190, 196, 204

D

Digital Divide 41, 42, 71, 112, 129, 134, 139, 141, 144, 146, 151, 158, 163, 165, 169, 183, 219, 233, 242, 244

Digital Literacy 12, 15, 24, 27, 42, 45, 47, 49, 52, 53, 58, 61, 63, 89, 107, 108, 114, 118, 122, 123, 124, 125, 131, 134, 135, 137, 142, 143, 144, 146, 152, 156, 158, 159, 160, 161, 163, 165, 166, 168, 170, 171, 174, 177, 179, 180, 185, 186, 190, 193, 200, 211, 212, 221, 223, 232, 238, 244

Digital Tools 19, 22, 29, 31, 62, 65, 66, 70, 71, 91, 105, 121, 125, 132, 134, 136, 151, 153, 154, 155, 163, 165, 169, 170, 185, 199, 200, 220, 221, 224, 225, 228, 230, 233, 237, 243

Digital Volunteering 6, 17, 18, 21, 22, 25, 28, 30, 35, 39, 41, 42, 43, 48, 53, 56, 65, 71, 72, 73, 74, 75, 77, 92, 121, 123, 128, 129, 132, 135, 138, 139, 140, 143, 144, 145, 147, 181, 236, 237

Digital Volunteerism 2, 4, 6, 7, 8, 10, 11, 12, 16, 19, 24, 25, 26, 29, 30, 32, 33, 41, 42, 43, 44, 45, 46, 47, 48, 49, 50, 51, 52, 53, 55, 56, 57, 58, 60, 61, 67, 68, 70, 71, 74, 83, 85, 115, 116, 117, 118, 119, 120, 121, 123, 124, 125, 126, 127, 128, 131, 134, 135, 136, 137, 138, 139, 140, 141, 142, 143, 144, 147, 149, 150, 151, 152, 153, 154, 156, 162, 163, 164, 165, 167, 168, 169, 170, 171, 172, 173, 174, 175, 178, 179, 180, 187, 188, 189, 190, 191, 192, 193, 196, 204, 206, 221, 233, 236, 238

Digital Volunteer Narratives 1, 2, 3, 5, 6, 7, 8, 9, 11, 12, 13, 14, 15, 16

Digital Volunteer Platforms 12, 21, 22, 23, 24, 25, 26, 27, 28, 29, 30, 31, 32, 33, 34, 35, 36, 37, 38, 40, 67, 170,

174, 237, 244

E

Educational leadership 2, 4, 5, 7, 12, 13, 14, 22, 23, 27, 34, 37, 39, 189, 190, 191, 192, 196, 209, 213, 214

Emotional Intelligence 47, 49, 52, 54, 71, 93

Engagement 1, 2, 3, 4, 5, 6, 7, 8, 9, 10, 11, 12, 13, 14, 15, 16, 17, 18, 19, 22, 23, 24, 25, 26, 27, 28, 29, 30, 31, 32, 33, 34, 35, 36, 37, 38, 39, 40, 41, 42, 43, 44, 45, 48, 49, 52, 53, 57, 58, 60, 61, 62, 63, 65, 66, 67, 69, 72, 73, 74, 76, 78, 82, 85, 86, 87, 88, 89, 90, 91, 92, 94, 96, 97, 100, 101, 102, 103, 105, 106, 107, 108, 113, 115, 116, 117, 118, 119, 120, 121, 122, 123, 124, 125, 126, 127, 128, 130, 131, 132, 133, 134, 135, 136, 137, 138, 139, 140, 141, 142, 143, 144, 146, 147, 149, 151, 152, 153, 154, 156, 157, 158, 159, 160, 161, 162, 163, 165, 167, 168, 169, 171, 172, 173, 174, 175, 176, 178, 179, 180, 181, 182, 183, 186, 187, 188, 189, 190, 195, 196, 197, 200, 204, 205, 215, 219, 220, 221, 224, 225, 226, 227, 228, 229, 230, 232, 235, 237, 240, 242, 243

Engagement Tools 157, 176

Enhancing Community Engagement Through Digital Volunteerism 149, 189, 190

G

Gamification 108, 136, 219, 224, 225, 226, 227, 229, 230, 237, 240, 242, 243

I

Impact Measurement 124, 126, 155, 225, 227, 232, 234

Inclusive Schools 115, 117, 119, 123, 124, 134, 135, 138, 141, 143

L

Leadership 1, 2, 3, 4, 5, 6, 7, 9, 10, 11, 12, 13, 14, 15, 16, 19, 21, 22, 23, 24, 25, 26, 27, 28, 29, 30, 31, 32, 33, 34, 35, 36, 37, 38, 39, 40, 75, 80, 85, 86, 87, 88, 89, 90, 91, 92, 93, 94, 95, 96, 97, 100, 101, 102, 103, 104, 105, 106, 107, 108, 110, 113, 115, 116, 117, 119, 120, 122, 123, 124, 125, 126, 127, 128, 131, 132, 133, 135, 136, 138, 139, 140, 141, 142, 143, 145, 146, 148, 166, 180, 187, 188, 189, 190, 191, 192, 194, 195, 196, 202, 203, 204, 205, 206, 208, 209, 211, 212, 213, 214, 215, 216, 217, 242

Leadership Development 11, 21, 22, 23, 24, 25, 26, 27, 28, 29, 30, 32, 33, 34, 35, 36, 37, 38, 110

M

Mixed-Methods 21, 22, 23, 24, 25, 26, 27, 28, 32, 33, 34, 35, 37, 38, 39, 40

N

Non-Governmental Organisations 42, 51

P

Project Management 31, 48, 53, 158, 163, 224, 226, 227, 228, 240

Q

Qualitative Research 1, 2, 4, 5, 8, 9, 16, 17, 18, 19, 39, 40

S

School–Community Bonds 1, 2, 4, 9, 15

School Leadership Capacity 21, 22, 23, 25, 26, 27, 31, 32, 36, 37, 38, 40

Skills 4, 6, 12, 14, 19, 22, 23, 24, 25, 26, 27, 28, 29, 31, 32, 35, 40, 41, 42, 43, 44, 45, 46, 47, 52, 53, 55, 64, 65, 66,

71, 82, 90, 91, 92, 110, 112, 130, 149, 150, 151, 153, 155, 159, 160, 161, 162, 163, 164, 165, 166, 170, 172, 177, 179, 180, 181, 183, 184, 185, 191, 193, 199, 200, 201, 206, 208, 224, 228, 230, 231, 235, 244

Strengthening Teachers and School Leadership Through Digital Transformation 187, 188, 191, 196, 204

T

Technology 3, 10, 18, 24, 29, 31, 36, 39, 41, 42, 43, 45, 46, 47, 50, 51, 52, 55, 57, 60, 62, 68, 71, 72, 75, 76, 77, 80, 82, 87, 89, 92, 93, 95, 96, 104, 105, 106, 107, 111, 112, 113, 115, 125, 126, 130, 132, 133, 134, 139, 141, 145, 149, 150, 154, 157, 168, 172, 175, 176, 177, 178, 180, 181, 183, 184, 185, 190, 191, 192, 194, 195, 196, 197, 199, 201, 202, 203, 204, 205, 208, 209, 210, 211, 212, 213, 214, 215, 216, 217, 219, 221, 222, 223, 227, 228, 232, 233, 234, 235, 236, 237, 238, 239, 241, 242

V

Virtual Collaboration 42, 47, 105, 179, 244
Virtual Engagement 44
Volunteerism 2, 4, 6, 7, 8, 10, 11, 12, 16, 19, 24, 25, 26, 29, 30, 32, 33, 41, 42, 43, 44, 45, 46, 47, 48, 49, 50, 51, 52, 53, 55, 56, 57, 58, 60, 61, 62, 65, 67, 68, 70, 71, 74, 75, 76, 79, 82, 83, 85, 91, 94, 100, 101, 103, 105, 106, 114, 115, 116, 117, 118, 119, 120, 121, 123, 124, 125, 126, 127, 128, 131, 133, 134, 135, 136, 137, 138, 139, 140, 141, 142, 143, 144, 146, 147, 149, 150, 151, 152, 153, 154, 155, 156, 162, 163, 164, 165, 167, 168, 169, 170, 171, 172, 173, 174, 175, 178, 179, 180, 183, 184, 186, 187, 188, 189, 190, 191, 192, 193, 196, 202, 204, 206, 209, 215, 219, 220, 221, 222, 230, 233, 234, 236, 237, 238, 240, 241, 242, 243, 244
Volunteer Retention 126, 137, 166, 230, 243
Volunteer Stories 1, 2, 4, 5, 10, 13, 14, 16